RENAISSANCE DRAMA

New Series XIX 1988

Renaissance Drama

NEW SERIES **XIX**

*Essays on
Texts of
Renaissance
Plays*

Edited by Mary Beth Rose

Northwestern University Press and

The Newberry Library Center for Renaissance Studies

EVANSTON **1988**

Editorial Note

RENAISSANCE DRAMA, an annual publication, is devoted to understanding the drama as a central feature of Renaissance culture. Coverage, so far as subject matter is concerned, is not restricted to any single geographical area. The chronological limits of the Renaissance are interpreted broadly. Essays are encouraged that explore the relationship of Renaissance dramatic traditions to their precursors and successors; have an interdisciplinary orientation; explore the relationship of the drama to society and history; and examine the impact of new forms of interpretation on the study of Renaissance plays.

Volume XIX (1988) includes essays concerned with the traditional issues of textual scholarship about Renaissance drama, as well as essays that explore questions of textual authenticity and canonization and examine the cultural environment in which the text is created, edited, and produced. This volume also includes the text of *Cupid's Banishment: A Masque Presented by Young Gentlewomen of the Ladies Hall, Deptford* (1617).

As editor I am very grateful to members of the Editorial Committee and to Assistant Editor Frances Dolan. Similar thanks are due to Manuscript Editor Alma A. MacDougall for her diligence and care.

Volume XX (1989) will include essays concerned with any topic related to Renaissance drama. For Volume XXI (1990), "Disorder and the Drama," we are seeking essays that discuss Renaissance dramatic representations of violence, crime, public strife, and political mayhem, and essays that explore the ways in which chaos is ritualized to contain and/or encourage social, political, and religious disorder. The deadline for submission is December 1, 1989. Manuscripts should be submitted with stamped, self-addressed envelopes.

Renaissance Drama conforms to the stylistic conventions outlined in the most recent *MLA Style Manual*. Scholars preparing manuscripts for submission should refer to this book. Submissions and inquiries regarding future volumes should be addressed to Mary Beth Rose, *Renaissance Drama*, The Newberry Library, 60 West Walton Street, Chicago, Illinois 60610.

Mary Beth Rose
Editor

Contents

RENAISSANCE DRAMA

New Series XIX 1988

Rebel Letters: Postal Effects
from Richard II *to* Henry IV

JONATHAN GOLDBERG

> In the beginning, in principle, was the post, and I will never get over it. But in
> the end I know it, become aware of it as our death sentence.
> —Jacques Derrida, *The Post Card*

I. On Deposit

MARJORIE GARBER offers a breathtaking start. Writing of the thematization of writing in Shakespeare, she asks, of 4.1 in *Richard II,* what is a deposition? "A 'deposition' is both a forced removal from office and a piece of testimony taken down for use in the witness's absence (as well as the term describing the lowering of Christ's body from the cross—Richard's view of the event). Richard here deposes at his own deposition..." ("Ghost Writers" 139).[1] Garber notes an undoubtedly repressed textuality in this scene, a repression so strong that the text itself remarks it. After Richard deposes himself, he asks, "What more remains?" (4.1.222), and is answered that he must read the document that details his crimes. So doing, he will be "worthily deposed" (227). Richard refuses to read the document and to turn his deposition into the written deposition demanded of him.

What he refuses to do in the play, he does, however, in Holinshed. There, according to a parliamentary document, he reads "a bill drawne of the said resignation, that he might be perfect in the rehearsall thereof," a bill that he in fact "desired to have ... drawne" (37). He insists, in

3

Holinshed's account, that his recited resignation be letter-perfect; when he deposes himself he reenacts a textual inscription. In Holinshed, then, the double meaning of deposition is explicit, and the duplication of terms points to the assumption that writing acts as a guarantee. The letter has a fixity and a permanence into which Richard inserts himself: "for the more suertie of the matter, and for that the said resignation should have his full force and strength, himselfe therefore read the scroll of resignation" (37). Richard does not merely read the scroll; he signs his resignation: "And for more record of the same, here openlie I subscribe and signe this present resignation with mine owne hand" (39).

Shakespeare's scene would seem to be constructed in the repression of the double meaning of deposition apparent in Holinshed. And when Richard declines to read, he launches an attack on writing, refusing to "ravel out" his "weaved-up folly" (228–29). "Weaved-up" offers an etymology for "text" that stresses its fabrication; as Richard describes it, a text that unkings him cannot be a sure text, for it unspeaks itself. Rather than that text, he asks his accusers to look at an (imagined) book that would describe their rebellious acts; if it contained "the deposing of a king" (234), that text would be "marked with a blot, damned in the book of heaven" (236). The text (for the imagined text is the very text the rebels would have him read, deposing him), as Richard describes it in his response, is therefore, by definition, a rebel text. Letters are not sureties or guarantees; to find oneself inscribed means to have been offered up to undoing.

Instead, Richard delivers (has already delivered) himself in speech:

> Now mark me how I will undo myself.
> I give this heavy weight from off my head
> And this unwieldy sceptre from my hand,
> The pride of kingly sway from out my heart.
> With mine own tears I wash away my balm,
> With mine own hands I give away my crown,
> With mine own tongue deny my sacred state,
> With mine own breath release all duty's rites.
> All pomp and majesty I do forswear;
> My manors, rents, revenues I forgo;
> My acts, decrees, and statutes I deny.
>
>   (203–13)

Yet, the speech that Richard delivers in which he undoes himself is, in fact, derived loosely from the bill in Holinshed; although hardly letter-perfect, Richard's speech of resignation is a version (a rewriting, as it were) of the written deposition he refuses to read afterwards:

I resigne all my kinglie dignitie, majestie and crowne, with all the lordships, power, and privileges to the foresaid kinglie dignitie and crowne belonging, and all other lordships and possessions to me in anie maner of wise pertein-ing.... And I renounce all right, and all maner of title of possession.... And also the rule and governance of the same kingdome and lordships, with all ministrations of the same.... And also I renounce the name, worship, and regalitie and kinglie highnesse, clearlie, freelie, singularlie and wholie, in the most best maner and forme that I may.... (38)

Richard's speech insists on his "own," yet his words have been written already. His speech (in both meanings of the word) enacts a textual suppression, and makes claims for the propriety of speaking. "Mark me how I will undo myself" (203); the written mark marks him, and the command "hear me" appears in a textualized form, as if audition were an act of inscription. "Are you contented to resign the crown?" Boling-broke had asked, and Richard replies: "Ay, no; no, ay; for I must nothing be; / Therefore no no, for I resign to thee" (200–02). Whereas in Holinshed, Richard signs when he resigns, here that doubled mark is marked in the duplicity of his response. Rather than the supposedly confirmatory doubling of Holinshed, Richard speaks within a textual duplicity. Saying yes and no at once, blotting himself out and insisting on himself, Richard speaks as if "resign" meant both to give away and to write again. In his duplicitous speech it does. So doing he speaks within a writing that lacks the monumentality and permanence of the text as represented in Holinshed.

Richard's deposition "speech" enacts a version of the repression of textuality to which many Shakespeareans have succumbed (not least in speech-act and metatheatrical analyses of the history plays).[2] For a representative instance, consider Terence Hawkes's *Shakespeare's Talk-ing Animals*. Guarding against the possibility that we might misappre-hend Shakespeare's plays as literature, Hawkes describes his book as a set of essays concerned with the ways in which the plays exhibit "a deep and almost certainly defensive commitment to language in its oral

dimension: to the ideal as well as the idea of man as the animal that
talks" (51). No doubt: Shakespeare's audience was not highly literate,
and literature, as the institution we readily name, does not apply to the
Shakespearean text. But no doubt, too, a relationship to an emerging
textuality is marked throughout the plays. Shakespeare writes scripts
which can, as the instance of Richard's deposition begins to exhibit,
repress that relationship. That repression, I would argue, serves an ideological function—and I would add "ideology" to Hawkes's listing of
the "ideal" and "idea" of the oral. Hawkes almost admits as much when
he describes the "Tudor 'revolution' " as "the establishment of the king
as the vital and unifying communicative link between man and deity
and man and man" (75), but by not interrogating that claim his argument repeats an attitude toward power (textual power) in the plays:
an insistence on living breath ("the vital and unifying communicative
link") rather than the claims of the text on speech—in this instance,
the text of Holinshed repressed in the deposition speech; the text of
that speech (the script which the actor "reads" as he speaks); and the
thematization of those linked repressions in the representation of textuality that Richard makes in his refusal to read the rebels' document.
In these multiple repressions, I would argue, can emerge a notion of
the text in Shakespeare and its relationship to the ideology of the second tetralogy.[3]

The ideological construction of textuality in Richard's speeches in
the deposition scene—or their repetition in Hawkes—are instances of
what Derrida calls logocentrism, confining "writing to a secondary and
instrumental function: translator of a full speech that was fully *present*
(present to itself, to its signified, to the other, the very condition of the
theme of presence in general), technics in the service of language,
spokesman, interpreter of an originary speech itself shielded from
interpretation" (*Gram.* 8). As Derrida argues, such characterizations of
writing are not neutral (although they formulate writing as, at best, a
neutrality, a representation that would ideally efface itself before living
speech). Rather, the hierarchization of voice and writing (in temporal
as well as evaluative terms) attempts to guard speech from the incursions of writing—precisely, then, the attitude of Richard refusing to
read the deposition or of Hawkes in his "defensive" characterization of
the primacy of oral communication. "Such is the breath of kings"

(1.3.215), however, that speech is invaded by what it would deny. Palpably, in Richard's citations of Holinshed. But more generally, as Derrida argues, since such incursions are systematic: they found speech (in an unfounding of the logocentric denials of writing). "Writing did not reduce the voice to itself, it incorporated it into a system" (*Gram.* 90), for, as Derrida demonstrates, from Plato on, discussions of writing, which have attempted to secure its merely secondary, derivative, fallen nature, have been haunted by the possibility that writing is as originary as speech (and if so that there is then no origin). He points "to the tradition that has always associated writing with the fatal violence of the political institution" (*Gram.* 36), a *usurping* incursion upon nature, life, breath.

Richard would ally writing to rebellion against the sanctity of the monarch and the breath and life of the king. But, as Derrida argues, such representations of power are ideological constructions couched in the devaluation of the very instrument that is allied to power and makes it possible—writing. Introducing a selection from the Shakespearean editor William Warburton's inquiry into the origins of language, Derrida exposes the ideological construction in which writing merely "befalls" power; rather, he insists (and demonstrates that despite itself, Warburton's text insists) on the complicity of writing and power. The relationship is, at one and the same time, effaced (in the logocentric devaluations of writing) and productive of the text. As Warburton writes the history of writing from hieroglyphics to phonetic transcription (a history toward writing effacing itself, since phonetic writing should efface itself before the sounds it represents), he also writes a history of script as an instrument of concealment, secrecy, power. The very arbitrariness of the relationship between phonetic script and sound (that is, that which should make script "invisible") is part of what makes script insistent and primary. It is not merely that phonetic script fails to provide a system that merely translates sound into another medium; script usurps voice ("mark me").

A writing made to manifest, serve, and preserve knowledge—for custody of meaning, the repository of learning, and the laying out of the archive—encrypts itself, becoming secret and reserved, diverted from common usage, esoteric. Naturally destined to serve the communication of laws and the order of the city transparently, a writing becomes the instrument of an abusive power, of a caste of "intellectuals" that is thus ensuring hegemony, whether its own or that of special interests: the violence of a secretariat, a discriminating reserve, an effect of scribble and scrypt. (Derrida, "Scribble" 124)

Derrida's summary of the enlightened horror of Warburton also characterizes Hawkes's attitudes, his attempt to rescue the Shakespearean text from the hands of the literary establishment. Warburton locates the moment in which the "fall" into phonetic writing occurred: in Egypt, when the king's secretary devised a script for the king that would not have the limits of hieroglyphics, a script for letters of state: "whence the name *epistolic:* '. . . as the government doubtless sought to keep the invention secret' " ("Scribble" 138). The Shakespearean text, as the deposition scene indicates, bears this duplicity too: it registers, in Richard's speech, the logocentric devaluation of writing as it is allied to an ideology of power; yet, it also is a written text (Shakespeare and Holinshed usurp Richard's "own"). Logocentric ideology, at one and the same time, effaces its relationship to that which establishes its power.

"What more remains?" (4.1.222). Richard's refusal to read the deposition is not the end of the deposition scene—and the remainder of the scene exhibits the relationship between the oral deposition (invaded by the mark) and the repudiation of the rebel text. For Richard does agree to read—himself, in a mirror—as if to affirm the presence of the body and the voice. "I'll read enough / When I do see the very book indeed / Where all my sins are writ, and that's myself" (273–75). For Hawkes, such reading is tantamount to a confession of failed kingship: "[H]e commands a mirror to be brought so that, as ever, he can look inward, not communicating directly with the world, with reality, but with himself alone, like a reader who studies alone, without communicating outside the realm of the printed page, abstracted from the warmth of oral-aural contact" (91). "Such 'writing,' " Hawkes concludes, reviewing moments in the play in which Richard is attached to script, "measures the extent to which, under that king, the vivid island language has indeed been grossly reduced" (103). But if, as I have been suggesting, the deposition scene stages relationships to a suppressed textuality, this scene of reading, in which Richard attempts to claim his "own" in the mirror, is, I would argue, the most explicit register of that suppressed textuality—a textuality that is one with power, not its fallen debasement.

For when Richard looks in the glass, that text refuses to confirm what
he would see there. It deposes him, too, beguiling him with a false
image; it refuses to deliver the present or to offer an outer image that
would correspond to what Richard supposes he will see:

> Give me the glass, and therein will I read.
> No deeper wrinkles yet? Hath sorrow struck
> So many blows upon this face of mine
> And made no deeper wounds? O flattering glass
> Like to my followers in prosperity,
> Thou dost beguile me!
>
> (276–81)

Richard's reading in the mirror disputes the solipsism that Hawkes sees
there. Rather, the mirroring reflection insists on a primacy that undoes
the lived reality of the body and the voice. Moreover, even that lived
reality is presented as textual—sorrow should have furrowed his brows,
imprinting them. And the mirror is like the gaze of some other upon
him (the flatterers of the past); it does not allow Richard to eye himself.
The circuit of one's own—everything that is entailed in what Derrida
calls presence—is shattered in this glass. Richard looks upon a mirror
for magistrates, and finds himself displaced and deposed by the image,
by the usurping secondarity of the reflection: the mirror or the text
(the equation is a Renaissance commonplace, of course),[4] which refuses to be merely a reflection, or to efface itself as writing supposedly
does in its relation to speech. The mirror, in every sense of the word,
makes Richard a subject—subject to the disseminative dispersal of a
textuality which refuses simply to mirror "reality." Rather, the signified
face is the signifying face. In the glass, Richard reads himself through
a textual citation:

> Was this face the face
> That every day under his household roof
> Did keep ten thousand men? Was this the face
> That like the sun did make beholders wink?
> Was this the face that faced so many follies
> And was at last outfaced by Bolingbroke?
>
> (281–86)

Richard's "self-discovery" is so entirely a matter of citation that the
mirror offers him a version of Marlowe's *Dr. Faustus* when he looks in

the glass. The flattering voice of the past includes, then, an author that
Shakespeare would put behind him. Richard is written within literary
history. And the relationship between Richard and Bolingbroke is signaled in the kingly title they share at this moment, as the hollow crown
passes from one to the other; depositioning describes the relationship
of signified to signifier.

This is, as Derrida claims, an economy of death. When Richard deposes, he is put on deposit, a virtual corpse as the glass shatters, an
actual corpse as the play ends. "Mark, silent king" (4.1.290), Richard
directs Bolingbroke: pointing to the shared economy of a shattering
textuality—for the *silent* king is no avatar of the oral-aural. "There lies
the substance" (4.1.299). There is no referent for "there." All shadow,
no substance. By the end of the play, Bolingbroke, who, as much as
Richard, turns the word against the word, is buried in the casket of
textuality: "within this coffin I present / Thy buried fear" (5.6.30–31).
As Garber comments about the deposition scene: "He is already a voice
from the past, and the disembodied voice, the ghost of Richard II, will
haunt the rest of the tetralogy with increasing power" ("Ghost Writers"
139).

But the subsequent plays are haunted too by what is put on deposit
in the deposition scene: the alliance of kingship with the repression of
textuality, and the ways in which the play both supports that logocentrism and undermines it. The rebel letter that Richard reads is dis-
seminated and displaced in the play that follows. It is the circuit of that
letter, put on deposit in *Richard II* and posted in *1 Henry IV,* that I
pursue here. It takes the breath away.

II. The Factor of Truth

Confirming Richard's logocentric alliance of writing with rebellion,
the rebels in *1 Henry IV* are associated with writing. The king holds
councils or confers privately with Prince Henry; he receives messen-
gers with news; he listens to stories. But when the Percies are alone,
Worcester offers to "unclasp a secret book" to his nephew (1.3.188),
the book that inscribes, in Hotspur's words, "a noble plot" (276), one
that will save the Percies from "the detested blot" (162) that threatens
to "fill up chronicles in time to come" (171). Worcester does not reveal

his plot to Hotspur; rather, he promises to "send you written" (261) his plan, and the scene ends with his assurance that the rebellion has been "ruminated, plotted, and set down" (271). Hotspur is told: "No further go in this / Than I by letters shall direct your course" (289–90), and, as if in confirmation of this textualization of rebellion, the next time Hotspur appears, he enters *"solus, reading a letter"* (2.3.0). When the rebels meet, their scene together (3.1) takes as long as the drawing of their indentures (3.1.80, 140, 258). "I'll haste the writer" (3.1.141), Glendower promises the impatient Hotspur, and when Mortimer agrees to hear his lady sing in Welsh, he justifies the delay: "By that time will our book, I think, be drawn" (221). And so the scene ends: "our book is drawn; we'll but seal / And then to horse immediately" (262–63). At the rebel front at Shrewsbury, Hotspur receives *"one with letters"* (4.1.12.1), and as the battle is about to begin, the post arrives again: "My lord, here are letters for you," a messenger says; "I cannot read them now" (5.2.79–80), Hotspur responds. Between these, an entire scene between the Archbishop of York and Sir Michael serves merely to display other rebels in a flurry of letter writing. "Hie, good Sir Michael; bear this sealèd brief / With wingèd haste" (4.4.1–2), the scene opens, and the Archbishop is still beseeching Sir Michael to speed as he exits to "write again / To other friends" (40–41).

Logócentric devaluation of writing is furthered by the contents of these rebel letters. Letters are so true to rebellion that they are rebellious, as shattering as the glass that Richard reads. This is apparent when Hotspur reads the first of the letters to arrive: " 'But, for mine own part, my lord, I could be well contented to be there, in respect of the love I bear your house.' He could be contented—why is he not then?" (2.3.1–4). Hotspur deciphers the equivocal and prevaricating letter; yet, true to the rebel form, he answers the letter with the letter: "Is there not my father, my uncle, and myself; Lord Edmund Mortimer, my Lord of York, and Owen Glendower? Is there not, besides, the Douglas? Have I not all their letters to meet me in arms by the ninth of the next month . . . ?" (23–28). Taking up the letter writer's devaluation of the "plot" as "light" (12), Hotspur counters, "our plot is a good plot as ever was laid" (15). When the messenger arrives with the first letter at Shrewsbury, it reveals Northumberland's "sickness"—he too "could be well contented to be there" and is not; by the time of the battle, none of the letter writers named in Hotspur's response to the letter of 2.3, save the Douglas, has arrived. The Archbishop of York's dispatches are letters of betrayal of the rebel plot. The indentures drawn with Owen Glendower secure nothing, like the map of England that the rebels also carve up, Hotspur opposing the "deep indent" (3.1.104) of the River Trent, and wanting to redraw the line on the map and on the land. Depending on letters, it is only letters that arrive at the battlefield: death is their destination.

From his father's letter, Hotspur learns the "truth" of the conventional definition of a letter, "the messenger and familiar speech of the absent," as Angel Day defines the letter in *The English Secretorie* (1), "a declaration, by Writing of the mindes of such as bee absent, one of them to another, even as though they were present," as William Fulwood puts it in *The Enemy of Idlenesse* (1–2).[5] Northumberland's letter represents and delivers his absence. This is true to the etymology of "epistle"—"upon (the occasion of) sending"—for the epistle is a dispatch put into the hands of time. And, as the epistolary handbook, of which Day and Fulwood are late exemplars, makes clear, letters have so little to do with their senders or receivers that they may be copied from a collection like Day's or Fulwood's, sent as the occasion dictates. Thus, while it is true to say that the rebel letters of *1 Henry IV* contain betrayal, it is also true to say that within the epistolary tradition of the letter, they could not do otherwise. Conveyers of absence, they cannot assure presence, neither the presence of sender or receiver. Nor could the words in the letter be one's own. To be true to the structure of the letter, in fact, they must be capable of dissemination. Hotspur seems entirely circumscribed by the letter. As he countered the rebel letter of 2.3 with the letters of his co-conspirators, so he responds to his father's letter by making the lying letter into a surety: "I rather of his absence make this use: / It lends a lustre" (4.1.76–77). Hotspur *calculates* with his father's absence; as the Douglas puts it, "we may boldly spend upon the hope of what / Is to come in" (54–55). He counts on time, the occasions that dictate letters upon which they are written. Absence is put on deposit to deliver a temporal remainder. The rebels have not yet "read / The very bottom" (49–50) of the letter, not until Hotspur dismisses the second letter-carrier at Shrewsbury: "O gentlemen, the time of life is short!" (5.2.81). Soon, it is over. Soon, that is,

Hotspur and his co-conspirators are only "blots" in the chronicle of time.

In part, this alliance of the rebels and writing can also be found in Holinshed. There the rebels draw up a set of "articles" and "by their writings and seales confirmed the same" (41). Letters are sent abroad and, at the battle of Shrewsbury, documents are delivered into the king's hand. But in Holinshed, unlike Shakespeare, the king also reads and writes. "But the king understanding their cloaked drift [the letters', which, as Holinshed comments, put a plausible face on the rebellion by detailing faults of the king], devised (by what meanes he might) to quiet and appease the commons, and deface their contrived forgeries; and therefore he wrote an answer to their libels" (42); indeed, they are able to meet him face to face at Shrewsbury because the king sends "letters . . . under his seale, that they might safelie come and go" (43). In Holinshed, then, the king is as deft as Shakespeare's Hotspur in deciphering the "cloaked drift" of writing; but like the rebels, too, he puts his guarantees into writing. Shakespeare's Henry IV does not read or write; the text of *1 Henry IV,* like the deposition scene in *Richard II,* seems complicit with an ideological and logocentric suppression of any connection between power and writing.

The king's, it appears, is a world of speech. He knows what the rebels "have articulate, / Proclaimed at market crosses, read in churches, / To face the garment of rebellion" (5.1.72–74), but never on stage does he read or write in reply. Rather, he sends Blunt to parlay with the rebels (4.3), and he meets them in conference. The Percies do not trust the king's word ("well we know the king / Knows at what time to promise, when to pay," as Hotspur puts it [4.3.52–53]), but they cannot produce his lying script. Rather, they offer the evidence suppressed in *Richard II* of the king naming Mortimer his heir. When they refer back to the past as written—and that means to *Richard II*—they cannot find Bolingbroke in his words. He was and is, for all his speech, a "silent king." Hotspur recalls his meeting with Bolingbroke, quoting lines from the earlier play: " 'Look when his infant fortune came to age,' / And 'gentle Harry Percy,' and 'kind cousin'— / O, the devil take such cozeners!" (1.3.251–53). Yet the cozenage Hotspur takes Bolingbroke to task for has no textual support; Bolingbroke does not say "kind cousin" to Hotspur in *Richard II* 2.3; misquotation of a nonexistent text is another rebel inscription. "My heart this covenant makes, my hand thus seals it" (2.3.50), Bolingbroke had told Hotspur; but there is no writing in that hand. "Look how we can, or sad or merrily, / Interpretation will misquote our looks" (5.2.12–13); thus Worcester defends the lie that condemns Hotspur to death. Characteristically, Worcester, who had first unclasped the "secret book," sees his face as an inscription, and sees seeing as reading. Rebel textuality is allied insistently to cozening texts that can only be misquoted.

Even in the most "oral" scene between the rebels—at Owen Glendower's, where the lady sings a seemingly untranscribable song—Glendower goes out of his way to insist that he is no illiterate magician, proclaiming his education and his literacy. And, as Mortimer hears his lady sing, he can praise her by claiming that her "tongue / Makes Welsh as sweet as ditties highly penned" (3.1.205–06). The rebels occupy a world that is always being textualized. A scrivener prepares a document offstage, and rebel speech turns speech into text. Unlike the rebels, the king, it appears, has no offstage secretaries writing letters for him, or preparing articles. No reader of letter manuals, with their insistence on the etymological link between secret and secretary, the king has no ties to script and its capacity to betray the writer. Hotspur dies mid-sentence at Shrewsbury, and Hal fills the absence, the living replacement of the dead letter.

That, at any rate, is how it may appear. For, as in *Richard II,* royal scenes of inscription and writing and reading have been replaced with scenes of speaking. Among their own, the rebels write; with the king, they speak. (Indeed, written "articles" in Holinshed are articulated in the scenes at Shrewsbury.) The play, from this evidence, would appear to be intent on an ideological project to secure the king's breath. Yet, in his first words in the play, Henry represents himself in a breathless figure:

> So shaken as we are, so wan with care,
> Find we a time for frighted peace to pant
> And breathe short-winded accents of new broils
> To be commenced in stronds afar remote.
>
> (1.1.1–4)

And Hotspur's "cozenage" is a charge that sticks; Henry himself, speaking to Hal, points to his kinship with the rebel leader. And, in the first scene, his dearest wish is that one Harry might replace the other. Such echoes in the play are commonplace in the criticism of *1 Henry IV,* and I do not plan to detail them here.[6] What does need to be remarked, however, is the way in which such relationships between the king and rebels share a textuality. The king may not be represented as the rebels are, literally engaged in inscription; but his very "being" is written: recall his sealing hand in *Richard II.* Note that the king's charge that the rebels have "face[d] the garment of rebellion / With some fine color that may please the eye" (5.1.74–75) describes their false writing in the same terms as the king had used to depict his performance to Hal: "I stole all courtesy from heaven, / And dressed myself in such humility / ... / Thus did I keep my person fresh and new, / My presence, like a robe pontifical, / Ne'er seen but wond'red at" (3.2.50–51, 55–57), echoing as well the equation of writing with defacement in Holinshed (42). In such metaphors, the king is literally invested, clothed in the garments of textuality within the logocentric devaluation of writing. Hotspur may appear in the battlefield besieged by letter carriers; the king on the battlefield is the letter: "The king hath many marching in his coats" (5.3.25). "What art thou / That counterfeit'st the person of a king" (5.4.26–27), the Douglas demands, and is answered, "The king himself." Henry's being is counterfeit; his person impersonation. The garb he wears—his presence—is a disseminative textuality.

Thus, the ideological structure of the play is not quite as dualistic as it first appeared to be. The rebel attachment to letters is the literalization—in letters and writing—of the textuality that marks the king, a textuality so secret that it is proclaimed openly. The emperor only has clothes; the naked body of the letter. "Has it ever been doubted that writing was the clothing of speech?" Derrida asks (*Gram.* 35); and is not such "exteriority" the attempt to secure being, life, presence against that which founds and unfounds them? In *1 Henry IV,* logocentric devaluation is everywhere haunted by what it represses, constituted by it. The king is never "in" in his words. He sees himself in Hotspur, and Hal as Richard; "in that very line, Harry, standest thou" (3.2.85), "thou, the shadow of succession" (99). For Hal truly to succeed his father, he must replace Hotspur; the line that will continue is a line of script. Hal

finishes Hotspur's sentence on the battlefield, as we noted before; but
not to replace death with life; rather, to continue the line.

  This is how Hal assures the king that he will "be more myself"
(3.2.93)—

> I will redeem all this on Percy's head
> And, in the closing of some glorious day,
> Be bold to tell you that I am your son,
> When I will wear a garment all of blood,
> And stain my favors in a bloody mask,
> Which, washed away, shall scour my shame with it.
>
> (3.2.132–37)

To be himself—to be the king's son—Hal must pass through the form
of Hotspur, face and body clothed in Hotspur's blood. The "shame"
here includes that textualization, and the washing away is the effacement of that which makes Hal himself. At the end of the line, the
"closing of some glorious day," Hal will come into his own by this
violent act of appropriation and effacement; he will emerge unblotted,
as if no passage through textualization had taken place. It is not merely
the metaphors of garment and mask that support such a reading of
these lines. Hal continues:

> Percy is but my factor, good my lord,
> To engross up glorious deeds on my behalf;
> And I will call him to so strict account
> That he shall render every glory up,
> Yea, even the slightest worship of his time,
> Or I will tear the reckoning from his heart.
>
> (3.2.147–52)

As much as Hotspur receiving the letter of his father's absence, Hal
calculates here—on the making-absent of Hotspur as the necessity behind his becoming-present. Yet, presence here is a coin that circulates;
what Hotspur has engrossed (bought up and monopolized as his own)
will be Hal's own. Such ownership is as dubious as Richard's claim to
speak his own. The agency here is explicitly that of the letter. "Factor"
is an agent, doer, maker, author. And "engross" has as its primary meaning the large and clear secretarial hand of the professional scribe pre-

paring a legal document. Hotspur is Hal's secretary, writing the script in which he will be written—written true, legal heir, on the line—so he will be accounted. To be engrossed is to be named in a document, written in a list of accounts—the "reckoning" that will occur on the day of reckoning when the violent effacement of Hotspur will "face" Hal's garment as he passes from one text into another and thereby into his own. Hal replaces Hotspur, his presence posited upon absence; he enters into textuality. The "deeds" of this "strict account" are written deeds in a legal register, an account book in which no one has his own.[7]

> HOT.
> O, I could prophesy,
> But that the earthy and cold hand of death
> Lies on my tongue. No, Percy, thou art dust,
> And food for—   [*Dies.*]
> PRINCE
> For worms, brave Percy.
>
> (5.4.82–85)

The hand of death on Hotspur's tongue is a hand writing; Hotspur's final sentence, spoken as if in another's text, names Percy in the third person. Only in writing can Percy say of/to himself, "Percy, thou art dust." The Prince, completing the sentence, enters into that reckoning.

Such reckoning is how Hal is characterized throughout the play, nowhere more so than in his soliloquy at the end of 1.2. Debates about Hal's character have always had come to terms with that speech and its uncanny echoes in the king's self-presentation in 3.2. "Hal's justification of himself," Stephen Greenblatt comments, "threatens to fall away at every moment into its antithesis. . . . Although we can perceive at every point . . . the potential instability of the structure of power, . . . Hal's 'redemption' is as inescapable and inevitable as the outcome of those practical jokes the madcap prince is so fond of playing" (30). In the speech, truth and falsity are allied as they are in the rebel letter, and, indeed, the images throughout the speech—economic, sartorial— are the images of the letter. Hal as "bright metal on a sullen ground" (1.2.200) offers himself as Hotspur takes his father's letter of absence and puts it on deposit for the final reckoning. As stamped coin, Hal's value is written.[8] And Hal's promise to "pay the debt I never promisèd"

(1.2.197) depends upon the "factor" of engrossment elsewhere. "By how much better than my word I am, / By so much shall I falsify men's hopes" (198–99); better and worse, true and false, exist in a counterfeit relationship to each other. And genuine "being," sunlike majesty, does not escape the textual order of simulation, eclipsing, clouding over a "heliocentric concept of speech" (*Gram.* 91). "Yet herein will I imitate the sun" (185). In which case, being itself would be counterfeit, the metaphor of truth, majesty, sun, revealed as the veil of truth.

The economy in which Hal offers himself is written within the metaphors in which writing is regularly devalued as the violent and rebellious letter incapable of truth. This is also the language of Hal's truth. If there is something "inescapable" here, as Greenblatt contends, it is not the play's inevitable support of constituted order. It is, rather, the inevitability of textualization. Hal's reckoning here plays with his being-absent, with the possibility of his insertion within a script. If Hal draws our assent, it is because he speaks within the truth of the already written, within a historical destiny that has written his lines.[9] He does not, as a character, know the future. He speaks rather within its already writtenness, charactered by the histories that proclaim his success and his succession. That is the inevitability in Hal's lines, a reckoning within a reckoning that has already been written. The present in which Hal speaks is "awhile" (183), and the future arrival as and into "himself" is one that "betters" his word only by falsifying it. It maintains a structure of veiling in which unveiling and re-veiling/revealing are one: "reformation, glitt'ring o'er my fault" (201). The structure, that is, of writing, in which truth is offered in the metaphor of (un)veiling; in which that veil, that metaphor, offers "the familiar acrobatics of the metaphor *of the truth*" (Derrida, *Post Card* 415).[10] The glittering truth put on deposit.

And delivered at Shrewsbury. "Glittering in golden coats like images" (4.1.100) is Vernon's phrase for the king and his troops, "gorgeous as the sun" (102), none more so than Harry "like feathered Mercury" (106), the trickster-god of the crossroads, where death and writing engross reality. Hermes, the letter carrier of the gods. So Abraham Fleming offers his *Panoplie of Epistles* (1576):

I give counsel to passe & repasse, to view and review, to take down and put on, to exercise and use, such weapons as he shall finde in this our Panoplie or house of furniture, and he shall feele him selfe in short space, fenced and strengthened to the purpose, against ignoraunce that ougly monster of many heades, an enimie of order, and a friend to confusion. (5v)

Fleming's letters are "warlike weapons," and the writer presents himself as "a *Mercurialist*" rather than a "*Martialist*" (5v). Or, rather, like Hal, as both—for instance, when he challenges Hotspur to single combat, speaking the rebel's praise "like a chronicle," making but "a blushing cital of himself" (5.2.57, 61). "Dispraising praise ... / ... became him like a prince indeed" (59–60). In the structure of giving and taking away, in a structure of the violence of the letter, Hal is *like* himself, present in "a 'dialectic' of protention and retention that one would install in the heart of the present" (Derrida, *Gram.* 67).

"At hand, quoth pickpurse" (2.1.46)

To summarize: the logocentric ideology of *1 Henry IV* is produced in a linking of two counter-procedures. The rebels are insistently attached to script literally, while the king is not; and, concurrently, the king is attached to script metaphorically. Hal's historical destiny in the play is the destiny of the letter; he will come to be, he already is, inscribed in the histories that assure his arrival. "To send, to destine, to dispatch" (*Post Card* 5); Derrida writes these as a series of appositions, and they concur in the career of the prince, whose telos is also within the scope of a Derridean equation: "*telos:* acquittal, exemption, payment, cost, expenditure, fee" (*Post Card* 56). Hal arrives at the point where his scripted being and his being scripted coincide—in the engrossment that puts him in the hand of the letter (so that his deeds are in the script of another) and puts that letter in his hand (so that when he speaks the end of Hotspur's final sentence his speech is within that text). The exchange, the arrival into his own, takes place through the agency of death.

If there *is* death within this economy, which is also the economy of life. "Engross" not only designates a script, it also means corporeal enlargement, life. The word also implicates Falstaff lying "dead" beside Hotspur as Hal completes his sentence, as the letter arrives. Falstaff evades the arrival in an equation of the counterfeit orders of death and life: " 'Sblood, 'twas time to counterfeit.... Counterfeit? I lie; I am no counterfeit. To die is to be a counterfeit ... ; but to counterfeit dying

... is to be no counterfeit, but the true and perfect image of life indeed" (5.4.112–18). Counterfeit in all this is Falstaff's claim to "true" existence; truth is produced in the "lie" and life itself is the "perfect image of life." Falstaff's evasions are written within the economy that embraces Hal, and which Hal embraces. Indeed, from his first words to Falstaff, Hal is writing him within his script:

Unless hours were cups of sack, and minutes capons, and clocks the tongues of bawds, and dials the signs of leaping houses, and the blessed sun himself a fair hot wench in flame-colored taffeta, I see no reason why thou shouldst be so superfluous to demand the time of the day. (1.2.6–11)

Hal here performs a reckoning, writes a bill; at the opening of 2.4, such reckoning is transferred—to Francis, whose rebellion he incites with the hopes of a thousand pounds, to Hotspur, inflamed with death: "his eloquence the parcel of a reckoning" (2.4.96–97). In these "trim reckonings" (to cite Falstaff's definition of the word "honor" [5.1.134] and the airy order of speech),[11] Hal's speech scripts others within the order of writing which also claims him, and which he (dis)claims.

III. The Purloined Paper

"Text" and its synonyms, as they have appeared thus far in this essay, are Derridean terms; yet, as I have argued elsewhere, the terms also ramify in their bibliographical meanings.[12] This inquiry into the representations of textuality within the Shakespearean text may also serve toward a consideration of the text—literally. Indeed, this might be the moment to return to the deposition scene in *Richard II* and to detail the bibliographical difficulties that it entails.[13] I choose, however, to stay with *1 Henry IV*, a text regarded generally as an unproblematic one. "The two 1598 quartos of *1 Henry IV* are ... among the cleanest and best-printed of all the Shakespeare quartos," David Bevington comments in his recent Oxford edition (87); they are the copy-texts for all modern editions of the play, the Folio having been set up from Q5 and exhibiting changes that reveal "literary meddling" (Bevington 101) without any authoritative source in authorial manuscripts or playhouse practices. Yet there is one F1 emendation accepted in virtually all modern editions, and I would like to examine it here. It may be one of only two moments when a piece of script is in Hal's hands, when, perhaps, he reads. The episode in the editorial tradition, to be examined here, participates precisely in the countermoves that I have described as structuring the logocentric ideology of *1 Henry IV.*

In Q1, the tavern scene (2.4 in F1) closes like this:

PRIN.

This oylie rascall is knowne as well as Poules: goe call him forth.

PETO.

Falstaffe: fast asleepe behind the Arras, and snorting like a horse.

PRIN.

Harke how hard he fetches breath, search his pockets.

He searcheth his pocket, and findeth certaine papers.

PR.

What hast thou found?

PET.

Nothing but papers my Lord.

PRIN.

Lets see what they be, read them.

Item a capon.	2.s,ii,d.
Item sawce.	iiii,d.
Item sacke two gallons.	v.s,viii,d.
Item anchaves and sacke after supper.	2,s,vi,d.
Item bread.	ob.

O monstrous! but one halfepeniworth of bread to this intollerable deale of sack? what there is else keepe close, weel read it at more advantage; there let him sleepe till day, ile to the court in the morning. We must all to the wars, and thy place shal be honorable. *I*le procure this fat rogue a charge of foot, and *I* know his death will bee a march of twelve skore, the money shall bee paid backe againe with advantage; bee with me betimes in the morning, and so good morrow Peto.

PETO.

Good morrow good my Lord. *Exeunt*

F1 prints this scene almost word for word, and with numerous variants in the accidentals: pointing, capitalization, and spelling. Its major substantive change is this: before the reckoning, Peto's name is inserted as the reader of the tavern bill; and a second speech heading below the list returns "O monstrous" to the Prince. Modern editions follow the Folio emendation; Peto (or sometimes Poins) reads the paper.

The emendation appears unarguable. "Read them" (2.4.510) sounds like a command to someone; it is parallel to "Search his pockets"

(505–06). As Bevington comments in a note to line 516, "The omission of a speech prefix ... before some quoted document to be read or proclaimed is not unusual" (206). The Folio "meddler" is simply spelling out the obvious. Or is he? As A. R. Humphreys remarks in his Arden edition of *1 Henry IV*, the one change that we can be certain of between the first staging of the play and the 1598 quarto was the substitution of names, Falstaff for Oldcastle, Peto for Harvey, Bardolph for Russell. A couple of slips, where the original names still appear in the text or in the speech headings, is evidence that someone went through the text and, in all but those few instances, made the changes. Thus, the absence of a speech heading for the reading of the tavern bill could mean that it had not been read originally by Harvey, for it has not been changed to Peto in Q1. The F1 emendation, according to this argument, would be unwarranted. It would be, even by an admission that Bevington makes: "literary meddling" (101) is his charge against the F1 changes in speech headings in 2.2. "They [the headings in that scene] read like literary meddling, and, in this important detail at least, do not inspire confidence in F1's report of staging or assignment of speeches." Yet Bevington trusts F1 at the end of 2.4. Fredson Bowers, on the other hand, does not; he believes what Q1 presents: "[T]he lack of a speech-prefix before the inventory and before Hal's subsequent speech ... indicates that Hal reads" (194n).

Bowers believes that Q1 represents a textual emendation caused by stage history. He claims that in the original version of the play, Poins was to have been left alone on stage with Hal at the end of the scene, another prank started in picking Falstaff's pocket. Then, according to Bowers, when the play was staged, it was found that the actor playing Poins was needed to take another part in 3.1, and so Peto was called upon to end the scene with Hal. Since it is hard to believe that Peto could read the tavern reckoning, Bowers argues, Q1 made Hal the reader; a proper edition of the play should therefore emend the scene so that Poins is the reader of the bill. Q1, in short, is not a reliable text for the end of 2.4; undoubtedly, erroneously, it does have Hal read.

Among modern editors, only Dover Wilson in the Cambridge text has Poins read the reckoning, although his argument is based on the assumption that the manuscript behind Q1 had the speech prefix *"Po"* for Poins, which was mistaken for *"Pe"* for Peto. (Wilson's argument

makes more sense than it might appear since an italic *e,* which would
be used in a speech heading, looks very like a secretary *o,* which would
be the hand in which most of the text was written, and would be the
ordinary hand that a scribe wrote; it will not explain how the Prince
comes to name Peto in the text of his speech, however.) Moreover, as
Dover Wilson and Bowers point out, the emendation from Peto to Poins
has good precedent. Malone did it; Dr. Johnson applauded it: "What had
Peto done that 'his place should be honourable' or that he should be
trusted with the plot against Falstaff? Poins has the Prince's confidence
and is a man of courage" (qtd. in Wilson 157n). And Bowers concurs:
"Dr. Johnson's instincts were sounder than the present-day veneration
for a theatrically altered text that violates the propriety of character
and of situation as Shakespeare had conceived it. An editor . . . can at
least give back to Hal his proper companion Poins, and keep Peto exclusively where he belongs . . . as a member of Falstaff's party . . . "
(195).

Dover Wilson and Bowers indulge fantasies about restoring Shakespeare's lost original text (so, too, do Gary Taylor and Stanley Wells in
their Oxford edition of the plays, in which "Harvey" appears at the end
of the scene—and as reader of the bill). Bowers's elaborate argument
about stage history and its role in shaping Q1 is quite clearly bent on
saving Hal from being sullied with low companions like Peto; it is
shaped by the royal contempt that can be read in the play. The Petos
of the world, Bowers insists, cannot read without being risible. Shakespeare cannot originally have wanted the Prince to have ended the
scene in his company. Modern editors, on the whole, are willing enough
to leave Peto there, and reading, as he does in F1; but they, too, share
similar suppositions. The Prince must not read. And perhaps the editorial emendation in F1 is a result of the ideological construction of
scenes of reading in the play; rebels read, but royalty do not.

There is one further point in favor of Poins that both Bowers and
Dover Wilson enlist, the Dering manuscript, a composite of both parts
of *Henry IV* put together for a private performance in the early 1620s.[14]
There, Poins shares the stage with Hal at the close of 2.4. But not
because the playscript has some access to Shakespeare's original; in the
editing that Edward Dering performed, the part of Peto has been eliminated from the play entirely. Moreover, in the Dering manuscript, al-

though Poins is there with Hal, no speech heading precedes the tavern bill. Hal, apparently, reads it; the Dering manuscript transcribes Q5, but with an eye to performance (the substitution of Poins for Peto in the scene is clear evidence of that); yet it allows Hal to read the reckoning. The manuscript does not, therefore, support Bowers's argument; it does, however, lend support to Q1.

This moment at the end of 2.4 is then a genuine textual crux, and the editorial problem it represents is fully complicit with the constructions of textuality within the play. Were Hal to read—and to read the reckoning that literalizes the accounting and calculating that marks his scripted being throughout the play—he would have crossed the line into rebel territory. The reckoning he began in his first exchange with Falstaff, reading him as if he were a tavern bill, would be realized literally, the purloined paper in his hand. And the robbing of that pocket would find its echo on the battlefield with Hotspur:

> O Harry, thou hast robbed me of my youth!
> I better brook the loss of brittle life
> Than those proud titles thou hast won of me.
>
> (5.4.76–78)

Not the proud titles, but the mean calculations that keep the body alive, would accrue to Hal in the robbing of Falstaff's pocket. "He fetches breath" (2.4.505) and searches his pockets.

If someone else reads at the end of 2.4, then Hal is protected from script. "What there is else, keep close; we'll read it at more advantage" (515–16). His hands are clean, although the lines could mean that he has read and puts further reading on reserve. The purloined papers are put into another "rebel's" pocket, at hand when the pickpurse demands it, secret otherwise (as script is in the occulted orality of the royal word). Ransacking the corpus of Falstaff, the monstrous body yields paper—rebel text—a reckoning of items consumed and payment due. Food for worms.

*   *   *

In 3.3 the jest comes home, Falstaff producing prodigious lies about what was in his picked pocket. Hal reveals that he knows just what was there, and Falstaff confronts him:

FALSTAFF

... You confess then, you picked my pocket?

PRINCE

It appears so by the story.

(3.3.161–62)

Hal confesses nothing, nor does he produce the paper. Rather, he reproduces it as speech, as the story. The heir apparent deals only in appearances; script has become the trim reckoning of air, a story. Logocentric ideology suppresses the text—history and the instability of the manipulable, deceiving, lying letter that goes under the name of truth. Yet, a moment after this oblique confession, Hal closes the scene with the one clear admission of the order of writing that goes hand in hand with power:

Go bear this letter to Lord John of Lancaster,
To my brother John; this to my Lord of Westmoreland.
Go, Peto, to horse, to horse.

(3.3.186–88)

Notes

1. Garber performs a similar inquiry in " 'Here's nothing writ'." An expanded version of "Ghost Writers" appears in Garber's *Shakespeare's Ghost Writers* (New York: Methuen, 1987). For a recent essay that further analyzes a thematics of textuality in *Richard II*—in ways akin to the exploration undertaken in this essay—see Pye, "Betrayal of the Gaze."

2. For example, Calderwood, *Shakespearean Metadrama* and *Metadrama in Shakespeare's Henriad;* Porter, *The Drama of Speech Acts.* In a number of recent essays, Harry Berger, Jr., has written in opposition to such speech- (and stage-) centered readings of Shakespeare, and in support of a version of textuality congruent with, but not identical to, the argument of this essay. For his theoretical statement, see "Bodies and Texts"; for studies of the issue in the second tetralogy, see "Psychoanalyzing the Shakespeare Text" and "Sneak's Noise."

3. For an incisive investigation of the ideology of Shakespeare's history plays—and the ideological suppositions of the criticism on them, see Holderness.

4. See Grabes, *The Mutable Glass.*

5. Day's manual first appeared in 1586; I quote from the 1599 expanded printing; Fulwood's book first appeared in 1568; I quote from a 1621 reprinting. For the history of the form in England, see Hornbeak and Robertson; for studies of the relationship of

Renaissance letter manuals to classical and medieval traditions, see Gerlo and Clough. Day's manual often translates Francesco Sansovino's *Del Secretario* (Venice, 1565).

6. On the economic metaphors, which I pursue here in their relationship to writing, see the classic New Critical essay by Dorius; cf. Rubinstein.

7. The verbal play in these lines is noted in Bevington's edition of *Henry IV, Part I,* although, in usual eighteenth-century editorial terms, "engross up deeds" is described as a "quibble" on "written legal instruments of purchase" and "brave acts" (229n148).

8. Compare Boethius's commentary on Aristotle, insisting that sound (*vox*) only becomes a word through an act of coin-like impression (qtd. in Shoaf, *Dante, Chaucer, and the Currency of the Word* 9–11).

9. I am grateful to Jeff Rodgers for this point.

10. On the veil of heliotropic truth see also Derrida, "White Mythology." "Facteur" in French also means postman, as Derrida stresses in "Le Facteur de la Verité," his reading of Lacan's seminar on Poe's "The Purloined Letter" in *The Post Card.*

11. On the relationship between Falstaff's catechism and Renaissance treatises on language, see Donawerth, *Shakespeare and the Sixteenth-Century Study of Language* 16.

12. See my "Textual Properties."

13. For a study that attempts this, see Jowett and Taylor, "Sprinklings of Authority," esp. pp. 152–55 for an argument that the "abdication episode" in the Folio may derive from a manuscript rather than from Q5, and pp. 194–98 for an argument that F1 does not offer the original scene expunged from Q1 but a later revision. Jowett and Taylor argue against the usual editorial estimation of F1 (this also extends to the text of *1 Henry IV,* as Taylor argues in "The Shrinking Compositor A"), but they are so intent on proving its value against Q1 that they ignore the real editorial problem of the "abdication episode"; although it appears in Q4 and Q5, texts which otherwise have no authority, those first printings of the scene differ from F1. Those differences cannot be attributed to corruptions of the text since they are the first versions of the scene we have. Their status is problematic, to say the least; Jowett and Taylor proceed as if the only version of the "abdication episode" we have is the one in F1. What complicates their argument is the fact that lines that they represent as only to be found in F1 are also found in Q4. Equally problematic, and symptomatic of the treatment of the episode, is the editorial principle announced by Matthew W. Black in the Penguin edition; Q4 is a printing that has a "faulty copy" behind it, he claims; nevertheless "many modern editions, including the present one, prefer some thirteen fourth-quarto readings" (636).

14. See the facsimile and transcription by Williams and Evans.

Works Cited

Allen, Michael J. B., and Kenneth Muir, eds. *Shakespeare's Plays in Quarto.* Berkeley: U of California P, 1981.

Berger, Harry, Jr. "Bodies and Texts." *Representations* 17 (1987): 144–66.

———. "Psychoanalyzing the Shakespeare Text: The First Three Scenes of the *Henriad.*"

Shakespeare and the Question of Theory. Ed. Patricia Parker and Geoffrey Hartman. New York: Methuen, 1985. 210–29.

———. "Sneak's Noise or Rumor and Detextualization in *2 Henry IV.*" *Kenyon Review* ns 6.4 (1984): 58–78.

Bevington, David, ed. *Henry IV, Part I.* The Oxford Shakespeare. Oxford: Clarendon, 1987.

Bowers, Fredson. "Establishing Shakespeare's Text: Poins and Peto in *1 Henry IV.*" *Studies in Bibliography* 34 (1981): 189–98.

Calderwood, James L. *Metadrama in Shakespeare's Henriad: Richard II to Henry V.* Berkeley: U of California P, 1979.

———. *Shakespearean Metadrama.* Minneapolis: U of Minnesota P, 1971.

Clough, Cecil H. "The Cult of Antiquity: Letters and Letter Collections." *Cultural Aspects of the Italian Renaissance.* Ed. Cecil H. Clough. Manchester: Manchester UP, 1976. 33–67.

Day, Angel. *The English Secretorie.* London, 1599.

Derrida, Jacques. *Of Grammatology.* Trans. Gayatri Chakravorty Spivak. Baltimore: Johns Hopkins UP, 1976.

———. *The Post Card: From Socrates to Freud and Beyond.* Trans. Alan Bass. Chicago: U of Chicago P, 1987.

———. "Scribble (writing-power)." *Yale French Studies* 58 (1979): 117–47.

———. "White Mythology: Metaphor in the Text of Philosophy." *Margins of Philosophy.* Trans. Alan Bass. Chicago: U of Chicago P, 1982.

Donawerth, Jane. *Shakespeare and the Sixteenth-Century Study of Language.* Urbana: U of Illinois P, 1984.

Dorius, R. J. "A Little More than a Little." *Shakespeare Quarterly* 11 (1960): 13–26.

Garber, Marjorie. " 'Here's nothing writ': Scribe, Script, and Circumscription in Marlowe's Plays." *Theatre Journal* 36 (1984): 301–20.

———. "Shakespeare's Ghost Writers." *Cannibals, Witches, and Divorce: Estranging the Renaissance.* Ed. Marjorie Garber. Baltimore: Johns Hopkins UP, 1987. 122–46.

Gerlo, A. "The *Opus de Conscribendis Epistolis* of Erasmus and the Tradition of the *Ars Epistolica.*" *Classical Influences on European Culture, A.D. 500–1500.* Ed. R. R. Bolgar. Cambridge: Cambridge UP, 1971. 103–14.

Goldberg, Jonathan. "Textual Properties." *Shakespeare Quarterly* 37 (1986): 213–17.

Grabes, Herbert. *The Mutable Glass: Mirror-Imagery in Titles and Texts of the Middle Ages and the English Renaissance.* Trans. Gordon Collier. Cambridge: Cambridge UP, 1982.

Greenblatt, Stephen. "Invisible Bullets: Renaissance Authority and Its Subversion, *Henry IV* and *Henry V.*" *Political Shakespeare: New Essays in Cultural Materialism.* Ed. Jonathan Dollimore and Alan Sinfield. Ithaca: Cornell UP, 1985. 18–47.

Hawkes, Terence. *Shakespeare's Talking Animals: Language and Drama in Society.* London: Arnold, 1973.

Holderness, Graham. *Shakespeare's History.* New York: St. Martin's, 1985.

Holinshed, Raphael. *Holinshed's Chronicles.* Ed. R. S. Wallace and Alma Hansen. Oxford: Clarendon, 1923.

Hornbeak, Katherine Gee. "The Complete Letter Writer in English: 1568–1800." *Smith College Studies in Modern Languages* 15 (1934): i–xii, 1–150.

Humphreys, A. R., ed. *King Henry IV, Part 1.* The Arden Shakespeare. New York: Methuen, 1974.

Jowett, John, and Gary Taylor. "Sprinklings of Authority: The Folio Text of *Richard II.*" *Studies in Bibliography* 38 (1985): 151–200.

Porter, Joseph. *The Drama of Speech Acts: Shakespeare's Lancastrian Tetralogy.* Berkeley: U of California P, 1979.

Pye, Christopher. "The Betrayal of the Gaze: Theatricality and Power in Shakespeare's *Richard II.*" *ELH* 55 (1988): 575–98.

Robertson, Jean. *The Art of Letter Writing: An Essay on the Handbooks Published in England during the Sixteenth and Seventeenth Centuries.* Liverpool: UP of Liverpool, 1943.

Rubinstein, E. "*1 Henry IV:* The Metaphors of Liability." *Studies in English Literature, 1500–1900* 10 (1970): 287–95.

Shakespeare, William. *The Complete Works.* Alfred Harbage, gen. ed. The Pelican Text Revised. Baltimore: Penguin, 1969.

Shoaf, R. A. *Dante, Chaucer, and the Currency of the Word: Money, Images, and Reference in Late Medieval Poetry.* Norman, Ok.: Pilgrim, 1983.

Taylor, Gary. "The Shrinking Compositor A of the Shakespeare First Folio." *Studies in Bibliography* 34 (1981): 96–117.

Wells, Stanley, and Gary Taylor, gen. eds. *William Shakespeare: The Complete Works.* The Oxford Shakespeare. Oxford: Clarendon, 1986.

Williams, George Walton, and Gwynne Blakemore Evans, eds. *The History of King Henry the Fourth, as Revised by Sir Edward Dering, Bart.* Charlottesville: UP of Virginia, 1974.

Wilson, John Dover, ed. *The First Part of the History of Henry IV.* Cambridge: Cambridge UP, 1958.

Back by Popular Demand:
The Two Versions of Henry V

ANNABEL PATTERSON

WHETHER OR NOT perceived as the last of Shakespeare's English histories, *Henry V* puts unusual strain on a historical understanding of the project that began with *Henry VI* and may or may not find its coda in *Henry VIII*. From the "cobwebs of topical allusion which the ahistorical and formalizing reader attempts desperately to brush away" (Jameson 34) we must reach to the largest and most challenging question of what a historical understanding itself might be, then and now; and the enterprise requires our juggling at least three meanings of "history" as a category of thought: the fifteenth-century history that Shakespeare took over from Holinshed and others and rewrote to his own specifications; the events in which he and his theater were environmentally situated in the 1590s and to some extent embroiled; and the subsequent history of the play's reception and interpretation, with which, for reasons which will become apparent, it is prudent to begin.

This third, critical history is sharply conflictual. More strikingly than almost any other play of Shakespeare's, and certainly more than any other "history," *Henry V* has generated accounts of itself that fall simply, even crudely, on either side of the line that divides belief from skep-

29

ticism, idealism from cynicism, or, in contemporary parlance, legiti-
mation from subversion. The topics, concepts, or institutions to which
such attitudes are directed are, manifestly, monarchy (of a certain populist style), nationalism, and militarism; and while it is usually stated
or implied that Shakespeare himself held or projected the attitudes that
the play supposedly articulates, it is often to be suspected that criticism, itself driven by historical imperatives, finds what it needs to in
the play by selective foregroundings and suppressions. The most extreme example of the idealizing view, the film directed by Sir Laurence
Olivier, was premiered in November 1944 in the context of the battle
of Britain and dedicated to the Commandos and Airborne Troops of
Great Britain, "the spirit of whose ancestors it has been humbly attempted to recapture" (Garrett, Hardison, and Gelfman 40). The Olivier film was contemporary, therefore, with E. M. W. Tillyard's study of
the history plays, closely followed, in 1947, by Lily B. Campbell's, which
to different degrees represented *Henry V* as the climax (successful or
unsuccessful) of Shakespeare's own version of the Tudor myth, with
Henry himself as Elizabeth's prototype.[1] As the nationalism of these
projects was implicit (compared to Olivier's production), so their influence was probably greater. Conversely, the age of nuclear deterrence
and of ethically ambiguous geopolitical alliances has produced a criticism, both in England and in the United States, that looks rather at the
tensions and contradictions in the Elizabethan ideology of ideal ruler,
unified state, and providential history.[2] And over the divide between
the idealist and skeptical positions is sometimes erected the conceptual
bridge of Shakespeare's supposed impartiality. As Anne Barton put it,
in the context of analyzing the tone of the famous night scene before
Agincourt, the dramatist seems "determined to stress the equivalence
of mutually exclusive views of a particular complex of historical events"
(102).

The critical record, then, highlights the problem of intentionality,
which will not be made to disappear by our focusing instead on the
intentions of Shakespeare's readers; and any attempt to recuperate
Shakespeare's own intentions must today grapple with the status of the
texts that are all we have to work with. Like almost everyone else,
Barton was looking at the Folio, which can possibly sustain the hypothesis of ideological confusion or deliberate ambiguity; whereas the

theses of Campbell and Tillyard could be better supported by *The Cronicle History of Henry the fift,* the first quarto version, which has long been ruled out of interpretive account by Shakespearean bibliographers, and placed in the evaluative category of the "bad quartos," that is to say, beyond interpretive reach.[3] Though less textually unstable than *Hamlet* or *King Lear,* where the quarto texts have strong claims for consideration, *Henry V* therefore presents a unique challenge to the new textual studies, since its publication history is ineluctably connected to the major critical disagreements over the play's meaning and cultural function.

For the first quarto version is not only shorter than the Folio but strikingly *different* from it. Among the most striking absences in the quarto are all five Choruses and the final Epilogue; hence, in the fifth Chorus, the non-appearance of the allusion to Essex's anticipated return from Ireland, which Gary Taylor has called "the only explicit, extradramatic, incontestable reference to a contemporary event anywhere in the canon" (*Henry V* 7); and with no epilogue, there is no final letdown, no admission that the legendary victory at Agincourt accomplished nothing, since in the following reign the regents for Henry VI "lost France, and made his England bleed" (Epi. 12; *Folio* 449, throughline-number [TLN] 3379). These last lines, which subsume the heroic moment in the recursive patterns of history, were also excised from the Olivier production, which otherwise retained most of the Choruses;[4] and even in 1623 the Folio arrangement of the English histories by chronology of reign rather than of composition submerges the skeptical effect and makes Henry the center rather than the last, inconclusive statement of the second tetralogy.

Also missing from the quarto is act 1, scene 1, where the bishops cynically discuss how they are to motivate the war and distract the House of Commons from their plan to reclaim ecclesiastical property; the Hostess's claim in 2.1 that Falstaff is dying because "The King has killed his heart"; almost all of the Harfleur episode, including the famous "Once more unto the breach" speech by Henry and most of his threats of violence upon the besieged citizens; much of the material in the scene before the battle of Agincourt, *especially* Henry's closing soliloquy on the hardships of kingship; several scenes in the French camp; all of Burgundy's speech on the damages suffered by France in the war; and much of the wooing scene between Kate and Henry. These differences are striking enough to demand serious interrogation, *especially* since there is nothing in the stage-historical records to refute the quarto's claim that it represents the play as it was "sundry times" acted by the Chamberlain's Company. It is generally assumed that the Folio text represents the acting version, and that, on the basis of choric references to staging, especially to the "wooden O" of the fifth Chorus, it was designed for the new Globe theater built in 1599; but it is equally assumed in other instances (such as *Hamlet*) that the Folio text was sometimes or always abridged in actual performance. We simply do not know, in fact, what the performative version of *Henry V* was like; and I shall argue that the quarto may very well be closer than the Folio to what the London audiences actually saw on the stage at the absolute turn of the century.

There are famous mysteries in the records of the quarto's production. The Stationers' Register for August 4, 1600, lists "Henry the ffift, a book to be staied," a phrase that could refer either to external restraint or to the internal workings of the publishers' trade. Most likely, given the innocuous group of plays which shared the staying order, it was merely what Peter Blayney has called a conditional entry, made in the absence of a warden to give the required signature. At any rate, by August 14 another entry records the transfer of an already-printed "historye of Henry Vth with the battell of Agencourt" to Thomas Pavier, who reprinted it in 1602. The first quarto, printed by Thomas Creede for Thomas Millington and John Busby, not only asserted its claim to be the version "sundry times played" by the Chamberlain's Men, but also counted for its sales upon public recognition of one of the play's comic characters. On its title page Henry himself and "his battell fought at Agin Court" appear "Together with Auntient Pistol" (524).

If the sixteenth-century story of the quarto's production is elliptical, its subsequent history has been massively obfuscated by the theory of the "bad quartos," a conception introduced in 1909 by A. W. Pollard, who took at face value the Folio editors' natural wish to devalue preceding editions, and especially their reference to "stolne, and surreptitious copies, maimed, and deformed by the frauds and stealthes of iniurious impostors, that exposed them" (A3r; *Folio* 7). A year later W. W. Greg introduced a new principle to support Pollard's—memorial reconstruction, or dictation from memory by one or more actors complicit with a piratical printer.[5] To the notion of an unreliable text, derived ultimately from the Folio's success in establishing its own authority, was therefore added the moral opprobrium associated with theft and treachery. These assumptions spread easily into subjective accounts of the *quality* of the differences observed, with the Folio versions of the plays, almost invariably, being designated as "artistically" superior, and they are only now beginning to be structurally undermined. In particular, the ethical issue would seem to have been resolved by a more skeptical view of the claims made by John Heminges and Henry Condell in promoting their own edition, and by Peter Blayney's persuasive attack on the piracy thesis. Blayney draws our attention to Humphrey Moseley's own advertisement for the Beaumont and Fletcher Folio of 1647, where, in the course of explaining why he has taken the trouble to acquire authorial manuscripts, he witnesses to an entirely reputable method of transmitting abridged playtexts to potential publishers:

When these Comedies and Tragedies were presented on the stage, the actors omitted some scenes and passages (with the author's consent) as occasion led them; and when private friends desired a copy, they then (and justly too) transcribed what they acted.

The parentheses here, "with the author's consent" and "justly too," speak to a theatrical practice of communal ownership of acting versions, and the open exchange, commercial or otherwise, of transcriptions made by the actors of those versions.

Memorial reconstruction may still be needed to explain those parts of a quarto text (fewer than has been claimed) which are patently so garbled as to resist even this new sociology of the theater, which allows for very considerable modification during production; but what this new theory does resolve unambiguously is an aspect of textual instability—the omission of whole scenes or large blocks of material—that was never adequately accounted for by adducing the bad memories of actors for parts other than their own. In the case of *Henry V,* the omitted materials are so crucial to the play's meaning and theatrical self-definition that hints have gradually emerged of the need for additional explanations. In 1954 John Walter, in the Arden edition of *Henry V,* defined the quarto as a memorial reconstruction based on the memory of the actors taking the parts of Exeter and Gower. But he also implied additional causes for its divergences from the Folio: "Certain omissions show that the play had been cut for compression, possibly for censorship, and to reduce the number of actors' parts. Generally there is a lowering of pitch, a substitution of cliché and the common currency of daily speech for the more heightened style of the Folio. In brief, the Q version may well be based on a cut form of the play used by the company for a reduced cast on tour in the provinces" (xxxix). There are at least three hypotheses here, each implying intention—the aesthetic ("cut for compression"), the political ("cut . . . possibly for censorship") and the socioeconomic ("cut . . . for a reduced cast on tour in the provinces")—which themselves may conceivably not be mutually exclusive, but which nevertheless derive from quite different critical assumptions and agendas; and poised uncertainly between them (by virtue of that floating "generally") is the inference that the style of the quarto version is more popular, in the sense of being *lower* and more *common* than the Folio. Looking backwards, and in one salient instance forwards, we can see where these hypotheses came from, and assess their usefulness to the pursuit of Shakespeare's intentions.

Three of the four concepts encapsulated by Walter were in fact developed simultaneously, by Alfred Hart in 1942. Seeking a new theory of the "bad quartos" that would take better account of major omissions, Hart argued at length that they were memorial reconstructions of *previous abridgments* of the plays prepared by Shakespeare's own company in accordance with theatrical experience. The differences, Hart thought, were often structurally (theatrically) intelligent but linguistically impoverished. The professional abridger "knew his audience loved an interesting story, packed with plenty of action and told in simple language, and rid the play of similes, amplificatory passages, platitudes, philosophic reflections, repetition, classical commonplaces, and literary ornament" (130). But even the best of the "bad quartos" (and *Henry V* is one of the best) reveal reportorial incompetence incompatible with the work of "an educated man":

Most of these [divergent] passages share certain characteristics in common— little elevation of thought, a certain coarseness verging on vulgarity, almost complete lack of fancy or imagination, dull, pedestrian and irregular verse, poor and overworked vocabulary, frequent errors in grammar and syntax, and a primitive type of sentence-construction. King, queen, cardinal, duchess, peer, soldier, lover, courtier, artisan, peasant, servant and child all speak alike.... Essentially each of these and many other speeches exhibit all the marks of garrulous illiteracy struggling amidst a maze of words to express what had been learnt or heard or recited or seen on the stage. (104)

From the newly self-conscious posture that a critic in the 1980s is privileged to adopt, one can see how deeply Hart's view of the "bad quartos" has collated the moralism of his predecessors in the field of bibliography with a class consciousness that distinguishes the "educated" text (one that endorses social hierarchies) from the "illiterate" reproduction that blurs them.

Hart's admitted concern, however, was to refute an alternative hypothesis to that of memorial reconstruction, to rescue Shakespeare from the possible charge of having begun with the "bad quartos," as first drafts, and expanded them into the Folio texts. From this agenda derive not only the contradictions between Hart's sense of good theater and good writing, but also an evolutionary struggle between his wished-for separation of Shakespeare from "badness" and the knowledge that within the theatrical practice of the Chamberlain's Men such separation was unlikely. Hart actually imagines a scene in which Shakespeare, having previously, "on fire with passion and emotions . . . filled *Hamlet* with 1,600 lines of long speeches," later heard them read aloud. He would then, Hart felt, "have shaken his head in critical disapproval and accepted the decision of his fellows to declaim less than a half of these speeches on the stage" (168). In this scenario, Shakespeare collaborates in the act of abridgment at least to the point of authorizing major cuts, a very different hypothesis, obviously, from the notion that they lapsed because minor actors could not remember them; and the notion of Shakespeare's "critical disapproval" of his own longer first draft runs counter to Hart's own critical disapproval of the "bad quartos" in general. And there is a still deeper incompatibility between the scenario of artistic collaboration between playwright and company in preparing the author's manuscript for actual production (a scenario which may now seem more plausible as the notion of the ideal, stable text recedes) and what Hart reveals elsewhere of his literary value system. "Every

scholar fashions for himself," he concluded, "a mental picture of the
master-poet at work, and to it subconsciously refers all that he thinks
or reads of him and his plays" (447). True; and the mental picture Hart
had formed, and that governed his theory of the "bad quartos," was of
a man incapable of revision, of his own work or another's. It is no
coincidence that Hart chooses as his peroration a passage from *A Midsummer Night's Dream* that implictly conflates Shakespeare with The-
seus and the Thesean definition of the artist:

> The Poets eye in a fine frenzy rolling, doth glance
> From heaven to earth, from earth to heaven.
> And as imagination bodies forth the forms of things
> Unknowne; the Poets pen turnes them to shapes,
> And gives to aire nothing, a locall habitation
> And a name.
>
> (5.1.12–17; *Folio* 177, TLN 1804–09)

With unconscious irony, Hart sets side by side Ben Jonson's neoclassical
assertion that Shakespeare "was not of an age, but for all time," that is
to say, unchangeable, with a passage from the Folio that, by the standards of later editors, is hopelessly misaligned and, in the wisdom of
time's passage, usually emended.

If Hart's confusions mark the transition from a Romantic aesthetics
of genius to a modern sociology of the theater, Walter's suggestion of
censorship as a motive for the quarto's reductions derives from a different set of critical concerns. In 1928, Evelyn May Albright argued
that the Folio "represents the text of a play intended for use on a
special occasion at the Globe before an audience of statesmen and
courtiers at the critical moment preceding the return of Essex from
Ireland in the autumn of 1599" ("Folio Version" 756). The Folio, therefore, is read as being broadly supportive of Essex and his policies,
whereas the quarto, intended for publication, was "shorn of the most
significant personal and political references" (753). She thus keyed the
play into a long and intemperate argument between herself and Ray
Heffner on the extent to which Shakespeare's work on English history
had any relation to the Essex conspiracy. At the heart of this debate is
one of the most celebrated (and most fully documented) exhibits of

performance history. I refer to the special production, on the eve of the earl of Essex's rebellion, of "the play ... of Kyng Harry the iiijth, and of the kylling of Kyng Richard the second played by the L. Chamberlen's players."[6] This episode, with its remarkable focus on Shakespeare's company and the use of an English history play, whether or not *Richard II,* for overtly political purposes, has long been a test of historicist criticism of Shakespeare. The Albright/Heffner controversy, marked by its quarrelsome tone and an obsessive focus on detail at the expense of procedural clarity, was characteristic of the old historicism at its worst; yet there is a mass of useful data which can be rescued from those quarrels and employed to broader effect. In contrast, New Historical critics have tended to focus on this event as proof that cultural artifacts do not passively reflect but actively construct their environment; yet such arguments tend to dead-end at the anecdote of Elizabeth's comment to William Lambarde, "I am Richard II, know ye not that," while occluding the complex of events that led up to the fateful performance, and other cultural calibrations of those events. They miss, therefore, an opportunity to explore the extraordinary environment created for and by the public theater at the precise moment on which Albright had focused, namely the "critical moment preceding the return of Essex from Ireland in the autumn of 1599," when we know (thanks to the allusion) that the play in its Folio version must have been constructed, and to which, in the Folio version, it explicitly drew its audience's attention.[7]

We will need to return to the fifth Chorus and the autumn of 1599. But there is another, more recent phase in the critical history of the texts of *Henry V* that must first be described and then, to some extent, contested. For Hart's conclusions were eventually recruited by Gary Taylor to the services of the new textual criticism of Shakespeare, which in the 1970s has sought to demonstrate that at least some of the "bad quartos" represent alternative *versions* of their plays, with the divergences explicable as authorial revision. For *Henry V,* however, Gary Taylor posited a more restricted theory, or rather developed one whose prior existence is reflected in Walter's reference to a "cut form of the play used by the company for a reduced cast on tour in the provinces" (xxxix). In *Three Studies in the Text of* Henry V, Taylor recalled Hart's proposal that the quarto represents a memorial reconstruction of a *previous* abridgment,[8] without specifying by whom that abridgment was likely to have been made (Wells and Taylor 75–111). Inspired, perhaps, by Hart's passing observation that this is also the quarto with "heavier reductions of the cast" (429) than any other, amounting to the disappearance of thirteen speaking characters (an observation which Hart subsumed under the category of blunder) Taylor developed a strenuous argument that abridgment was required not by the attention span of the London audiences but by the economic constraints on a company traveling (like the tragedians in *Hamlet*) in the less remunerative provincial towns.

Despite its semi-adoption by Walter in the Arden edition and subsequent reappearance in Taylor's own single-volume edition of *Henry V* in the new Oxford series, there are problems with this hypothesis. The fact of the omission of the Choruses seems too striking, in its reformation or deformation of the play's tone, genre, and general address to the audience, to be adequately explained by the premise that, once casting exigencies ruled, the Chorus could not be played by any of the other parts, who all appear in too close proximity for him to change costumes.[9] But more importantly, Taylor himself admits that casting difficulties cannot explain the omission of the very first scene, which throws such a cynical light on the motives for the war against France (*Three Studies* 80), or of the Jamy and MacMorris episode, which was either "omitted to shorten the play or censored, because of King James's recently expressed irritation at dramatic ridicule of the Scots" (85). Taylor also admits that the substitution of Clarence for Bedford "has nothing to do with limitations of cast, and the reason for the change can only be aesthetic" (101); that the substitution of Bourbon for the Dauphin is not only an aesthetic improvement, but must have antedated the abridgment, and was therefore made by Shakespeare himself; and that some of the omissions in the Harfleur scene are evidence of "deliberate and coherent" theatrical cutting "in the interests of simplifying the play into patriotism" (130). This mixed reasoning, invoked whenever the primary hypothesis cannot stand the test of its own rules of application, is a useful witness to what, I believe, should be a cardinal rule governing the *interpretation* of textual divergences between quartos and folios; namely, that no single hypothesis is likely to be able to explain all the instances of textual divergence; and that it is better to admit this in advance than be forced to introduce exceptions that shake the primary hypothesis at its roots.

Even more telling is Taylor's casual suggestion that the abridgment of the Harfleur episode indicates an intention to simplify the play "into patriotism." For by this standard we might *also* comprehend the quarto's omission of the cynical first scene with the bishops that undermines their case for the "just war" against France; Burgundy's missing lament for the despoliation of the French countryside, for which Holinshed provides no mandate; and especially the radical alterations in the scene most crucial to Henry's characterization, the disguised visit to the common soldiers in the night before Agincourt. As Taylor himself observes, the Folio creates a striking contrast between the "populist morale-building walk" *described* by the Chorus and what we actually see. Henry makes "no attempt to cheer his soldier," but rather picks a fight with Pistol, enters the conversation with Bates and Williams disingenuously, putting them at a serious disadvantage in the discussion of the limits of military loyalty and the rectitude of the cause for which they fight, and then "launches into a long and bitter soliloquy on the agony of his own condition, disregarding the fate of the army" (88). In the quarto text, bereft of the contrast between the idealized choric view of the occasion and its actual representation, the king's disguise loses some of its disingenuity, while without the closing soliloquy the scene concludes with "good-natured Henry joking with his men, as they walk away." "What," Taylor asks, "was the impetus behind this series of alterations?" (90). Given his own thesis, he is forced to propose that they were triggered by the prior decision to omit the Chorus for reasons of casting economy. We might rather feel that Taylor's brilliant analysis here of the changes requires another conclusion altogether, one that makes primary and purposive the desire to simplify the character of Henry for a certain type of audience, performance or readership. While Taylor is certainly aware that no single bibliographical explanation is likely to assume holistic force, there are enough exceptions here to the primary hypothesis—that abridgment was set in motion by casting exigencies—to shake the entire argument at its foundation.

In Taylor's edition of *Henry V* the casting hypothesis remains unqualified, except by the suggestion that "some of [the quarto's] omissions almost certainly derive from the practice of Shakespeare's own

London company, and therefore arguably from Shakespeare himself"
(23). The casual inference about simplification in the direction of patriotism, originally attached merely to the Harfleur episode, however,
becomes a statement linking a whole series of omissions whose effect,
Taylor now sees, "is to remove almost every difficulty in the way of an
unambiguously patriotic interpretation of Henry and his war" (12). Yet
the conflict between this perceived pattern of abridgment and its supposed motives—reducing the cast—is hereby exacerbated; and the textual theory, deriving from an earlier stage of Taylor's thinking, is never
synchronized with the new, more plausible account of the play as a
whole that this edition offers. Indeed, those adaptations that Taylor
associates with an effort to make it "more uncomplicatedly patriotic"
are designated the least textually authoritative (23), whereas those,
like the quarto substitution of Bourbon, which Taylor accepts on *qualitative* grounds, are actually incorporated, in defiance of editorial precedent, into his own Oxford edition.

As Taylor's struggles with the evidence reveal, bibliographical arguments, when isolated from historical or cultural criticism, will tend,
when the going gets tough, to fall back on subjective standards of value.
The resistance of the textual evidence to holistic solution suggests, at
the least, that the quarto/Folio relationships are greatly more interesting, more demanding of procedural cautions, and more intellectually
challenging in the *range* of explanatory categories they seem to invoke,
than bibliography has so far been able to accommodate. Once one
accepts the thesis that the quarto text represents a theatrical abridgment, which has suffered some textual garbling in its passage from
promptbook to printed text, it may fairly be asked what motivated *this*
abridgment, these particular omissions. Hart proposed dramatic
compression for reasons both pragmatic (restricting the performance
time) and dramatic (eliminating tedious ornaments and speeches). Taylor, at various stages of his thinking, proposed casting exigencies, with
occasional minor instances of possible censorship, authorial second
thoughts (in the treatment of Bourbon and the Dauphin), and nonau-
thorial, inauthentic simplification into patriotism. In my view, this last
theory explains the greatest number of the most significant divergences, with two provisos. The first is that it too cannot be assigned
holistic explanatory force. It cannot, for instance, explain the removal

of the Chorus, whose voice might itself be thought to embody the essence of an idealizing, unquestioning nationalism, whose silencing would seem to work in the opposite direction.

The second proviso is that we abandon as misdirected the Hart/Taylor assumption that Shakespeare had no hand in the abridgment. This protective impulse derives from the stigma attached to the "bad quarto" hypothesis, and can now be abandoned. Shakespeare's status as a writer is scarcely endangered if, for example, we posit that the abridgment was a tactical retreat from one kind of play to another, from a complex historiography that might have been misunderstood to a symbolic enactment of nationalist fervor. In the next stage of the argument I focus on the circumstances that plausibly would have dictated such a retreat, relocating the relationship between quarto and Folio in their larger, mutual relationship to events, persons, and cultural practices.

II

This environment included the practice of writing and rewriting history, in whatever genre. Historiography, in the sixteenth and early seventeenth century, was no academic discipline but a matter of public interest, both in the sense that the material of English history was popular material for the emergent national theater, and because (for a set of reasons which included this same popular appeal) the government regarded English historical materials as subject to its own control. Witnesses to this attitude are:

1. The mid-sixteenth-century *Mirror for Magistrates,* a collection of lugubrious tales of prominent historical figures who came to a bad end during the same period (the fifteenth century) that Shakespeare's histories themselves encompassed. When the *Mirror* appeared in 1559, at the opening of Elizabeth's reign, its preface pointed out that "The wurke was begun, & part of it printed .iiii yeare agoe, but hyndred by the lord Chauncellor that then was" (8).

2. The censorship of the 1587 edition of Holinshed's *Chronicle,* especially in those sections which dealt with Scottish history and reflected the semi-republican influence of George Buchanan (Donno).

3. The inspection by Sir Edmund Tilney, Master of the Revels, of the manuscript of *Sir Thomas More,* and his marginal instructions to the

company, whichever it was, to "Leave out ye insurrection wholy & ye cause theroff & begin wt Sr Tho: More att ye mayors session wt a reportt afterwards off his good servic don being Shrive off London uppon a mutiny agaynst ye Lumbards. Only by a shortt reportt & nott otherwise att your own perrilles."[10]

4. The publication of Shakespeare's *Richard II,* first and second quartos, in 1597 and 1598, with the deposition scene removed.

5. The scandal over Sir John Hayward's *History of Henry IV,* which was published in February 1599, with a dedication to the earl of Essex. Three weeks later the archbishop of Canterbury ordered the dedication to Essex cut out. At Easter Hayward published a second edition with an "Epistle apologetical," which at Whitsun was called in and burned, while Hayward was confined to the Tower.

6. The Bishops' Order of June 1, 1599, which included, along with its prohibition of satire, the injunction that "noe English historyes be printed excepte they bee allowed by some of her maiesties privie Counsell."

This pattern of official surveillance continued into James's reign. When Fulke Greville wished to write a history of Elizabeth's reign, he was prevented by Cecil from getting access to the necessary documents, on the grounds that he might "deliver many things done in that time, which might perchance be construed to the prejudice of this" (Greville 239). Sir Walter Ralegh's *History of the World,* which had been begun under Prince Henry's patronage, was published in 1614 after the prince's death while Ralegh was in the Tower on a charge of treason, and promptly called in by James (Racin; Tennenhouse). Ralegh's *History* suffered both from the vagaries of patronage and the overdetermined hermeneutics that particularly affected historians.[11] For underlying the official scrutiny of historiography, which included, of course, the possibility of commissioning histories or inducing historians to serve the agendas of particular monarchs, was the concern that the public appetite for knowledge of the past should be satisfied only by such *versions* of history, official history, that the government could itself regard with complacence.

The question raised, then, by Shakespeare's English history plays in general, and by *Henry V* in particular, is whether they do, as Tillyard, Campbell, and others assumed, belong in the category, if not of official history, at least of such historiography as could be reckoned supportive of the system and the dominant ideology. It is not enough simply to dismiss these critics as naively mistaking an official ideology for a "world view" shared by the entire society. I have elsewhere suggested that any broad general notion of the hegemonic, especially as it applies to the theater, needs to register more subtle distinctions, such as the variant positions on theater's usefulness to the government expressed by Montaigne, Heywood, and Davenant (Patterson). But we need here additionally to register both the special constraints under which *history* plays operated, and the indeterminacy of the materials—earlier English history and its historiographical presence in the culture—on which Shakespeare chose to focus for the last decade of the sixteenth century. It is not always recognized that, by basing his plays on the 1587 edition of Holinshed's *Chronicle,* Shakespeare must necessarily have observed a historiographical shift away from providential and dynastic history toward something at least more open-ended. In 1548 the title page of Hall's *Chronicle* had been able to read the Wars of the Roses as an essay on "union," and the dynastic struggles between different stems of Edward III's family tree as culminating naturally in Henry VIII, "the indubitable flower and very heir of the said lineage." In 1580, Stow's *Chronicles,* dedicated to the earl of Leicester, presented history to the "gentle Reader" as a "discouragement of unnaturall subjects from wicked treasons, pernitious rebellions, and damnable doctrines" (iiiir), and fifteenth-century history, in particular, as a design (featured in an ornamental frontispiece) in which Elizabeth replaces Henry as "the indubitable flower . . . of the said lineage," placed symmetrically above the stem that went nowhere, representing Richard II. But already by 1580, and certainly by the 1590s, when Shakespeare turned to Holinshed for his account of the fifteenth century, the most obvious lesson offered by the English chronicles was that they continually invoked their own supplementarity. History did not stop where one would like it to; worse, it would continue when the Tudor dynasty, for want of a lineal descendant from Elizabeth, would itself be cut off like the stem descending from Richard.

This fact alone is sharply registered by Shakespeare in the Folio epilogue to *Henry V,* where the choric effort to delineate the reign an epic success succumbs to history's resistance to closure:

Thus farre, with rough, and all-unable Pen,
Our bending Author hath pursu'd the story . . . .
(*Folio* 449, TLN 3368–69; italics added)

But it was not only in its lost capacity for closure that English history
exuded anxiety. The 1587 edition of Holinshed, which continued the
story through Elizabeth's reign to the end of 1586, is a calendar of
woes. It foregrounds natural disasters, local crimes and their punishment, instances of treason and their punishment, leading ineluctably to
the Babington Plot and the hideous execution of the conspirators,
whose complicity with Mary Queen of Scots leads to *her* trial and
condemnation. The supplement thus reveals a design, if not a desire,
for a downbeat ending, a dying fall. And as earlier sections of Holinshed
had incorporated the poems recited at formal entertainments for Elizabeth, these later chapters include the verse elegies for Sir Henry Sidney, proleptically standing also for his son, who before he died at Zutphen
had served as a focus of national hope and expectation; and, on a more
sinister note, the poem known as "Tichborne's elegy," written by one
of the Babington plotters in the Tower, recently recuperated as one of
the most authentic and powerful of Renaissance poems on death (Stein
76–83). Supporting the extensive moralization against "malcontents"
is, as one would expect, an organicist description of the English state,
stressing the *natural* principle of community and collaboration in the
animal kingdom, where all creatures can be observed "seeking after
fellowship of like with like to live together" (Holinshed 910), though
each of the animal species cited, including, of course, the bee, has its
own natural king. Yet undermining this appeal to Nature are two cruel
fables, the first attributed to Babington himself, comparing the law to
a shepherd who, in order to control his flock, killed a sheep a day in
full view of the others; the second, a dramatic version of the Aesopian
fable of the *Frogs Desiring a King,* is presented by the chronicler as
"A prettie apolog allusorie to the present case of malcontents." Its overt
message is, not surprisingly, "to be content when we are well, and to
make much of good queene Elizabeth, by whom we enjoie life and
libertie" (Holinshed 922). Its uncontrollable content, as the frogs are
devoured by the stork, was something entirely different: "(Will they,
nill they) the herne should rule over them."[12] Holinshed, then, marked
a stage in the development of English historiography that was already

marked by stress, that already, in today's parlance, revealed the cracks in the dominant ideology; and particularly by admitting the contrast between organicist images of orderly "natural" polities and those raw emblems of power and powerlessness that the fable tradition provided, this later chronicle should warn against any naive reading of the famous beehive speech in *Henry V* as an unproblematic key to the "Elizabethan world picture."

III

Late Elizabethan historiography, then, having discovered providential history, had difficulty in preventing it from becoming rebarbative. But there was one phase of earlier English history that, as Sir John Hayward discovered, was a particularly dangerous one for the historian to explore, especially if, as Hayward also discovered, he keyed his version of fifteenth-century history into current affairs. By dedicating his *History of Henry IV* to the earl of Essex, Hayward indicated, intentionally or unintentionally, a connection between the popular local hero that Essex had become and the Lancastrian usurper who made himself king at the expense of Richard II. There seems little doubt that Hayward's difficulties were caused by widespread acceptance of this analogy, and exacerbated two years later when, on the eve of Essex's rebellion, his steward Gilly Merrick arranged for that special performance of "the play . . . of Kyng Harry the iiijth." Whether or not that play was *written* by Shakespeare, a question that now seems undecidable, the most important point for our purposes is that the performance was *connected* by contemporaries to Hayward's *History,* and the two were assumed to have had similar subversive motives. William Camden, himself a historian of repute, wrote in his *Annals:*

Merrick was accused . . . that he had . . . procured an old out-worne play of the tragicall deposing of King Richard the second, to be acted upon the public stage before the Conspirators; which the lawyers interpreted to be done by him, as if they would now behold that acted upon the stage, which was the next day to be acted in deposing the Queene. And *the like censure given upon a Booke of the same argument,* set forth a little before by Hayward a learned man, and dedicated to the Earle of Essex, as if it had beene written as an example and incitement to the deposing of the Queene; an unfortunate thing

to the author, who was punished by long imprisonment for his untimely setting
forth thereof, and for these words in his preface to the Earle: *Great thou art
in hope, greater in the expectation of future time.* (192–93; italics added)

In Camden's view, manifestly, it is far from always or certainly the case
that history, as Stow had claimed in 1580, serves to discourage "unnaturall subjects from wicked treasons, pernitious rebellions, and
damnable doctrines" [iii]).

The quarto text of *Henry V* was published between August 4 and 14,
1600. As a publishing event, therefore, it fell smack into the middle of
the Hayward/Essex crisis, to which Shakespeare's own company was
connected, at least on the night of February 7, 1601. We might argue
indefinitely whether they were acting in ignorance of the meaning of
their performance of a play about Henry IV (an unlikely possibility of
which they apparently managed to persuade the Privy Council). But a
decision to print another English history, or to let it be printed, could
not possibly have been unwary, given the Bishops' Order in June 1599
restricting precisely such publication, and undoubtedly in part an official response to Hayward's indiscretion. The quarto was, moreover,
registered one month after the imprisonment of Hayward in July 1600,
which in turn followed closely upon the preliminary examination of
Essex at York House in June 1600, during which his possible complicity
in Hayward's project was mentioned as one of the lesser charges. I
suggest that the text that was published is itself testimony to such
wariness as these closely linked events induced. The *Cronicle History*
that made it to the stationer (past the temporary "stay") was in fact a
Lancastrian history that would pass the closest inspection. It had nothing to do with deposition, and very little with rebellion. Rather it presented an *almost* unproblematic view of a highly popular monarch
whose most obvious modern analogy was Elizabeth herself. In a benign
political semantics, "popularity" replaces "obedience." Elizabeth had
had great success in working the cultural signs of popularity, through
the myth of the virgin queen, the progresses, the Accession Day cele-
brations, and the symbolic icons. And, as Roy Strong has shown, the
older she grew, and the greater grew the public anxiety about the
succession, the more welcome to her were symbolic portraits and emblems of unqualified power and vitality. Yet the eyes and ears on her
mantle in the "Rainbow" portrait (dated 1602 by Strong) were a none-

too-subtle reminder that the myth needed the support of public surveillance, that the cultural forms of late Elizabethanism took the form
they did because the queen and her ministers were watching. And if
the quarto *Henry V* could be read as presenting yet another symbolic
portrait of her, and one that was, by regendering, consistent with her
own heroic rhetoric at Tilbury, it could only improve the credit of the
Chamberlain's Men, who, the quarto asserted, had "sundry times" been
loyally staging this story. Since the publication of the quarto had preceded their examination by the Privy Council on the dangerous matter
of the performance of the *other* Lancastrian history play on February 7,
1601, then it may have helped them establish their innocence.

The Folio text, however, was a very different matter, since it spoke
directly, at least in the fifth Chorus, to Elizabeth's last and most dangerous challenge by a rival allure. Precisely at the moment of *Henry V*'s
composition, in fact, she was locked into a competition for public vis-
ibility and popular sympathy with Essex, who had the charismatic advantages of youth, personal attractiveness, great physical height, a list
of military successes at Rouen, Cadiz, and the Azores, and above all his
masculinity. Already in Thomas Heywood's *Fair Maid of the West* the
stage had recognized in Essex a symbolic focus for national self-esteem.
The play opens with this popular perception:

> .... Most men think
> The Fleet's bound for the Islands.
> .... Nay, tis like
> The great success at Cales, under the conduct
> Of such a noble General hath put heart
> Into the English: they are all on fire....
> ....
> How Plymouth swells with gallants; how the streets
> Glister with gold! You cannot meet a man
> But trick'd in scarf and feather, that it seems
> As if the pride of England's gallantry
> Were harbor'd here.
>
> (1.1.3–15)

A contemporary engraving was prepared by Thomas Cockson in connection with the earl's departure for Ireland on March 27, 1599, showing Essex on horseback (the imperial posture), against a background

of the campaigns at Rouen, Cadiz, and the Islands, with Ireland sym-
bolically on the horizon (McCoy).

The Folio version of *Henry V* shares with this portrait an extreme
form of topicality, a moment of historical expectation that can be dated
with precision, and whose very poise on the edge of the unknown is
central to the meaning and function of the artifact. In the summer of
the previous year, 1598, Essex had quarreled with the queen in the
Privy Council over who should command the Irish campaign, and she
had given him (in a scandalous moment that immediately entered the
circuitry of national gossip) a box on the ear, precipitating his retirement to Wanstead and the imprudent letter he wrote to Lord Keeper
Egerton, full of anger and insurrectionary language:

No storme is more outragious then the indignation of an impotent Prince. The
Queenes heart is indurate, what I owe as a subject I know, and what as an
Earle, and Marshall of England: To serve as a servant and a slave I know not....
Cannot Princes erre? Can they not wrong their subjects? Is any earthly power
infinite? (Camden 127).

In February 1599 Essex, having made a temporary submission and
returned to court, was himself given the Irish commission that he had
sought, with at least mixed motives, for Sir George Carey; but everyone
knew that this was a dangerous commission for him to accept, a final
test of his usefulness to the regime and of Elizabeth's abilities to harness
both his militarism and his popularity to her service. On September 28,
1599, with the campaign a shambles, Essex made his unauthorized
return to England, and in forty-eight hours was committed to custody.
By late November he was facing charges of misgovernment of the Irish
campaign. "Libels" in his support were circulated in London (Historical
Manuscripts Comm. 2: 132, 146). On December 29 preachers at Paul's
Cross prayed for Essex by name, and attacked the government (*Calendar of State Papers, Domestic Series* 365; cited in Albright, "Folio
Version" 742). More significantly, as Richard McCoy has shown, the
supporters of Essex were developing a rival iconography of leadership
and popularity, of which the queen was forced to take notice. On February 2, 1600, Thomas Cockson's heroic engraving of Essex was circulating, "with all his titles of honor, all his services, and two verses

underneath that gave hym exceeding praise for wisdom, honor, worth" (Historical Manuscripts Comm. 2: 435; qtd. in McCoy 324). By the end of August the Privy Council had moved to suppress not only this "picture" but also any other "pictures of noblemenn and other persons ... sett forth oftentimes with verses and other circumstances not fytte to be used":

Because this custome doth growe common and indeed is not meete such publique setting forth *of anie pictures but of her most excellent Majesty* should be permytted yf the same be well done ... [the archbishop of Canterbury] will give direccion that hereafter no personage of any noblemann or other person shalbe ingraven and printed to be putt to sale publiquely, and those prints that are already made to be called in. (Dasent 619–20; qtd. in McCoy 326; italics added)

"Pictures" thus joined the list of cultural forms identified in the Bishops' Order of June 1, 1599, as under special surveillance. In the meantime, Essex's *Apology,* or defense against the charge of excessive militarism, which had been circulating in manuscript while he was still in Ireland, was published (in May 1600), along with that damning letter to Egerton in which he had questioned Elizabeth's infallibility. Its very publication may have been part of the challenge to Elizabeth's authority that would culminate in the special showing of "the play ... of Kyng Harry the iiijth, and of the kylling of Kyng Richard the second," followed by the actual insurrection of February 6, 1601.

This evidence, taken together with the furor over Hayward's *History,* indicates that from February 1599 to February 1601 England witnessed a struggle not only for the popular imagination but also, obviously, for control of the media by which that imagination was stimulated. And during the summer of 1599, while Essex was in Ireland with the results of his campaign as yet unknown, Shakespeare, we know, was at work on a version of *Henry V* that included the Choruses. If the earlier Choruses are written in the mood of chivalric celebration and enthusiasm (being "on fire") that *The Fair Maid of the West* associated with Essex's earlier campaigns:

> Now all the Youth of England are on fire,
> And silken Dalliance in the Wardrobe lyes:

> Now thrive the Armorers, and Honors thought
> Reignes solely in the breast of every man.
> They sell the Pasture now, to buy the Horse;
> . . . .
> For now sits Expectation in the Ayre . . .
>
> (2.Pro; *Folio* 426, TLN 463–70);

the fifth Chorus pinpoints the Elizabethan moment of "Expectation" more exactly, and explicitly connects it to the theme of popularity that the *Henry IV* plays had inaugurated. By a strenuous act of the visual imagination which must substitute for the deficiencies of dramatic representation, the reader/audience is invited to "now behold":

> In the quick Forge and working-house of Thought,
> How London doth powre out her Citizens,
> The Maior and all his Brethren in best sort,
> Like to the Senatours of th'antique Rome,
> With the Plebeians swarming at their heeles,
> Goe forth and fetch their Conqu'ring *Caesar* in:
> As by a lower, but by loving likelyhood,
> Were now the Generall of our gracious Empresse,
> As in good time he may, from Ireland comming,
> Bringing Rebellion broached on his Sword,
> How many would the peacefull Citie quit,
> To welcome him? much more, and much more cause,
> Did they this *Harry.*
>
> (5.Pro; *Folio* 445, TLN 2872–85)

Almost every term in this extraordinary passage bristles with innuendo and intellectual challenge. In the leisure provided by the "Forge and working-house of Thought," however quick, as distinct from the instant reception that staged drama imposes, these ambiguities can be unfolded. Not the least of them is Shakespeare's invocation of an artisanal metaphor for thought itself; but the governing peculiarity is that he should have chosen to insert so tendentious a passage into a play already, by virtue of its historical pretext, generically suspect. Nor was it only that he had chosen to make a connection with Elizabeth's intransigent favorite only weeks after Hayward's *History* had been called in for doing the same thing. In thematizing the *popular* and its role in earlier historical events (both Roman and English) Shakespeare made visible what the story of Hayward's *History* only reveals if one follows its details, that much of the anxiety it generated in official circles was connected to *its* popularity, its unusually wide circulation and distribution.[13] Hayward, as much as Essex, had courted the public and succeeded. In the examination of Wolfe, the printer of Hayward's *History,* it was part of his defense that he yielded to popular demand for a second edition:

> The people calling for it exceedingly ... 1,500 of these books being almost finished in the Whitsun holidays of 1599, were taken by the wardens of the stationers, and delivered to the Bishop of London ... The people having divers times since called to procure the continuation of the history by the same author. . . . Since the last edition was suppressed, a great number have been for it. (*C.S.P.D.* 450–51)

The same inference is drawn from the records of Essex's trial, where one of the accusations is that, when Hayward originally sent him a copy of the *History,* Essex had waited to see how many copies would sell, and then sent it to Archbishop Whitgift to have it suppressed, *in order* that the market might thereby improve still further. The *Directions for Preachers* published on February 14, 1601, warning the clergy not to express support for Essex from the pulpit, claimed that "the Earl, knowing hundreds of them to be dispersed, would needs seem the first that disliked it" (*C.S.P.D.* 567); and Bacon's speech at the trial claimed that he wrote "only a cold formal letter to the Archbishop to call in the book ... knowing, that forbidden things are most sought after" (Birch 2: 450). These official concerns with numbers, invaluable for establishing the degree to which the entire crisis was a matter of informed public concern, and for providing statistical content to the then-still-living metaphor of *publication,* contribute a powerful gloss on Shakespeare's own emphasis on "how *many*" would have flocked to welcome Essex back from Ireland, an emphasis, however, that the Folio text is prepared to leave, by means of a question mark, indeterminate.[14]

Note also the care with which this passage establishes its own protocols as metaphor, and the posture in which the metaphor is offered. The analogy between Henry's return from France and Essex's return from Ireland is "a lower, but loving likelyhood"; lower, in that Essex is *not* the victorious monarch, but only the "Generall of our gracious

Empresse"; loving, in that the playwright offers the analogy not as the
kind of challenge suspected in Cockson's engraving, and unmistakable
in Essex's letter to Egerton, but as an expression of loyalty and a recognition of structural differences. The syntax, too, is distinctively conditional, positing not only the moment of "Expectation," but a cautious
optimism ("As in good time he may").[15]

Yet even within these self-imposed controls, the language is provocative. The city may be peaceful, but the welcoming crowd "quits" that
stable environment for the liminal territory of the shore. The analogy
between Essex and Henry is *preceded* by that between fifteenth-century
England and "antique Rome," an analogy that points to a major structural difference between them, since "conquering Caesar," by definition
Julius, was still the military agent of a republic (however pushing at
those limits), as distinct from the imperial model established by Oc-
tavian and repeated by "our gracious Empresse." The very presence of
the plebeians, "swarming" at the heels of the senators, reminds that
empress of the popular "many" to whom she herself had deliberately
appealed and on whose labor, as in the beehive metaphor invoked by
Henry's Archbishop, the welfare of the hive depends.[16] Swarming, bees
notoriously desert the hive under the leadership of another monarch.
It so happens that another of the cultural artifacts pertaining to this
crisis is a manuscript poem attributed to Essex himself, which plays on
the beehive metaphor as a trope of his own condition. Dated 1598,
and probably written during his retirement to Wanstead, the poem
is a complaint, actually a "Buzze," which Essex made "upon some
discontentment":

> It was a time when silly bees could speak,
> And in that time I was a silly bee
> Who fed on thyme until my heart 'gan break,
> Yet never found the time would favour me.
> Of all the swarm I only did not thrive,
> Yet brought I wax and honey to the hive.[17]

Resenting the fact that "the lazy drone" lives off the thyme, the bee
complains to the "king of bees"; but the monarch replied succinctly,
"Thou'rt bound to serve the Time, the thyme not thee." The uninten-
tional silliness of this exchange should not deprive it of explanatory

force in the extraordinary situation we are investigating, in which symbolic forms of communication were of paramount significance. And if Essex were buzzing in the queen's ear in the fall of 1598, by the summer of the following year, when *Henry V* was being constructed, his capacity to lead a rival swarm was more clearly in evidence.

This fact alone makes sense of the representational instability that Shakespeare has introduced into *Henry V,* not merely by praising Essex at a time when a dedication to him could result in imprisonment, but by allowing the analogy between Essex and Henry to confuse the more "natural" analogy between Henry and Elizabeth. As Jonathan Dollimore and Alan Sinfield have argued, the legend of Henry's reign was "a powerful Elizabethan fantasy simply because it represented a single source of power in the state,"[18] the fusion of monarch and military hero in a single, popular archetype. The allusion to Essex destabilizes that fantasy, along with that other Elizabethan myth propagated at Tilbury, that the queen herself could play both roles. The Archbishop's metaphor of the beehive (pending the discovery that bees have *queens*) accomplished the same feat; but the suppressed metaphor of the swarm works rather to distinguish general and empress, by signifying their competition for popular support and approval.

The quick-thinking imaginative forger who wrote this Chorus would also have known, surely, that "bringing Rebellion broached on his Sword," a phrase that editors have difficulty glossing,[19] was truly ambiguous, a self-fulfilling prophecy which would be unavoidably recognizable as such by February 1601. And even in mid-1600 its status was identical with that of Hayward's dedication to Essex as "great in hope, greater in the expectation of future time." Since in Hayward's case, the records show, the authorities translated expectation into hope, it is hardly surprising that the published (quarto) text of the play makes this interpretation unreadable by erasing it.

What Shakespeare intended by creating the ambiguity in the first place is, of course, another question altogether. For what audience was this complex strategy designed, superimposing two historical eras (or three, if we include the gesture toward antique Rome) and two structures of analogy which contradict each other? Had he imagined a warning to Elizabeth, which would imply that the warning was capable of reaching her, if not by court performance, for which there is no evidence, then by oral report from the public theater? Or rather, in some version of the Albright hypothesis, had he planned an encoded incitement to Essex, intended for private performance before some audience of "malcontents"? Or was the Folio version a well-meant but ill-advised attempt at mediation, with the public stage conceived as the liminal territory where the playwright and actors took no sides, creating "loving likelihoods" in the national interest? The representational slipperiness, then, by which Henry could configure *both* Elizabeth and Essex, at the end of a play whose protagonist was, if peerless, certainly not flawless, would not merely register Shakespeare's much vaunted objectivity and disinterestedness. Rather, it would contribute to an argument for a pragmatic reconciliation between general and empress, pragmatic in the sense that "history," by refusing to settle their rivalry, provided no basis for decisively altering the current allocations of power and lines of authority.

I lean to the third alternative, as a basis for ascribing intention in the *writing* of the Folio text. Theoretically, an imagined mediation of a local, contemporary crisis gives substance to a term currently fashionable in neo-Marxist criticism but does so precisely by reinstating the human factor, individual agency, that Marxist criticism generally occludes and that cultural criticism must insist on. Yet we know from events (the deletion of the Choruses, the rebellion itself) that such a mediation was never effected. That failure must also be incorporated into our theoretical model of how one text became another. I assume that the environment (as redescribed here) would have been peculiarly stimulating of self-consciousness, encouraging a dramatist to assess, but not necessarily accurately, the conditions of constraint that defined his medium, the degree of his freedom to operate within those constraints.

In the Folio text of *Henry V,* which by my account must have registered a still hopeful view of that freedom, a vision of national unity is posited, not, as in such comedies as *A Midsummer Night's Dream,* as a festive community, but as tenable only within a sober historical perspective. As Henry himself is observed by the French Constable to have advanced beyond the "Whitsun morris dance" which was the Dauphin's metaphor for his tavern phase (2.4.25), the Folio version of his story produces at the level of consciousness what the earlier plays in both tetralogies merely produced—an image of the nation-state as an ideal

that survives the continuous struggle for power of competing aristo-
crats, and of the hegemonic, therefore, as the master code of history.
What the Folio text does *not* produce, however, is an idealized model
of unity, *except* in Archbishop Chichele's beehive speech, in the Folio
firmly qualified by our prior recognition that the Archbishop is cynical,
self-serving, and elitist.[20] That the beehive speech survived in the quarto,
while the negotiations of the first scene disappear, is both a further
testimony to the relation between abridgment and a simpler form of
patriotism, and a reminder that the play was written in the context of
the Bishops' Order, for whose implementation Archbishop Whitgift was
responsible.

In place of organicist political theory and the coating of self-interest
with rhetorical honey, the subdued voice of "our bending author" offers, penultimately, only the sexual and dynastic version of union, granting a festive and erotic color to France's and Katherine's capitulation,
providing we only take the story "thus far" and no further. And while
the image of "antique Rome" with its crowds of swarming plebeians
anticipates *Coriolanus,* the play in which Shakespeare would a decade
later reexamine the political structure through the lens of classical
republicanism, in *Henry V* this inquiry is sporadic. The Folio text remains committed, though not without moments of distaste, to the system of government endorsed by centuries of English, rather than Roman,
history, and willing to entertain, though not without framing it as extreme imaginative effort ("Work, work, your thoughts"), a commitment
to ideas of national greatness and agreement. What happened after the
turn of the century was, and produced, another kind of story.

IV

There are two last textual questions that deserve attention here. The
first is an oddity that sharply refocuses the problems of interpretation
posed by the appearance of Essex in the fifth prologue. For this may
not be the only marked topical allusion to the crisis that began in 1598
when Elizabeth and Essex quarreled in public, and Essex received the
famous box on the ear. It happens that the Folio text of *Henry V* also
features a box on the ear, whose importance is recorded by repetition
(4.1.220, 4.7.130, and 4.7.176; *Folio* 439, TLN 2064, 443, TLN 2658–59,

444, TLN 2702). It complicates the allusion, if it is one, that while the intended recipient of the box is Henry, and therefore arguably either Essex or Elizabeth (or both), the deliverer is Michael Williams, common soldier, commonly referred to in the speech prefixes as "Will." Given that the entire episode was invented by Shakespeare with no precedent in the sources, and given that all of the speeches in which this phrase was embedded survive in the quarto, although in reduced form, it is telling that in all three occurrences the more colorful (and hence memorable) "box on the ear" is replaced by the generic and nonspecific (respectively "strike," "strike," and "harm" [Allen and Muir 540, 545, 546]). A reading of these textual differences that privileges historical circumstances will not only see the *disappearance* of the "box" as the strongest demonstration of its topical force, but will have to wrestle, once again, with the play's unstable representational field. If "Will," as the testimony of the sonnets would suggest, is Shakespeare's own signature (Fineman 26–27, 289–96), his appearance as the voice of the common man in the crucial scene before Agincourt (and his disappearance, as a name, from the quarto) still further complicates the reception of this scene and its direction of audience sympathy. Is Williams, then, another repository of the popular voice, a common man whose relation to Shakespeare himself is uncommonly close, and who therefore competes for exegetical control with both the Chorus and "our bending author"? If so, two opposed (though symmetrically related) conceptions of the popular are here, in this scene of ideological density, set in fully articulate contest with each other: the national leader whose populist style has established the mandate (if not the justice) of his cause, and the (un)common critic of that cause whose intelligence prohibits a simple submission of his will to the idea of popular leadership, merely because it is in the national interest.

The last textual item may also claim the privileged status of self-referentiality. I refer to Archbishop Chichele's speech on the Salic law as a rationale for the French campaign, which bibliographers have raised to the status of a crux. Both Hart and Taylor make much of the fact that the Folio and quarto derive this speech, with remarkable fidelity, from Holinshed, or, more precisely, that the Folio derives from Holinshed and the quarto, substantially abridged, from the manuscript behind the Folio. As always, at stake in the debate are questions of intention and value: what does it mean that Shakespeare relied here so extensively on the actual words of Holinshed? Was he merely copying because the scene was insignificant, or faithfully transcribing because its materials were crucial to his purpose? Is the length of the Salic law speech disproportionate, and was the quarto therefore wise in its abridgment? Or was its length intended to be parodic (a position taken in Olivier's film production)?[21] According to Hart, the quarto's divergences from the Folio are merely obtuse blunders, ruining the historical logic of the set piece; for Taylor, while in one instance the quarto removes an "arithmetical blunder" derived from Holinshed (*Henry V* 37), abridgment in general works against Shakespeare's intentions in this speech, whose length and slow pace are required, he argues, for dramatic suspense, withholding the excitements promised by the Chorus. And Taylor utterly rejects the hypothesis of parody as "uncharacteristically indiscreet" (34).

It need hardly be said by this point that Taylor's own arguments elsewhere, and all of mine in this essay, make such an assertion unnecessary. Yet we do not even need to posit parody to explain the Salic law passage (whether good or bad theater) and its retention (more or less) in the quarto. For if anything in *Henry V* might be seen as meta-commentary, as the playwright's statement of methodological self-consciousness, it might be this historical instance of how "history" can be manipulated for political purposes. Its *retention,* then, albeit in an abridged form, might be seen as the quarto's moment of self-knowledge, and also of its resistance to the very conditions that produced it, to the authorities who, at the turn of the sixteenth century, were dictating what form the stories of English national experience, past and present, should take.

Notes

1. Tillyard (304–14) took a less sanguine view of *Henry V* than Campbell (255–305), regarding it as a routine and formulaic performance without the energies invested in the two parts of *Henry IV.*

2. See, for instance, Greenblatt (42–45), and Dollimore and Sinfield. Earlier skeptical readings were primarily characterological in focus, including that of Gerald Gould, who

in the immediate aftermath of World War I revolted against the "more hideous 'Prussianisms' with which Shakespeare has endowed his Henry" (42).

3. For both quarto and Folio texts, I have used the facsimile editions (quarto, Allen and Muir; Folio, Hinman).

4. See Garrett, Hardison, and Gelfman 134: the film's final words are as follows:

> Small time: but in that small, most greatly lived
> This star of England: Fortune made his
>   sword: and for his sake . . .
> In your fair minds let this acceptance take.

5. Greg, *Merry Wives;* his theory was refined in *Two Elizabethan Stage Abridgements.*

6. See the confession of Sir Gilly Merrick, Essex's steward, on March 5, 1601, *Calendar of State Papers, Domestic,* 1598–1601, 278, art. 78, p. 575.

7. While G. P. Jones (99) points out that Essex's departure for Ireland was expected as early as November 1598, citing the letters of John Chamberlain, nine of which relate to Dudley Carleton the progress of the commission, it is hard to see why this argues an earlier compositional date for the play, given the Chorus's precise emphasis on return, rather than departure. Perversely, Jones himself was arguing that the Choruses as a group were added much later, for a royal performance in James's court, supposedly in the Royal Cockpit, sometime in 1605. By this logic (which equates Henry with Prince Henry, producing an entirely different analogic structure), the fifth Chorus has to be read as an exception and given an earlier date than the others.

8. See also, for earlier versions of this theory, Price, Okerlund, and Greg, *First Folio.*

9. For alternative, unpersuasive explanations for the problem posed by a text without the Choruses, see Jones; Smith, who sought to prove that the Choruses were a later addition, that the allusion in the fifth prologue was not to Essex but to Lord Mountjoy, who took over his commission; and Law, who effectively refuted Smith's proposal.

10. See Greg, *Sir Thomas More* (xiii–xv), and, for a recent analysis of the textual and chronological problems posed by this note, McMillin.

11. See Tennenhouse 235: "The *History* failed as an act of clientage because, following the death of its original patron, it was subjected to a tendentious reading by the King"; and 252: "Readers sympathetic to Ralegh read it as an honest history. . . . Hostile readers read it as a malcontent's complaint, an attack on the present times by a man . . . who dared insinuate he had been unjustly punished. . . . James construed it as a personal attack."

12. This darker meaning is made especially available by Holinshed's description of the earlier state of the frogs, as "living at libertie in lakes and ponds, would needs (as misliking their present intercommunitie of life) with one consent sue to Jupiter for a king." This behavior is further identified as "longing after novelties." The two appearances of "libertie" in this passage are, therefore, diametrically opposed to each other.

13. I derive these details and their original citations from Heffner, who, however, was so busy attacking Albright and attempting to disprove any connection between Shakespeare and either Essex or Hayward that he overlooked the most interesting aspect of Hayward's case—the extraordinary evidence it supplies as to the conditions and

control of publication, the testimony as to the *History*'s popularity, and the focus of the authorities precisely on this issue as exacerbating, if not constituting, the primary offense.

14. Compare Albright, "Folio Version" 734, on the connection between this stress on numbers in Shakespeare's Chorus and the figures later cited in testimony about the rebellion.

15. Taylor (*Henry V* 7) suggests that the qualifier, "much more, and much more cause," is a "sting in the tail" that limits the "unquestionably complimentary" import of the metaphor proper. I agree that it may limit, by gradation, approval of Essex, but not that the phrase prevents our developing any "biographical fantasies" that Shakespeare was "an admirer of Essex, with Henry V modelled upon him." Whether or not admiration is the appropriate term, the representational slippage that this passage accomplishes cannot be so undone by a single qualification.

16. It is important to note the connection, in the Folio text, between this suppressed metaphor of the swarm and the military emphasis of the Archbishop's beehive, which clearly anticipates the post-Agincourt spectacle:

> Others, like Souldiers armed in their stings,
>
> Make boote upon the Summer's Velvet buddes:
>
> Which pillage, they with merry march bring home;
>
> To the Tent-royal of their Emperor.
>
> (1.2.193 –96; *Folio* 425, TLN 340 –43)

17. See British Museum Sloane Ms. 1303, "The Earl of Essex his Buzze, which he made upon some discontentment."

18. Dollimore and Sinfield 220. They add that this formula, unique in earlier British history, avoids the "structural problem of the over-mighty subject—the repeated theme of other plays." They apparently do not perceive the effect of the Essex allusion in reintroducing this structural problem in an excessively topical context; and their reading of the play hews the neo-Marxist critical line that literature can only critique ideology unknowingly: "[I]n this play, which is often assumed to be the one where Shakespeare is closest to state propaganda, the construction of ideology is complex—even as it consolidates, it betrays inherent instability" (211).

19. Compare Albright ("Folio Version" 732–33) on the ambiguous semantics of "broach." The term was clearly used in connection with fears of civic unrest. Compare *1 Henry IV* 5.1.21: "A portent of broached mischief to the times"; while Lord Henry Howard, referring to the Essex conspiracy itself, wrote in a letter that "All the partisans of the last tragedy resorted to Southampton without impeachment . . . and new practises were set on broach" (Stopes 248 –49).

20. It is worth remembering that Holinshed's report of the parliament of 1414 was clearly sympathetic to the bill which proposed that "the temporal lands devoutly given, and disordinately spent by religious and other spiritual persons" should be appropriated by Henry to provide for national defense and relief of the poor. In the Folio, Canterbury's beehive metaphor admits this populist theme for a moment, when the monarch surveys "the poore mechanicke Porters, crowding in / Their heavy burthens at his narrow gate"

(1.2.200 –01; *Folio* 425, TLN 347 –48); but in the quarto version these two lines alone
are, significantly, missing from the speech.

21. It is tempting to speculate what motives or anxieties lie behind Olivier's decisions
as to how to handle the war's claims to be *just*. Where one might have expected suppression of the opening scene with the bishops, followed by serious treatment of the Salic
law speech, Olivier retained the cynical motivation and directed the public rationalization as high farce. This strategy has caused his commentators some difficulties. See
Geduld 28 –29: "The distortion . . . for comic effect serves, intentionally, to obscure the
actual words of the two prelates. Olivier does not want us to become too aware of the
duplicities and complex motivations behind the 'justifications' that the Archbishop offers. . . . [He] leaves in the specious justification for Henry's invasion, but plays the scene
so that we hardly notice its speciousness amid the comedy." This reading reminds us
forcibly that rationalization of the troublesome is as much a part of the critical process
as it is and was of public policy.

Works Cited

Albright, Evelyn May. "The Folio Version of *Henry V* in Relation to Shakespeare's Times."
      PMLA 43 (1928): 722 –56.
———. "Shakespeare's *Richard II* and the Essex Conspiracy." *PMLA* 42 (1927): 686 –720.
———. "Shakespeare's *Richard II,* Hayward's History of Henry IV, and the Essex Con-
      spiracy." *PMLA* 46 (1931): 694 –719.
Allen, Michael J. B., and Kenneth Muir, eds. *Shakespeare's Plays in Quarto.* Berkeley: U
      of California P, 1981.
Barton, Anne. "The King Disguised: Shakespeare's *Henry V* and the Comical History."
      The Triple Bond: Audience, Actors, and Renaissance Playwrights. Ed. Joseph G. Price.
      University Park: Pennsylvania State UP, 1975. 92 –117.
Birch, Thomas. *Memoirs of the Reign of Queen Elizabeth.* 2 vols. London, 1754.
Blayney, Peter. "Shakespeare's Fight with *What* Pirates?" The Folger Institute, May 11,
      1987.
Calendar of State Papers, Domestic Series. Vol. 5. *Elizabeth, 1598 –1601.* Ed. M. A. E.
      Green. London, 1869.
Camden, William. *The Historie of the . . . Princesse Elizabeth. . . . [Annals.]* Trans. R. Norton.
      4 pts. fol. London: Fisher, 1630.
Campbell, Lily B. *Shakespeare's "Histories": Mirrors of Elizabethan Policy.* San Marino:
      Huntington Library, 1947. 3rd ed., London: Methuen, 1964.
Dasent, John Roche, ed. *Acts of the Privy Council of England.* London: HMSO, 1905.
Dollimore, Jonathan, and Alan Sinfield. "History and Ideology: The Instance of *Henry V.*"
      Alternative Shakespeares. Ed. John Drakakis. London: Methuen, 1985. 206 –27.
Donno, Elizabeth Story. "Some Aspects of Shakespeare's Holinshed." *Huntington Library
      Quarterly* 50 (1987): 229 –48.

Essex, Robert Devereux, earl of. *The Poems of ... Robert, Earl of Essex.* In vol. 4 of *Miscellanies of the Fuller Worthies' Library.* Ed. A. B. Grosart. Edinburgh: Blackburn, 1872.

Fineman, Joel. *Shakespeare's Perjured Eye: The Invention of Poetic Subjectivity in the Sonnets.* Berkeley: U of California P, 1986.

Garrett, George P., O. B. Hardison, Jr., and Jane R. Gelfman, eds. *Film Scripts One.* New York: Appleton, 1971.

Geduld, Harry M. *Filmguide to* Henry V. Bloomington: Indiana UP, 1973.

Gould, Gerald. "A New Reading of *Henry V.*" *English Review* 29 (1919): 42–55.

Greenblatt, Stephen. "Invisible Bullets: Renaissance Authority and Its Subversion, *Henry IV* and *Henry V.*" *Political Shakespeare: New Essays in Cultural Materialism.* Ed. Jonathan Dollimore and Alan Sinfield. London: Methuen, 1985. 18–47.

Greg, W. W., ed. *The Book of Sir Thomas More.* Malone Soc. Reprints. London: Malone Soc., 1911.

———. *The Shakespeare First Folio: Its Bibliographical and Textual History.* Oxford: Clarendon, 1955.

———, ed. *Shakespeare's* Merry Wives of Windsor, *1602.* Oxford: Clarendon, 1910.

———. *Two Elizabethan Stage Abridgements:* The Battle of Alcazar *and* Orlando Furioso. Malone Soc. Reprints. Oxford: Malone Soc., 1923.

Greville, Fulke. *The Life of the Renowned Sr Philip Sidney.* London, 1652.

Hall, Edward. *The union of the two noble and illustre famelies of Lancastre & Yorke ... proceadyng to the reigne of the high and prudent prince Kyng Henry the eight, the indubitate flower and very heire of both the sayd linages.* London, 1548.

Hart, Alfred. *Stolne and Surreptitious Copies: A Comparative Study of Shakespeare's Bad Quartos.* Melbourne: Melbourne UP, 1942.

Hayward, Sir John. *The first part of the life and raigne of King Henrie the IIII.* London, 1599.

Heffner, Ray. "Shakespeare, Hayward, and Essex." *PMLA* 45 (1930): 754–870.

Heywood, Thomas. *The Fair Maid of the West, Parts I and II.* Ed. Robert K. Turner, Jr. Lincoln: U of Nebraska P, 1967.

Hinman, Charlton, ed. *The First Folio of Shakespeare.* The Norton Facsimile. New York: Norton, 1968.

Historical Manuscripts Commission. *Report ... Penshurst.* Ed. C. L. Kingsford. London: HMSO, 1934.

Holinshed, Raphael. *The first and second volume of Chronicles.* London, 1587.

Jameson, Fredric. *The Political Unconscious: Narrative as a Socially Symbolic Act.* Ithaca: Cornell UP, 1981.

Jones, G. P. "*Henry V:* The Chorus and the Audience." *Shakespeare Survey* 31 (1978): 93–104.

Law, R. A. "The Choruses in *Henry V.*" *Texas Studies in English* 35 (1956): 11–21.

McCoy, Richard C. "'A dangerous image': The Earl of Essex and Elizabethan Chivalry." *Journal of Medieval and Renaissance Studies* 13 (1983): 313–29.

McMillin, Scott. *The Elizabethan Theatre and* The Book of Sir Thomas More. Ithaca: Cornell UP, 1986.

The Mirror for Magistrates. Ed. Lily B. Campbell. Cambridge: Cambridge UP, 1938. New York: Barnes, 1960.

Okerlund, Gerda. "The Quarto Version of *Henry V* as a Stage Adaptation." *PMLA* 49 (1934): 810–34.

Patterson, Annabel. " 'The very age and body of the time his form and pressure': Rehistoricising Shakespeare's Theater." *New Literary History* 20 (1988–89): 83–104.

Pollard, A. W. *Shakespeare's Folios and Quartos: A Study in the Bibliography of Shakespeare's Plays, 1594–1685.* Cambridge: Cambridge UP, 1909.

Price, Hereward T. *The Text of* Henry V. Newcastle-under-Lyme: Mandley & Unett, 1921.

Racin, John, Jr. "The Early Editions of Sir Walter Ralegh's *History of the World.*" *Studies in Bibliography* 17 (1964): 199–209.

Smith W. D. "The *Henry V* Choruses in the First Folio." *Journal of English and Germanic Philology* 53 (1954): 38–57

Stein, Arnold. *The House of Death: Messages from the English Renaissance.* Baltimore: Johns Hopkins UP, 1986.

Stopes, Charlotte. *The Life of Henry, Third Earl of Southampton, Shakespeare's Patron.* Cambridge: Cambridge UP, 1922.

Stow, John. *The Chronicles of England, from Brute unto this present yeare of Christ, 1580.* London, 1580.

Strong, Roy. *The Cult of Elizabeth: Elizabethan Portraiture and Pageantry.* London: Thames, 1977.

Taylor, Gary, ed. *Henry V.* The Oxford Shakespeare. Oxford: Clarendon, 1982.

Tennenhouse, Leonard. "Sir Walter Ralegh and Clientage." *Patronage in the Renaissance.* Ed. Guy Fitch Lytle and Stephen Orgel. Princeton: Princeton UP, 1981. 235–58.

Tillyard, E. M. W. *Shakespeare's History Plays.* London: Chatto, 1944. New York: Macmillan, 1947.

Walter, J. H., ed. *King Henry V.* The Arden Shakespeare. London: Methuen, 1954.

Wells, Stanley, and Gary Taylor. *Modernizing Shakespeare's Spelling, with Three Studies in the Text of* Henry V. Oxford: Clarendon, 1979.

Plays Agonistic and Competitive: The Textual Approach to Elsinore

JOSEPH LOEWENSTEIN

> ... what Players are they?
> ROSIN.
> Even those you were wont to take delight in the Tragedians of the City.
> HAM.
> How chances it they travaile? their residence both in reputation and profit was better both wayes.
> ROSIN.
> I thinke their Inhibition comes by the meanes of the late Innovation?
> —*The Tragedie of Hamlet,* F1, Oo3v[1]

I N ALL EDITIONS of *Hamlet* with a complete textual apparatus, the actors approaching Elsinore get tangled in footnotes. The Folio text includes some tart, but by no means straightforward, comments on "the late Innovation" (happily, "the late Innovation?") and the intrusion of "an eyrie of children" on the London theatrical scene, and, since a good deal of this topical material is absent from the second, or "good," quarto, an editor has a considerable amount of explaining to do.[2] It turns out that a number of important arguments are focused on this passage. Conclusively to explain its appearance in F and its substantial absence in Q2 would be to date *Hamlet,* to describe the copy-texts for both the Folio and the good quarto, and above all to establish whether or not Shakespeare ever blotted a line, to divine how he revised and when. As the reviewers have made clear, neither Harold Jenkins in the new Arden Shakespeare nor Philip Edwards in the New Cambridge Shakespeare have finally solved these matters, for discussions of the passage inevitably set simplicity of explanation at odds with the need to accommodate all the data. And yet there is even more at stake than

63

a date for *Hamlet,* an account of its textual transmission, and an assessment of Shakespeare's habits of revision. To enter this thicket is to track the various "authorizations" or institutionalizations of this play. One may begin here to describe both performance and text as works, intellectual properties, and to describe the particular modes of competition in which they participate. I must make it clear at the outset that I am not about to accomplish a resolution of the editorial crux— in fact, I suspect that resolution is *practically* impossible—although I do intend to summarize what has been argued.[3] My procedure here is the application of textual criticism to thought; my thesis is that in these lines Shakespeare makes *Hamlet* the sign of important authorial and historical emergencies; my goal is to describe, not what happens in *Hamlet,* but what *Hamlet* happens, specifically how these lines locate the play in what can, without terminological strain, be referred to as the cultural *economy* of the English Renaissance.

I

ROS.
I thinke their inhibition, comes by the meanes of the late innovasion.
HAM.
Doe they hold the same estimation they did when I was in the Citty; are they so followed.
ROS.
No indeede are they not.
HAM.
It is not very strange, for my Uncle is King of Denmarke, and those that would make mouths at him while my father lived, give twenty, fortie, fifty, a hundred duckets a peece, for his Picture in little, s'bloud there is somthing in this more then naturall, if Philosophie could find it out.

—Q2, F2v

To begin with the traditional address to the passage: all attempts to date the play have had to make their peace with the reference in these lines to "the late innovasion." Some traditional glosses, ones that have grown more fashionable recently, find a reference here to the Essex rebellion or to the June 1600 Privy Council order for the restraint of the theater, but what I believe to be more responsible criticism has settled on the rise of the children's companies, beginning in December 1600 with the performance of Jonson's *Cynthia's Revels.*[4] A few lines later in F comes the more explicit reference to the way this "ayrie of Children, little Yases . . . [who] are now the fashion" have "be-ratled the common Stages" and thus provoked "much to do on both sides" (F1, Oo3v–Oo4), the so-called War of the Theaters.[5] I will have a good deal to say of this "War" in what follows. The War of the Theaters does not considerably assist in the dating of *Hamlet,* for it is difficult to suppose it to have been perceptibly underway before the performance of Jonson's *Poetaster* in the spring of 1601 (it lasted only a couple of seasons); indeed, the war doesn't seem to have had more than one side until later in the year, when Marston and Dekker, who had been much mocked in *Poetaster,* replied to it—and to other Jonsonian plays—in *Satiromastix.* This only complicates the dating of *Hamlet,* since many critics believe *Hamlet* to have influenced Marston's *Antonio's Revenge* (performed in the winter of 1600–01), one of the plays satirized in *Poetaster,* which would give us a chain of influence proceeding from *Hamlet* into the War of the Theaters and thence *back* to Rosencrantz's remarks on "the eyrie of children" who "are now the fashion"—"Innovation?" indeed. Though some may find no charm in the idea that in a way *Hamlet* influenced itself, this is actually a reputable theory.[6] I invoke it at the outset since it can help to point the particular emergency of the contested lines. However the problem of glossing these lines be solved—even if the fall of Essex impinges on the wanderings of this theatrical troupe—the passage, insofar as it *dates* the play, inevitably locates it within a primarily theatrical calendar. Rosencrantz bears news from a new *theatrical* world.

Would that discussion of the passage could be left off here, with the recognition that *Hamlet* is explicitly embroiled in theatrical fashion. But there is a *textual* crux as well as a calendrical one to be dealt with, and bibliographic argument has whirled around this passage. Q2 lacks the references to the little eyases and to the contentiousness of the London stage. Attempts to resolve the crux represented by the variation of these texts have been part of an old campaign to establish a single "good" text of the play, *Hamlet* "as Shakespeare wrote it." I have little to add to the recent critique of this bibliographic *desideratum.* Nor is it my purpose in the following account of the several arguments concerning the textual transmission of *Hamlet* to provide some final resolution of those arguments. Instead I wish to ascertain what the absence in Q2 of references to the War of the Theaters can tell us about the significance of *Hamlet* as an event in Early Modern literary culture. The evidence concerning this crucial textual variation is extremely confusing, and in what follows I can spare the reader only some of the details, for in matters of Shakespearean textual studies one cannot be brief, diplomatic, and compelling—two out of three would be the best one could hope for. [The reader with no patience for bibliographic argument may wish to skip to the last three paragraphs of this section.] The textual details, which combine variously—even promiscuously—with the external evidence, conduce to a variety of textual hypotheses of which three general ones have commanded the greatest esteem.[7] The first and oldest hypothesis is simply that the play went into production without any allusion to the War of the Theaters and that the passage (roughly corresponding to 2.2.335–58 according to the lineation in the new Arden edition) was soon added but without affecting the copy-text for the second quarto. Thus Q2 is held to be very close to the originally performed version of the play, F is held to be very close to a later performance text, and *Hamlet* may be thought to have influenced itself. Though this hypothesis is now recovering a certain degree of prestige—and G. R. Hibbard's single-volume edition for the Oxford Shakespeare will no doubt secure it even more—its adherents were a shrinking minority until quite recently.[8]

One reason for the earlier loss of prestige is that some bibliographers, perhaps ambitious to penetrate the mysteries of Shakespearean creativity, sought to trace the state of these lines in Q2 to the vexed surface of the poet's own manuscript. According to a second hypothesis, Shakespeare added this passage late in the history of his composition of the play, before the promptbook was prepared or at least before the play went into production. This modification not only brings us closer to Shakespeare's study, it also helps to explain, without recourse to a theory of two distinct versions performed by the Chamberlain's Men, how the copy for Q2, usually described as closely derived from foul papers, could generate a printed text without the reference to the little eyases and to the consequent War of the Theaters; either the foul papers were supposed to make no mention of the child actors, or, more elaborately, the foul papers included such references but apparently as an after-thought. This latter version of the hypothesis provides that these lines *seemed* to be excrescences and were therefore passed over by either the compositor or the scribe who prepared copy for the compositor.[9] Indeed, this version of the hypothesis has been substantially and mag-isterially adapted in Harold Jenkins's new Arden edition of the play, where he combines the first and second hypotheses, giving us early performances of *Hamlet* without the topical material, and a later ver-sion performed with the material inserted, but a text of Q2 that records only *some* of the insertions.[10]

But the variations of F and Q2 admit of a completely different sort of explanation. Instead of two acting versions represented by the two texts (first hypothesis), or a revision leading to a single acting version (second hypothesis), or two acting versions the first of which is quite badly represented by Q2 (Jenkins's hybrid)—all theories of how the text of the play *grew*—one can entertain a theory of how the play shrank, a hypothesis based on the idea of deliberate excision.[11] In the case of a third hypothesis the textual critic need not suppose that the topical material entered the play while it was still in draft; indeed, this third hypothesis, making no trespass on the privacy of authorship, mod-estly concentrates its attention on the business of the acting company. According to this third hypothesis, at some point, either during re-hearsals or after the play had run for a while—suppositions concerning this moment will depend on how one weights the information regarding the date of the play—at some point, the company decided to cut some of the topical material preserved in F. That is, F is taken as a tentative production version prior to Q2; Q2 is taken to be a *subsequent* (and perhaps somewhat faulty) performance version. (Note that the com-pany—in this case a rather fidgety company—*can* still be supposed to have added the material recorded in F after early performances of the play without it; what the third hypothesis needs is simply a decision to omit the material, or some of it.) The textual critic might prefer to fix the moment of excision before the run begins, or at least before the promptbook is prepared, so that the excision can be marked, however casually, on that messy text, either foul papers or a close descendant of foul papers, which is the immediate ancestor of Q2. We can then suppose Q2 to have been printed from foul papers (or a copy of foul papers) marked up for preparation of the promptbook.[12]

To be sure, this third hypothesis has its inconveniences. While it enables us to describe a copy-text for Q2 that is both very close to foul papers and also proximate, with respect to the topical material, to the promptbook, it leaves us with a slight bibliographic embarrassment when we turn our attention to the copy-text for the Folio. Because of its particularly theatrical character, F *is* generally thought to be derived from the promptbook, yet F stands as our chief source for a passage supposed, according to our third hypothesis concerning the copy for Q2, to have been cut from performance. That is, the hypothesis proposes a theatrical cut in a copy-text close to foul papers in the case of Q2 and the absence of a theatrical cut in a copy-text close to the promptbook in the case of F. No wonder W. W. Greg remarked (charmingly), "On the whole it seems to be a rather queer prompt-book, if prompt-book it is, that lies behind F" (323).

J. M. Nosworthy (163, 182–85) and Philip Edwards (20) have suggested that the copy for F is itself just preliminary to the promptbook, which solves this last problem, though now *both* texts of *Hamlet* have drifted, at least in the bibliographic imagination, away from the promptbook and the stage. Note that a hypothesis that emphasizes theatrical cutting can tend to extremely radical formulations. Consider the following argument, a common one. Q1 is a very poor representative of what Shakespeare wrote for the Chamberlain's Men, but Nicholas Ling had it printed, knowing that it could pass as a playbook; garbled as it is, it is the right *length* for a play—2,154 lines. The same cannot be said of the other two versions. The title page to Q2 advertises a text "enlarged to almost as much againe as it was"—not far off, really, since the text is 3,674 lines long. It is quite possible that Q2 is, in fact, unactably long. The same might be said of F, which is only about 200 lines (net) shorter than Q2. What I referred to as the "embarrassment" of the third hypothesis—that it proposes theatrical cuts in a text printed from a close descendant of foul papers and the retention of passages ostensibly cut from performance in a text printed from a close descendant of the promptbook—is simply a particularly awkward exposure of the difficulty of explaining these *texts* merely as records of theatrical activity. They are too long for the theater, but they have "theatrical" cuts; they are records of performance, but we must assume that they record the author's imaginings before they were constrained by theatrical exigencies (to put it this way reveals some of the implicit romanticism of textual criticism), or (perhaps this phrasing will sound tougher) they are reconciled with Shakespeare's fullest, thoroughly impracticable working-out of the play.[13] However difficult it is to date this play and to account for the variations of its text, it seems clear that many of the variations are deliberate, and that the texts record attempts to mediate between what may be called a transcript and that copious dramatic pretext that might be called a "poem unlimited." Attempts to save the third hypothesis put the critic under some pressure to suppose that the lines were preserved in a playhouse manuscript the fidelity of which to Shakespeare's own foul papers was cherished, for some reason, by the company, cherished despite the fact that this text was no longer regarded as an acting version.[14] Despite its weaknesses, the third hypothesis, because it tends to reinforce the idea of a "literary," counter- (or trans-) theatrical *Hamlet* manuscript whose existence may be traced within the Folio text, is probably destined to thrive under our professional attention.

At any rate, these are the three essential textual arguments: (1) two performance versions of the play, one without, a second with the topical passage (Shakespeare, the master of the theatrical moment); (2) a draft without the passage, but an unbroken tradition of performance with the passage in (Shakespeare, the painstaking reviser); (3) rehearsals or early performances with the passage included, and its excision accomplished early in the theatrical history of the play (the copious poet and the pragmatic company). Actually, the hypotheses are legion; I have been condensing, summarizing, assimilating. In the spirit of proliferation, let me propose a fourth hypothesis; I offer it as an elaborate, second-best alternative to the first hypothesis (which is not only the simplest but also, I think, still the best). This fourth supposition can stand as an apotheosis of the trans-theatrical theory. Suppose Shakespeare to have included the crucial lines in the text presented to the company—we need not concern ourselves with the moment of their composition. Again comes the decision to cut the passage. But suppose now that the cut was never, or seldom, actually observed in performance, that the decision to cut was reversed. Thus, one might surmise,

these lines were *marked* for cutting in a messy, pre-promptbook theatrical text, which is why Q2 fails to print them; but they were actually
performed when the play went into production—or back into production—which is why the Folio prints them.[15] But it has not been my
chief concern to resolve the textual crux. Rather I wish that the reader
might discern within the various, and variously unsatisfactory, attempts
at textual explanation the nagging emergency of the passage.

A summary of the attempted explanations: *either* the playwright added
these lines (or the bulk of these lines) early in the production history
of *Hamlet* (hypotheses 1 and 2), or the passage, whenever it was
composed, was cut but preserved in the playhouse archives in a version sufficiently esteemed to survive for two decades and to reassert
itself in the copy-text for F (hypothesis 3), or the members of the
company wanted most of these lines cut from this already remarkably
long script, but a more persuasive theatrical intelligence wanted them
in, and *got* them in (hypothesis 4). Notice that it becomes even more
clear why a cultural historian might wish to bestir her- or himself over
these details if we ask, not simply "How may we infer Shakespeare's
intended words from the printed texts of *Hamlet?*" but, more precisely,
"Why, ultimately, are details of the theatrical life in London so unob-
trusive in Q2?" The question elicits a slightly different sort of summary:
either because the relevance of certain new aspects of theatrical life to
Hamlet did not immediately strike Shakespeare (hypothesis 1 or 2 will
admit of this argument) or other acute intelligences within the company (hypothesis 1); or because theatrical life in London had not yet
achieved its relevance to *Hamlet* when the copy for Q2 was finished
(hypothesis 1) or at least when that copy was in its cleanest condition
(hypothesis 2); or because explicit reference to theatrical life in London, in the first performances of *Hamlet* or perhaps only in the manuscript of the play, was thought to have lost its relevance or to lengthen
the play unnecessarily (the—weak—hypothesis 3 or, if the thought was
discounted, hypothesis 4).[16] What deserves some lingering attention is
the fact that hidden behind the various hypotheses about copy-texts is
a critical consensus that the printed texts of *Hamlet* record a deliberate
adjustment, very likely a deliberate adjustment worked out in quite
particular consultation with the acting company.[17] That is, according
to *each* attempted solution of the textual crux, the topical is embraced

by intense authorial or authoritative intentions.[18] Surely criticism can aspire to make sense of the deliberation, the embracing intentions here.

I do not wish to propose that the original creative deliberations surrounding this passage had anything like the intensity of the bibliographic squabbles issuing from them. My point is simple. Something was happening in the London theatrical scene that accorded with issues embedded in a script either already in performance or in a draft that was probably very fully realized; the thinking-through of that accord is registered in the Folio text of the play. What has now subsided into mere textual crux was once—if only momentarily—considered theatrically crucial, so that even if the theatrical passage to Elsinore begins with the lower criticism it must work its way up to the higher.

II

ROSIN.
... But there is Sir an ayrie of Children, little Yases, that crye out on the top of question; and are most tyrannically clap't for't: these are now the fashion, and so be-ratled the common Stages (so they call them) that many wearing Rapiers, are affraide of Goose-quils, and dare scarse come thither.

HAM.
What are they Children? Who maintains 'em? How are they escoted? Will they pursue the Quality no longer then they can sing? Will they not say afterwards if they should grow themselves to common Players (as it is like most if their meanes are not better) their Writers do them wrong, to make them exclaim against their owne Succession.

ROSIN.
Faith there ha's bene much to do on both sides. . . .

—F1, Oo3v–Oo4

If in fact the state of Q2 is telling us that for some reason the company wanted to remove all references to the children's companies, to excise any mention of the condescension of the Blackfriars playwrights to the "public" playwrights, to delete all reference to theatrical competition, then the company was only anticipating the anti-topicality of most classroom practice and of most criticism. (The gloss to these lines will refer us to those pages in the Introduction that deal with the dating of *Hamlet,* or with its text; and we reassure our students that they need

not concern themselves with these dreary pages.) Critics have occasionally legitimized the "intrusion" of the passage by delimiting its
reference: the sudden rise of London's child actors to favor is constrained to participate both in a "larger" thematic of usurpation or to
render the hero's obsession with fickleness (actually it is Rosencrantz
who raises this issue). We can widen the reference of this passage
considerably, but the interests of legitimization, of reclamation, cannot
long be served.

It would be securely within the tradition of reclamation, for example,
to propose that Hamlet finds in the usurping children an image of his
own infantile rebelliousness; it would be more than reclamation to
propose that *Shakespeare* stages his own considerable rebelliousness
here. The Danish past is, after all, erased here by an English present.
(Later in the play, the England that is here invoked will be represented
as the land of a genuine lunacy antithetical to the false lunacy of representation. And England will cleave to Denmark, such that one must
be the land of the living, the other the land of the dead.)[19] This rebellion is a bit of public, but anti-mimetic, theatricality; it cannot be so
easily reclaimed. Anti-mimetic rebellion will be staged again in the next
act, when Heminges (probably), playing Polonius, reminds Burbage,
playing Hamlet, that "I did enact Julius Caesar. I was killed i'th' Capitol.
Brutus killed me" (3.2.102–03). Observing that this later passage "contains extra-dramatic meanings," E. A. J. Honigmann ("Date" 30) toys
with the idea that Polonius's accompanying reference to playing at the
university might itself be extra-dramatic. He points out that the title
page of Q1 refers to performances of *Hamlet* at Oxford and Cambridge,
argues that Polonius's lines are unlikely to be a late interpolation, and
then arrests his interesting chain of inference. He seems to be leading
toward Nosworthy's proposition that *Hamlet* was drafted in anticipation of university performances.[20] A wonderful thought: like the players
in Elsinore, the King's Men offer a road show. Certainly in the performances to which the Q1 title page refers—with Hamlet in exile from
the university and *Hamlet* in exile to it—in such performances, the
hero's earlier question, "How chances it they travaile?" would be theatrically anti-dramatic.

And the passage obtrudes even more intransigent, more specifically
anti-dramatic matter. Economic constraints have forced the players to
their provincial tour in Denmark:

ROS.

Faith, there has been much to do on both sides; and the nation holds it no sin
to tar them to controversy. There was for a while no money bid for argument
unless the poet and the player went to cuffs in the question.

HAM.

Is't possible?

GUILD.

O, there has been much throwing about of brains.

(2.2.350–56)

Poets and players are laboring within a newly competitive economy;
Rosencrantz brings news from the theatrical marketplace which was
the front lines of the War of the Theaters. The problem of dating *Hamlet,* the nature of its emergency, will depend on how many skirmishes
may be supposed to have been waged within this war, on where *Hamlet*
comes in the sequence of theatrical skirmishes that culminate in Jonson's *Poetaster* and in Dekker's (and Marston's?) *Satiromastix,* a public
squabbling that pits public theaters against private, Henslowe interests
against Burbage, the Blackfriars Jonson against the Paul's Marston. One
play indisputably set Hamlet's favorite company on the road to Elsinore,
and that is Jonson's *Cynthia's Revels.*

Cynthia's Revels comes early in the War of the Theaters. Hence,
although it satirizes contemporary theatrical practice, it does so without much animus. It begins with one of Jonson's most unsettling In-
ductions, in which the brilliant boy-actor, Salamon Pavy, draws straws
for the right to speak the Prologue with an equally ambitious fellow-
actor. When he loses he seeks revenge on the Author—as if Jonson had
exploited his power by scripting Pavy's own bad luck. His revenge is
to reveal Jonson's plot "and so stale his invention to the auditorie before
it come forth." The threat is momentous, and crucial here for what it
implies about the status of dramatic authorship and theatrical dissemination. Jonson's Pavy begins a drift toward the representation of a
dramatic script as a theatrical property, of drama as commerce. After
the avenging plot summary, and some mild mockery—possibly aimed
at Marston, possibly at Shakespeare—of playwrights who meddle in the
operations of acting companies, Pavy undertakes to negotiate with the
playwright on behalf of his audience. He encourages modesty of diction,
ingenuity of sentence, and, above all, genuine originality. Speaking for
the coterie audience, Pavy begs that playwrights "would not so penu-

riously glean wit, from everie laundresse, or hackney-man, or derive
their best grace (with servile imitation) from common stages" (Induction 180–82). The War of the Theaters will thrive on the energies of
class competition invoked here, will relish the thematics of the *impoverished* imagination.

Moreover, it will fasten on plagiarism as its central issue.[21] Pavy ends
his attack on plagiarism with a figure that surely seized Shakespeare's
attention:

they say, the *umbrae,* or ghosts of some three or four playes, departed a dozen
yeeres since, have bin seene walking on your stage heere: take heed, boy, if
your house bee haunted with such *hobgoblins,* 'twill fright away all your
spectators quickly. (Induction 194–98)

The passage is enough to send an editor of *Hamlet* into a frenzy. Jonson
is almost certainly referring to Henslowe's 1597 revival of *The Spanish
Tragedy* (though this was old news when *Cynthia's Revels* was staged)
and more generally to the fin-de-siècle revival of the revenge play form
spearheaded by Marston. Before he left off his association with the
Chamberlain's Men for a more upscale relationship with the Children
of the Chapel, Jonson must have heard that they too were going to try
bringing back the old revenge plays of the previous decade, that Shakespeare was even considering reworking the outmoded *Hamlet*-play of
1587 (probably by Kyd), complete with the neo-Senecan ghost of the
Ur-Hamlet and a version of the play-within-a-play of Kyd's *Spanish
Tragedy*.[22] It is entirely characteristic of Jonson to direct his most scath-
ing attacks at degraded versions of his own principles: here what is
singled out for abuse, manufactured as the central issues of the War of
the Theaters, are plagiarism and slavish nostalgia.[23] Notice the perti-
nence of these issues for *Hamlet*. What Jonsonian psychopathology
selects as the central vices of contemporary theatrical practice provides
the essential conceptual framework for theatrical practice at Elsinore.
Recognizing this framework will enable us to say more articulately, to
mean, what we have been saying all along, which is that *Hamlet* is
haunted by theatricality.

My remarks here are to a great extent influenced by William Empson's
"*Hamlet,*" a much revised version of his 1953 essay, "*Hamlet* When

New."[24] Empson sees *Hamlet* as a specific response to the revenge revival; his achievement is to recognize the engagement of this play in the pragmatics of revival.[25] That insight can be elaborated, for Shakespeare meditates not only on the pragmatics of revival, made a matter of special contention by the warring theaters, but on the poetics of revival as well. That is, Shakespeare not only conjures up the "ghosts of some three or four plays," impersonating them in the ghost of Hamlet I and the ranting Laertes; he rises to the specific issues of the Jonsonian challenge as soon as he gets his cry of players onto the Danish scene. Almost immediately Hamlet asks for a recitation from a very Jonsonian play, Jonsonian in its slavish neoclassicism: "one speech in't I chiefly loved," says Hamlet, " 'twas Aeneas' tale to Dido—and thereabout of it especially when he speaks of Priam's slaughter" (2.2.442–44).[26]

Shakespeare insists here on the full reach of the play's cultural memory, the full scale of its ambitions. The speech that follows will, of course, provide one of the play's myriad analogues for Hamlet himself, in this case an imago in which the filial avenger is conflated with the bloodthirsty murderer of fathers. The oedipal fantasy is overdetermined, for by recalling Virgil's most explicit recollection of Homer, the speech places Shakespeare in an agonistic relationship with the only precursors whom one tradition of criticism finds worthy of him. All of *Hamlet* is perhaps adumbrated in the hesitation with which the *Aeneid ends,* but in the particular suspended moment before Pyrrhus strikes, one can easily find a furiously empowered effacement of all distinction between Trojan Homer, Trojan Virgil, and Trojan Shakespeare. Canonization was a favorite activity for Elizabethan cultural apologists; *Hamlet* joins here in the procedures of such critical texts as *The Arte of English Poesie, Palladis Tamia,* and *The Apologie for Poesie,* although in this instance we have something very close to what Jonathan Freedman calls autocanonization, "those moments in which popular or mass culture adopts the canonizing strategies of high or official culture in order to legitimate itself" (213).

My application of Freedman's notion wants some clarification. Most obviously pertinent is Freedman's emphasis on *self*-canonization. Just as Virgil authenticates himself in his hero's Homeric telling, so Shakespeare canonizes himself here by opening tragedy to epic. By detailing its lineage, Shakespeare is plainly announcing exactly how important this play is.[27] But my application of Freedman's term also forces me to ask what kind of transaction this scene represents in the commerce between official and popular culture. To an extent, the London theater already partakes of official culture, if not securely; that is why Francis Meres can canonize popular dramatists in *Palladis Tamia*. But surely the "rugged Pyrrhus" speech renders the partaking problematic; *that* may be learned from the long-standing critical dispute over whether the speech is any good or not. What continues to bother critics, what clearly caused sleeplessness in A. C. Bradley, was that Coleridge found disdain for the speech "beneath criticism." I trust it is not dismissive simply to say that the speech *conflates* the manner of ranting tragedy and of Virgilian epic. This is *contaminatio,* practiced in such a way that it elides the distinction between *imitatio* and the adoption of stylistic fashion. To be as clear as possible: no particular idiom is being lampooned (interrogated, subjected to critique); what suffers under the solvent of Shakespearean polemical cunning is the idea of a gross sequestering of "popular" idiom from neoclassical stylistic canons. The "Pyrrhus speech" accomplishes an assault on discursive strata—say, the official and the popular—*per se,* an assault that has remained critically unassimilable: in *Hamlet* 2.2 official and popular are made to be imperfectly distinguishable. Whatever the genetics of the text of this scene in F, the imaginative activity that produced it was powerfully integral. The deliberation that welds the report of the War of the Theaters to the report of a war in Troy provides for a concordance of many discords.

To remark that authorial agon has been intentionally situated within the sphere of theatrical competition is in many ways to recapitulate the analysis that Robert Weimann has performed on Hamlet's advice to the players. He writes of that speech:

Its theme is neither exclusively that of Renaissance rhetoric or neoclassical poetics nor that of Elizabethan theatrical practice, but one in which the demands of the former are viewed in relation to, or in collision with the latter. (280)

This merits only a minor correction: for Shakespeare, to view neoclassical poetics "in relation to" Elizabethan theatrical practice entails a denial that the former is "in collision with" the latter.[28] This implicit denial is, I think, the essence of the theatrical management instituted in *Hamlet*.[29]

These are still matters of public theatricality. Yet there is a good deal more to say of this speech, business to conduct closer to home. Nothing in *Hamlet* so betrays the tiger's heart of its upstart poet than its initial comparison:

> *The rugged Pyrrhus, like th'Hyrcanian beast—*
>
> (2.2.446)

This tentative line, this trial, at once recalls both Marlowe's *Dido* (5.1.159) and Greene's stinging insult from his *Groatsworth of Wit* and puts down that which is recollected as a misremembrance: " 'Tis not so."[30] The tiger's heart is replaced, or perhaps only disguised, by the sable arms, overshadowed by an epic heraldry both more gentlemanly and more dismal. It is not enough that Shakespeare should inscribe himself here within a genealogical fiction that establishes him as the heir to Homer and Virgil; he also recalls, with casual negligence, those former competitors whom he has outstripped and outlived. Kyd's generation is buried even as this line is spoken and canceled. That is, even in the Q2 *Hamlet,* where references to the children's companies are hard to detect and references to the War of the Theaters are nowhere to be seen, Shakespeare has already implicated contemporary theatrical competition in the more rarefied struggle with Homer and Virgil. In one sense, then, the emergence of theatrical news into the text of *Hamlet* is what was meant all along. In another sense, Jonson provokes the emergency, for Shakespeare has inserted his theatrical news where it can most unsettle the quite anxious Jonsonian distinction between neoclassical *imitatio* and opportunistic plagiarism. The hobgoblins of plagiarism consort with the *umbrae* of *imitatio.* The deliberation that produces the text of this scene in the Folio *Hamlet* is a thinking-through in the context of a particularly lively theatrical economy of the poetics and pragmatics of revival.

III

The rugged *Pyrrhus,* he whose Sable Armes
Blacke as his purpose, did the night resemble

> When he lay couched in the Ominous Horse,
> Hath now this dread and blacke Complexion smear'd
> With Heraldry more dismall: Head to foote
> Now is he to take Geulles, horridly Trick'd
> With blood of Fathers, Mothers, Daughters, Sonnes . . . .
>
> —F1, Oo4

Aeneas's tale to Dido once again pulls representation in *Hamlet* away from a Danish scene to an English stage, and matters of public theatricality drift toward private meditation as he marks the pastness of the immediate past. *Hamlet* is more than an oedipal plot; here the play hints at the oedipal character of the cultural marketplace. Indeed, oedipal structures are essential to the "extra-dramatic meanings" of this play. Stephen Dedalus, before Ernest Jones, remarked these structures, proposing in the communications between the Ghost and Hamlet a dialogue between Shakespeare and his lost son: Joyce's oedipal *Hamlet* is more elegiac and more witty than is Jones's.[31] I think Joyce the better critic here, if only because he is willing to hazard a description of theater so private that it can barely be recaptured for the Danish scene. It is indecorous, but historiographically appropriate to guess at the private logic that binds the reflections on the child actors to the autocanonization of *Hamlet*.

According to Dedalus, Shakespeare speaks with the purgatorial voice of the father in 1.5. I suppose him to impersonate the father once more when Rosencrantz announces the arrival of the London theatrical scene at Elsinore. Shakespeare, for years the impersonator of dignified old men, may be said to exclaim against his own succession here: the little eyases parody his own licensed and professional usurpation of the roles of old men. But another late innovation has erased the merely professional nature of Shakespeare's usurpation, for Shakespeare in this antidramatic present displaces, and here stages the displacement of, an English father who—it depends on the dating—has just died, is dying, or is to die within a few months. The meditation on John Shakespeare's death and the anxious yearning for apt paternity may be said to continue in Aeneas's tale to Dido, where the deaths of pettier elders are recorded and a new lineage chosen: Marlowe, Greene, and Kyd are rejected for the benign and distant parentage of Homer and Virgil. In the description of Pyrrhus charged with the burden of his father's furious honor, we again see, not only Hamlet, but Hamlet's maker; and all swell here with self-transforming power, a power, by no means absolute, to defend the father, which is, however limited, a power over the father. That Pyrrhus's power is a power to confer a new coat of arms is by no means fortuitous. John Shakespeare had wanted one since 1568; only in 1596 was his son sufficiently eminent and influential to secure this honor on his father's behalf. Pyrrhus figures the violence implicit in filial service.

Shakespeare's coat of arms was not *only* a private matter. As a gauge of the social position of poets and men of the theater it engaged other jealous minds.

They are growne licentious, the rogues; libertines, flat libertines. They forget they are i' the *statute* [Eliz. 39:4, making players, officially, vagabonds, *not* gentlemen], the rascals, they are *blazond* there [in the statute, not in the College of Heralds], there they are trickt, they and their pedigrees; they need no other *heralds,* I wisse. (*Poetaster* 1.2.52–55)

Here is another good reason for wishing to fix the date or dates of *Hamlet*—so that one could begin to assess whether Jonson's attack in *Poetaster* on upstart playwrights provoked or was provoked by the implications of this scene in *Hamlet.*[32] If Q2 is an early draft or performance version, and if it precedes *Poetaster,* then issues of canon and genealogy came up together, but without the stimulus of the slap from Jonson. If F is prior, as Dover Wilson thought, then Jonson himself may have motivated the *braid* of meditations on theatrical, cultural, familial, and social competition. Again, the "Flourish for the Players" at Elsinore is a concordance of discord; a serious swordplay of goose quills; a suspension, not a solution, of competition.

Jonson, for his part, would aspire to a solution, if not an evasion, of competition, and he worked it out quite differently, retreating to the private theaters, to Whitehall, and to the vagaries of noble patronage, on the one hand, and to the quiet confines of the Folio *Works* on the other; his effort is to displace competition by means of an anti-agonistic laureation.[33] Shakespeare works otherwise, confirming agon in competition. What he expresses at this juncture is nothing less than the construction of Early Modern authorship, in which the humanist prestige of canonicity is *coordinated with* the economic logic of success.

Rosencrantz's remark that "there was for a while no money bid for argument unless the poet and the player went to cuffs in the question" is not a simple one to construe. It is not clear whether he means that now poet and player go to cuffs over the poet's fees or that the only plays that sell are those that stage hostilities between poet and playwright. What is clear is that the players have retreated to Elsinore from a specifically *competitive* theatrical environment; only in such an environment could Jonson force plagiarism as the central issue of the War of the Theaters. Within the heavily capitalized London theater, jokes, plots, habits of diction had attained the status of intellectual property. There, as in most emergent spheres of an economy, property relations were drastically unsettled. Where once a playtext had been a mere means to the productive labors of an acting company, it had come to have autonomous value. Contest over this emergent property is expressed variously—in injunctions to "those that play your clowns [to] speak no more than is set down for them," in the vogue for plays that stage (as does *Cynthia's Revels*) a coming-to-blows of actor and author, itself clearly an intellectual property dispute.[34] It is impossible to say how much animus fired the explosions in the War of the Theaters (Jonson was clearly nettled, but his anger almost always exceeds circumstance); animus is not important to this competition. In the previous decade, the University Wits had succeeded in transforming the ancient tradition of flytting into a marketable commodity. The warring playwrights exploit this new principle of London's cultural marketplace—Insult Sells.

The war economy was, happily for the playwrights, inflationary. As playtexts began to acquire autonomous value, their price began to rise. During the 1590s the price that acting companies paid for plays hovered around six pounds, but by 1602 eight pounds was not uncommon, and by 1612, prices ranged from ten to twenty or twenty-five pounds. The beginnings of this inflation must have been palpable in the years just before *Hamlet* was written (Albright 221). And this is not the only evidence for revaluation of playtexts. In the years before *Hamlet* there developed the novel procedure of "staying registration." Opinion is now divided about the function of such registration. A. W. Pollard believed that such registrations enabled acting companies to translate their "stage rights" in plays into a rudimentary copyright, by paying an individual stationer to register a given text for publication. No one had any intention of publishing the text at that moment: the printer had *eventual* claims on the playtext, while the acting company, having thus protected the text from unauthorized publication, could now control the occasion of its publication. According to more recent counter-arguments (Cairncross; Johnson), staying registration was itself a *means* to unauthorized publication, an unscrupulous stationer's method of securing rights to printing *despite* the wishes of the acting company. Either way, staying registration was a means of stabilizing a market in theatrical property that was both quickened and threatened by the late innovation of piratical publication. The threat of such piracy is itself crucial evidence of the new commercial pressures in the theater, for piratical publication seems to depend on yet another novel develop-ment in the theatrical economy, the piracy of playtexts by acting com-panies, unscrupulous companies seeking cheap texts as they left the competitive urban theatrical scene and set out on a season of provincial touring. In more ways than one, then, *Hamlet* is a product of the late innovation. Though some mysteries persist in the case, we surely have an instance of staying registration when, in July of 1602, James Roberts "entred for his Copie" in the Stationers' Register "a book called the Revenge of Hamlett Prince [of] Denmarke as yt was latelie Acted by the Lord Chamberleyne his servantes"; we surely have an exemplar of a pirated text in Nicholas Ling's first quarto of 1603. Theatrical labor had precipitated new forms of competition—new commercial transactions and new forms of theft—all of which transformed the institutional status of the dramatic text. The text acquired new economic value, so that a fine pragmatic imagination could comfortably invest it with other values. "Thus o'ersized" it could become a sphere of great cultural claims, the theatrical text commensurate with epic, the public text adequate to the most intense private fantasies. Jonathan Goldberg has recently argued that, in *Hamlet,* "the pen produces the character, the letter, and the person" (323); perhaps it is more than supplementary for me to observe that a competitive press and a competitive theater produce the playwright, the playbook, and the author.[35]

Perhaps this historiography of the text can prove more generally useful to students of English Renaissance culture, promoting new forms of attention and enabling new forms of discrimination. In Jonson's case, the printed playtext is an anti-theatrical monument, whereas for Shakespeare, print was coming to be coordinated with theatrical interests. The Chamberlain's Men had successfully diversified: they had built their own playhouse and may even have secured the cooperation of friendly printers, thus assembling a cartel of disseminative apparatuses. Recent criticism has inscribed the English theater within a dialectic of tense dependence on the interests of the new monarchy, so that the drama has been represented as oscillating between ideological collusion and ideological resistance; historical criticism needs to correct this model by recognizing the degree to which English theatricality invented and improvised within spheres relatively autonomous from the ideological productivities of the court. The textual approach to Elsinore leads us away from the English court, back to the city, to the bookstall, the printshop, the box office, and the stage.

Notes

1. I cite the First Folio from Charlton Hinman's facsimile edition, the second quarto from W. W. Greg's facsimile; except where otherwise indicated, however, I cite *Hamlet* from the new Arden edition of Harold Jenkins. I silently adjust the facsimile texts to accord with modern typographic and orthographic norms in the use of *u* for *v, v* for *u, i* for *j, j* for *i;* long *s* is changed to short *s.*

2. Here I'm going against Jenkins's identification of the "innovation" with the Essex rebellion; this is not to say that Jenkins's reading could not have *become* accurate. In this (and much else) I follow Fredson Bowers (Review), who notes that one source of Jenkins's appetite for the reading is that it will help him date the play; to this might be added the vogue in finding the Essex rebellion everywhere in late Elizabethan texts. For more on the reference of "innovation," see below, notes 4 and 6.

3. On the matter of insolubility, see the final pages of Werstine. The first version of the present essay suffered from its having been delivered in the winter of 1987, before I had the benefit of reading Werstine's essay. I concur with his assessment of the theoretical obstacles, obstacles that are essentially epistemological, to the resolution of the textual arguments affecting *Hamlet*—or any other text; I would add that there are genuinely significant obstacles to resolution that are a matter of the sociology of knowledge.

4. This line of argument is usually bolstered by arguments that Gabriel Harvey knew the play, probably from having seen a performance, and probably before the fall of Essex in February of 1601; *Cynthia's Revels* was produced during the previous year. Another line of argument discounts the limitation *ad quem* of February 1601, and proposes that the topical moment in *Hamlet* refers to Jonson's *Poetaster.*

It should perhaps be noted that persuasive arguments *can* be marshaled on behalf of the Privy Council ruling as the "innovation": by virtue of its having limited the number of playhouses to two and the number of weekly performances at those theaters to two, the ruling could easily have inhibited theatrical business; see Honigmann, "Date." That the ruling proved ineffectual does not itself seem to me to be sufficient grounds for rejecting this interpretation, for since the scene is straddling the fictive and the real it does not seem an inordinate supplementary imposition to ask an audience to imagine an actual—and notorious—ruling having its intended effects, to accept an inconsequential fact as if it were consequential.

What does seem an obstacle to this interpretation is that Rosencrantz has spoken of an innovation as a means to an inhibition. Though it is easy enough to conceive of the Privy Council ruling as an "innovation," it is far easier to think of it as an "inhibition." The latter term, present in the sentence to designate a distinct *result* of what is referred to as an innovation, seems to block reception of "innovation" as anything like a distinct attempt to inhibit theatrical activity. The sentence "His recovery came by means of a remarkable cure" seems a useful analogy: though we can construe "remarkable cure" as a restoration to health, we may be expected to construe it as a kind of therapy, since "recovery" clues us to look for an *alternative* construction for "cure." This is not positive evidence. I am simply pointing out that the line makes it difficult for an audience to construe "innovation" as "the official inhibition of theatrical activity"; we would expect the lines that follow to relieve the difficulty and secure such a reference, which they do not. Nothing in the dramatic structure of the scene seems to provide a context for riddling from Rosencrantz at this juncture. (And see the discussion of "innovation" in the Kittredge *Hamlet.*)

5. The War of the Theaters has received little new attention in twentieth-century scholarship. Small may be recommended cautiously as an introduction to the subject; the most useful work done since then may be found in Campbell, Harbage (90–119), Omans, and Talbert.

6. It is also the theory that I am most inclined to accept. More important, it is quite *close* to the theory that Jenkins espouses, though he believes that "innovation" refers to the Essex rebellion. Jenkins holds that *Hamlet* responds to the War of the Theaters in its comments on the "throwing about of brains" in the professional urban theater; this, he believes, is what marks *Hamlet* as subsequent to *Satiromastix* (presumably Jonson's early splutterings don't count until they provoke Marston and Dekker's response). Still, Jenkins also wishes to accommodate a reference to *Hamlet* in marginalia found in Gabriel Harvey's copy of Speght's Chaucer, marginalia to which it is difficult to give a date subsequent to late February of 1601. (Leo Kirschbaum attempted to remove that temporal limit; he is refuted in Honigmann, "Date.") The Harvey note seems to require a version of *Hamlet* antedating *Satiromastix*. (If the truth be told, it'd be far easier to give a date of late 1598 or early 1599 to Harvey's marginalia, a date to which almost everything in the passage points, except that *that* would require a very early date for *Hamlet,* one not only well before the War of the Theaters, but before one or two other generally accepted *termini a quo.*) So Jenkins accepts the possibility of minor additions

to the play later in the year, noting that this lends some support for arguments (Bowers, "Pictures"; Smith, Pizer, and Kaufman) that the juxtaposition of the portraits of two Horaces in *Satiromastix* imitates *Hamlet*. (It is worth noting here that in 4.1 of *Satiromastix,* Tucca says "my name's Hamlet revenge." He *need* not be taken as alluding to Shakespeare's play, for "Hamlet, revenge" seems to have been the most notorious line in the *Ur-Hamlet* of the previous decade; cf. Thomas Lodge's reference in *Wit's Miserie* [1596] to "the Visard of the ghost which cried so miserably at the Theator, like an oister wife, Hamlet, revenge" as well as the much later allusion in *The Night Raven,* by S. R., "I will not call Hamlet Revenge my greeves.") Jenkins is wise, I think, to rest nothing on this particular piece of evidence, since in this case influence may well flow in the other direction; see my note 27 below. If that were so we would have not only a hypothetical cycle of influence that proceeds from *Hamlet* to *Antonio's Revenge* to *Poetaster* to *Hamlet* (with new material on the little eyases and the late innovation now included) but also one that proceeds from *Hamlet* to *Satiromastix* to *Hamlet* (with new material on the comparison of the portraits of Hamlet I and Claudius now included in 3.4). Of course, these "derivative" *Hamlet*s are purely hypothetical revisions. (The arguments for an acting version of *Hamlet* without the remarks on the trouble caused by the little eyases will be taken up below in the discussions of the first and third textual hypotheses.) The hypothesis of a version of *Hamlet* without the references to the little eyases, circulating in manuscript or actually in performance, should be recognized as a response to only three evidentiary tugs: Harvey's marginalia, the text of Q2, and Marston's supposed indebtedness in *Antonio's Revenge*.

7. For a useful introduction to how the theories of textual transmission evolved under what has been called the New Bibliography, see chap. 2 (and its appendices) of Honigmann, *Stability* 7–21.

8. See Hibbard's introduction to *Hamlet:* he displays not only the simplicity of this hypothesis, but also its explanatory power, for he argues that the unusual choice of copy-text for F—theatrical text instead of a quarto edition—may be *explained* by the inadequacy of Q2 to contemporary theatrical practice. But note that this argument might also be invoked in defense of the second hypothesis, discussed below.

It is worth noting that Fredson Bowers, in an important review of Jenkins, has implied that he holds this to be the best explanation, at least as far as this passage is concerned. He appears to recommend as the simplest explanation (though he offers this explanation entirely in the subjunctive) that the play went into production in late 1600 or early 1601 with this section of 2.2 more or less as Q2 gives it (i.e., with lines 335–58, according to the new Arden lineation, absent) and that these lines were added later in 1601; see below, notes 9 and 10, and Bowers, Review 284–88.

Bowers proposed this possibility less formally in 1962; see his "Established Texts and Definitive Editions," collected in *Essays.* He and Hibbard have not been alone in recent advocacy of this position. Steven Urkowitz has argued that Q1, Q2, and F *Hamlet* each represent distinct versions of the play, each with distinct Shakespearean authority, a position from which he has retreated to the extent that he no longer regards Q1 as authoritative ("Three *Hamlet*s").

9. Here the difficulty will involve a supposition that authorial additions to an authorial manuscript appeared to lack authority. The hypothesis can be sophisticated—by supposing a fair copy to have intervened between the completion of a version prior to the "innovation" and the making up of the promptbook so that a subsequent authorial addition to that fair copy really seems an excrescence or the addition to have been written hastily, in another ink, or to have been dictated to someone writing another hand.

The *hand* in which copy for Q2 was written, once firmly believed to be Shakespeare's—this is Jenkins's position still—may not necessarily be so. In his review of Jenkins, for example, Bowers summarizes Jenkins's assertion and passes on cagily, "granting so much and granting it gladly" (284); in his review of the state of textual scholarship in 1971, "Seven or More Years?," he is more definite: "[I]t seems to me inconceivable, now that we know that the same two Roberts' compositors set *The Merchant of Venice* as well as Q2 *Hamlet,* that anyone could fancy both manuscripts were holograph as was generally assumed before the era of compositor analysis" (58).

The many variants of the second hypothesis tend to depend on the assumption that copy for Q2 was illegible in places, and that is itself a dubious assertion; Roberts' compositors are more than likely to have had scribal fair copy in their hands. In general, far too much has been made of the "indecipherable copy" of Q2. Bowers believes that the compositors consulted Q1 when that copy proved problematic (and that Q1 and F ultimately derive from the same promptbook). Jenkins believes very strongly that the copy for Q2 was frequently indecipherable and argues against an intervening fair copy. (Peter W. M. Blayney implies, however, that setting without fair copy would have been quite uncommon.) My own sense is that where Jenkins claims an indecipherable copy to explain nonsense he would be as well off, perhaps better off, with the hypothesis of nonsensical fair copy. Compositors are not idiots, though they make mistakes: illegibility will not so easily explain Jenkins's first piece of evidence (38) on behalf of illegible printer's copy, to wit, at 349, *the umber* for *thumb.* One is very much more likely to choose "your fingers and thumb" over "your fingers and the umber" when illegible copy offers even the hint of choice, whereas a fair copy that offers the latter reading only will have an authority that is difficult to resist. (On 46 Jenkins supposes that copy read "th[*half-space*]umbe". Compositor Y, the more careful of Roberts' two workmen, was setting here: why he should deliberately transform nonsensical "th umbe" into "the umber"—even supposing two expansions, first to "the umbe" and thence to "the umber"—in this textual circumstance eludes me.) I am not proposing that this error in Q2 *must* be scribal in origin, for it seems to me to be explicable as compositorial error of a sort that by no means requires the hypothesis of illegible copy (though I should think that supposing the copy to have read "th umbe" will not help here). (The same might be said of those instances that Jenkins cites as "what appear to be author's first thoughts corrected *currente calamo*" [41]; the Roberts compositors who set Q2 were very good, but most of the errors Jenkins cites seem to me to be attributable to imperfect compositorial proof-correction.) My first point is that it is usually extremely difficult to distinguish compositorial confusion over a manuscript reading from scribal confusion, since the key unit of work is usually roughly the same—both scribe and compositor absorb copy in phrasal units (except where difficulties of comprehension, as when one is reproducing technical, extremely idiosyncratic, or foreign language, reduce the unit of temporary memorization). From what Blayney has argued we are as likely to find this sort of error in books set from fair copy as from "foul." It is worth quoting him here; he is discussing the use of press variants to deduce copy, but his conclusion is appropriate to any attempt to ascertain the nature of copy based on bibliographic arguments from the appearance of the printed page: "With a few very trivial exceptions, the uncorrected state agrees with the manuscript . . . , and it is the manuscript that is in error" (289, and see 265–66). My second point is simply that Jenkins, following in the line that descends from Dover Wilson, wants very much to have at least one text of *Hamlet* which involves a printer's attempt to construe William Shakespeare's own handwriting. Where Q2 shows signs of playhouse marking the book-keeper is supposed to have been marking up William Shakespeare's own autograph manuscript, and not, which would be a bit more likely, marking up a transcript.

It might be added that a *fair copy* of the Q2 copy-text will help explain how it is that in portions of Q2 in which the printed text results from some form of conflation of Q1 and ms. copy clear textual errors independent from Q1 are to be found (as in Jenkins's example [48] of 1.5.55–56). Q1 should have been more persuasive than illegible copy, but Q1 was clearly resisted, and in lines where it has been consulted; the readings offered by Q2 are, then, either compositorial errors—never to be discounted—or signs of confidence in ms. copy, in which case one should assume that it appeared to deserve it.

10. In a sense this is a deep sophistication of the first hypothesis, with the distinction that Jenkins's Q2 is *not* a record of the early performances. Because his Q2 fails to reproduce a performance version, and fails because the foul papers record in confusing fashion the transition from the first to the second stage-version, Jenkins may be situated in the tradition of the second hypothesis.

Because of the current authority of his edition, I am obliged to indicate why Jenkins's textual arguments must be regarded as inconclusive, if only to explain why the various arguments for the transmission of *Hamlet* are presented here as still competing. The tendency of Jenkins's arguments may be traced to Dover Wilson's influential *The Manuscript of Shakespeare's* Hamlet. It was Wilson who first thinned out the ranks of those willing to entertain the first hypothesis. He did so by arguing (1: 96ff.) that the absence of a reference to the children's companies in Q2 seems to involve a *deletion* of at least some version of the material preserved in F. Wilson maintained, that is, that Q2 was both historically secondary to F and logically faulty; it could not be supposed to preserve— or at least not to preserve accurately—a version of *Hamlet* in circulation or performance prior to that version represented in F.

For neither Bowers (Review 287) nor, earlier, Honigmann are the signs of omission compelling. Honigmann argued ("Date") for the first hypothesis, largely on external evidence, taking comfort that the most recent bibliographical scrutiny of Q2, by John Russell Brown, had issued in the same hypothesis ("Date" 31). Bowers, who has objected stringently to the complexity of Jenkins's textual hypotheses with respect to this passage, also believes that Q2 makes good sense here, and can easily represent a performance version. Holding that "the late innovation" refers to the rise of the children's companies, he suggests (Review 288) that the long passage on the eyrie of children (335–58) is a later addition which begins simply by *elaborating* a subject that was already present in the first performance version, and presumably in the foul papers, present in the allusion to the late innovation, and then proceeds to discuss the consequences of this innovation, namely the War of the Theaters. ("[T]here is no reason in the world why the 'late innovation' lines or Hamlet's caustic comment on Claudius's popularity need have been part of an addition and so not present in the original foul papers. If Shakespeare later added a topical reference to the War of the Theatres which therefore could not have been printed in Q2, it would have been no more than II.2.335–58, which we know from F"; Bowers, Review 288.)

It is instructive to consider the buried rationale of Wilson's argument. Despite the fact that he regarded the lines on the late innovation (in both Q2 and F) as a reference to the Essex rebellion and therefore as a reference distinguishable from the discussion of the little eyases (in F only), he regards the two references as derived from a single stage of composition—topical references, however distinct, are effectively treated as the same sort of thing. Thus, Wilson regarded Q2 as defective, as logically fragmented, because the "topicalities" had been sundered. Hence, wherever Wilson has held sway, the state of Q2 has been regarded as conspicuously inaccurate, insofar as it represents neither any distinct stage of composition nor any particular performance text.

At any rate, Wilson has obviously influenced the way in which Jenkins makes use of the second hypothesis. Wilson taught Jenkins to blame supposed faults in Q2 on supposed compositorial confusion. Jenkins's achievements in this line of argument are not overwhelming—this is not seriously to impugn a magnificent editorial labor—for he is vague on the mechanics of such complex textual transmission. A theory of revision may provide for layered copy-texts, but if one is convinced that there are *signs* of omission in Q2, gaps, the hypothesis of copy-text with *logical* layering of textual strata has only limited explanatory power. Still, neither the second hypothesis nor Jenkins's appropriation of its logic is fundamentally despicable: a topical interpolation might have required complex adjustments at its boundaries to the prevenient version of the play, and the scribal or compositorial attempt to leave out what had been added might well have resulted in the preservation of some of those accommodations.

Jenkins's argument could surely be strengthened by detailed recourse to Q1. Copy for the bad quarto, registered in July 1602, is usually regarded as a memorial reconstruction; it contains an abbreviated version of the topical material, which suggests that the actors who performed the reconstruction knew a performance version of the play that included references to the late innovation ("noveltie" in Q1), specified as "private playes, / And ... the humour of children" (Q1, E3), but which lacked any allusion to the War of the Theaters. Thus Jenkins might have argued that the allusion to the War of the Theaters is a late addition, that cuts were made to accommodate it—"the humour of children" scratched to make way for the "little eyases"—and that Q2 records the accommodating cut but fails to reproduce the (once interleaved?) interpolated material.

11. Bowers points out that arguments here can be reversible; we can speak with comparable ease (or difficulty) of cuts or additions (Review 287–88).

12. The supposition that copy for Q2 is a descendant of foul papers just antecedent to the promptbook accommodates one particular piece of evidence very nicely (for others, clearly marshaled, see Hibbard 93–102). At 4.1.40, Q2 is missing a half-line, in which would have appeared the subject that would have given grammatical completion to the sentence fragment in the three and a half lines that follow it; F deletes the full sentence. One may postulate that the deletion was intentional, and that in F the excision is a clean one, whereas in Q2, the cut was marked in the copy-text, or a near ancestor to it, but that a scribe or a compositor transmitted a text with only the first half-line of the doomed passage removed. (That is, both F and Q2 show evidence that the sentence was to have been removed; since Theobald, editors have been trying to figure out ways to preserve it, even though this requires them to give the sentence an entirely conjectural subject. They have traditionally inscribed their own bad faith here by making their emendation a hypermetrical one.)

Wilson, Bowers, and Jenkins—a considerable bibliographic consensus—concur that a non-Shakespearean fair copy intervenes between the foul papers and the promptbook, though they have some differences about whether theatrical markings preliminary to preparation of the promptbook were written on the foul papers or on this intermediate fair copy. Bowers points out that "this basic hypothesis . . . prevents any suggestion that in single readings an F variant from Q2 could represent an authorial revision" (Review 284); it does not prevent any suggestions about the evolution of Shakespeare's drafts or about the possibility of theatrical cutting (or failure to cut, for which see my fourth hypothesis below).

Because of the logical difficulties in tracing *late* theatrical cuts to the copy for Q2, it is easy to see why Jenkins is so unenthusiastic about political explanations for the absence of the topical material in Q2 (44–45). A 1604 excision for political purposes would come awfully late to influence foul papers. Bowers has useful things to say about the omissions in Q2 as theatrical cuts marked, if not necessarily executed, in the promptbook or a pre-promptbook fair copy—and about theatrical cutting in general; see his Review 284–85. However he is, I think, injudiciously hostile to the possibility "that the Q2 manuscript was edited (and censored) especially for printing in 1604. If one may credit this latter speculation," he continues, "then the way is opened for all sorts of conjectures that can only muddy waters that are murky enough without idle roiling anew" (285). This looks like an argument from editorial convenience. It is true that simplicity of explanation is to be preferred in scientific modeling, but simplicity of models is by no means a guarantee of the "truth" (or future utility) of an explanation. Without entering into the dodgy business of verification in historical research, I would only wish to point out that Bowers does not in fact offer a detailed account of why these particular cuts were selected to speed particular actions.

13. Nosworthy makes this argument from line count as strenuously as anyone has done (165–66).

Edwards, with a weary but not unwarranted imprecision, surmises that the copy for both Q2 (19) and F (21–24) are long drafts, Q2 far more tentative, but F also unfinished; both precede prompt copy and both possess an easy amplitude that will be chastened in the creation of a more spartan promptbook, now lost. (Thus we have a combination of the second and the third hypotheses, a slowly evolving series of drafts and an excising acting company.)

14. Jenkins as well as Edwards credits the company with reverence for the idea of an authoritative super-*Hamlet,* a manuscript more copious than either F or Q2. He concludes that the copy for F was a transcript based on Q2 and corrected against a ms. influenced by the promptbook (or by "stage practice"), but representing a somewhat longer version of the play than that actually acted by Shakespeare's company. Jenkins has considerable tolerance—and perhaps a certain enthusiasm—for bibliographic complexity; if such a model of the textual situation resembles the last stages of Ptolemaic cosmology, it must be conceded that this model similarly saves most of the appearances, that *Hamlet* is notoriously difficult to edit, and that the cultural stakes in saving the textual appearances are extremely high.

15. This would also explain why the actors who "reported" the copy for Q1, probably in 1602, knew a version referring to the child actors, as Q2 does not (because F was in fact the acting version in 1602 *and thereafter*). This hypothesis derives the "topicalities" of F simply from the promptbook rather than from foul papers to which the promptbook was accommodated when the copy for F was prepared.

This hypothesis is not altogether an amateur production, since it is substantially derived from Nosworthy's argument about Q2: "[T]he Q2 manuscript was very much an author's final draft which had been handed to the company in all its untidiness. . . . [I]t is evident that the playhouse scribe recognised certain markings in the original manuscript (brackets in the left-hand margin) as deletions and that the Q2 compositors did not" (139). I have taken over this argument from illegible copy-text and simply relocated the origins of illegibility from author to acting company. But note that Nosworthy goes on to assert that the passage on the War of the Theaters was itself a last-minute addition and not an omission.

Hibbard also seems to believe that the Folio text is somehow a *defended* text. Like Nosworthy and Edwards he holds that copy for F is just preliminary to the promptbook; he holds (against the powerful consensus of Bowers, Jenkins, and Wilson) that Shakespeare himself was responsible for that copy—indeed that the misreadings in F are authorial misreadings. But the misreadings he cites in support of this argument involve a special clinging to the language of the foul papers, what Wilson calls "anticipation," as in "The vertue of his feare: but you must feare" for "The vertue of his will, but you must feare" in Q2. One might call this, tropically, "hyper-prolepsis" or "Miser-Poet's Foreclosure."

16. It will be noticed that I do not include the possibility that the omissions in Q2 are the result of editing for publication. That oddly common argument is briefly entertained by Jenkins and rejected (44–45). (Bowers concurs, and with excessive vehemence; see note 12 above.) If, for example, discussion of the War of the Theaters is excised

to avoid insult to a company now under Queen Anne's patronage (by a company now under King James's patronage?), one must wonder why so scrupulous an editor failed to excise the reference to the habitual drunkenness of Danes. No other rationale for excision has been proposed to date.

17. The idea of deliberations with the company concerning cuts and revision is by no means fanciful: in line with the literary critical arguments of H. Resch, J. D. Wilson, and T. S. Dorsch, Brents Stirling has argued, on bibliographic grounds, that such deliberations have left their traces on the text of *Julius Caesar;* but cf. the counterarguments in Jowett.

By emphasizing deliberate adjustment I will seem to be shadowing what has become a trend in recent criticism of *Lear.* Michael Warren, in his seminal article "Quarto and Folio *King Lear,*" Urkowitz (*Revision*), and Honigmann ("Revised") have employed traditional methods of textual criticism in order to articulate a history of deliberate revision, either by Shakespeare or by some other theatrical intelligence associated with the King's Men; this approach to *Lear* has since been monumentalized in a collection of essays on the "revisionary" theory, *The Division of the Kingdoms* (Taylor and Warren). If I am offering what is to some degree a comparable argument, I do so advisedly. The bibliographic assumptions and procedures of their approaches have received both explicit and implicit criticism, and to some extent their descriptive work has suffered by comparison with the powerful intricacies of Blayney's arguments.

My scruple over the recent revisionary readings of the *Lear* texts is far less significant than Paul Werstine's, since he is himself one of the contributors to *The Division of the Kingdoms.* Werstine specifically doubts the security with which one can argue for Shakespeare's having deliberately and extensively revised *Lear,* yet he can still entertain the possibility of what I have been calling "theatrically intelligent" revisions of both *Lear* and *Hamlet.* He attempts to describe the effective theatrical differences between the Q2 *Hamlet* and the F *Hamlet,* arguing that the Folio Laertes is more worthy of Hamlet's empathy than is the quarto Laertes and that the Folio Claudius is more cunning, "a stronger adversary" (22). Of the change he sees in Laertes I am unpersuaded; as for Claudius, he seems a more *voluble* adversary in F, though not necessarily a stronger one. But surely Werstine is right to see some access of generosity in the Folio Hamlet, for he is not so very much *after* Rosencrantz and Guildenstern as he is in the quarto. The most important achievement of his essay is not, however, a simple matter of practical criticism. It comes when he admits that the discrepancies between the texts do not all add up, and insists that one can characterize the effect of some of the differences without claiming a totalized conception of those differences, much less an intentional logic of differences.

This tends to a useful editorial argument. The advocates of authorial revision participate in the quest for the one true text; they complicate, but do not transform, the bibliographical hunger for origins (and cf. Urkowitz, *Revision* 14). Urkowitz believes that he has avoided the critical lapse in which Werstine's criticism seems to implicate him. Werstine believes, and surely he is correct, that a richly descriptive account of the differences between Q2 and F has essential editorial utility, even in the absence of a convincing bibliographical etiology of those texts. Werstine has doubts about our ability to account for all the textual differences between the two versions—as who could not who had read the last chapter of Blayney?—and his doubts seem to extend to our ability to construct a compelling general description of the copy for these two texts, but he does hold that the texts are different in ways that demand editorial recognition, that, although one text *may* serve to improve a reading in the other, it continues to be an editorial folly to attempt to collapse one text into the other. (In the essay that essentially opened the topic of the revised *Lear,* Warren describes a passage in which modern editors, by conflating quarto and Folio of *that* play, conjure into existence "a reading that has *no* authority" [98].) Revisionary bibliography has transformed the rhetoric of the True (or Authoritative) into a rhetoric of authorial Preference, a considerable improvement, but so far the revisionists still labor under what Werstine regards as a deluded faith in the possibility of inferring authorial intention. Citing Foucault—and apparently having benefited from some crisp breezes from a Derridean climate of opinion—he suggests that the quest for authorial intention has distracted us from discriminate address to discriminable texts.

18. To my knowledge, no bibliographer has proposed what might be called indeterminate error on the part of the compositors of Q2: the absence of the topical material from the quarto has been plausibly assumed to have been *motivated*.

19. See Margaret Ferguson's observations (300) about Claudius's dumbfounded query "What should this mean?" (4.7.47), when a letter comes to him from, apparently, "the undiscover'd country, from whose bourn / No traveller returns" (3.1.79–80). Like the passage on the theater in London, Claudius's exhortation, "Do it, England" (4.3.68), seems a moment when the play attempts to rouse itself from what the play itself keeps insisting on, the nightmare inauthenticity of representation: again, an England of deadly action would be an obverse of a Denmark of deadened recall.

20. Nosworthy, chap. 11. It is unfortunate that he weakens his case by simply ignoring F. S. Boas's vigorous argument (chap. 1) against an Oxford performance (though this still leaves Cambridge as a possibility). Yet Nosworthy is concerned primarily with urging the probability of a Cambridge performance in 1600 or 1601 (168).

21. That Jonson anticipated that the central issue of the War of the Theaters would be one of intellectual property, that he wished to *make* it the central issue (because of its centrality to his own sense of poetic identity) is even more obvious in *Poetaster.* The Marston-figure in that play, Demetrius, attacks Jonson's Horace for being a translator (Jonson was himself not only an imitator but a translator of Horace, albeit not until 1604) and, for Demetrius, translation is simply plagiarism, thus:

> And (but that I would not be thought a prater)
> I could tell you, he were a translater.
> I know the authors from whence he ha's stole,
> And could trace him too, but that I understand hem not full and whole.
>
> (*Poetaster* 5.3.310–13)

22. Jonson's Pavy goes on to attack precisely those theatrical nostalgias to which the Chamberlain's Men were catering, conjuring the satiric portrait of one "(whom it hath pleas'd nature to furnish with more beard, then braine)" and who "prunes his musstaccio,

lisps, and with some score of affected othes) sweares down all that sit about him; *That the old Hieronimo* (as it was first acted) *was the onely best, and judiciously pend play of Europe*" (lines 206–11).

23. As Anne Barton points out, Dekker and Marston responded with a *tu quoque:* in *Satiromastix,* Jonson is mocked as an erstwhile actor of Hieronymo; in additions for the printed version of *Antonio and Mellida,* as a reviser of *The Spanish Tragedy.* One might specify a description of the War of the Theaters by describing it as a contest over the inheritance of Kyd's literary properties. The little eyases made their most pointed intervention in this contest sometime between 1599 and 1604 with *The First Part of Hieronimo,* "a full-blown theatrical burlesque of *The Spanish Tragedy*"; see Reibetanz.

It should also be noted here that revival was not necessary to raise questions about the originality of revenge plays. In his epistle to Greene's *Menaphon,* one of the texts that seems to link Kyd most securely with the *Ur-Hamlet,* Nashe makes an attack on the tendency to unreflected neoclassicism in the form: "English Seneca read by Candlelight yields many good sentences, as 'Blood is a beggar,' and so forth; and if you entreat him faire in a frosty morning, he will afford you whole Hamlets, I should say handfuls, of tragical speeches" (474). Revival, then, seems to compound a problem recognized considerably earlier in the history of Elizabethan revenge tragedy.

24. The essay is full of good ideas—also of lively but baseless suppositions, which *may* be why it has been so unjustly neglected. The suppositions do not much compromise the essential argument, which is exquisitely attuned to the relation of the play to theatrical currents at the very turn of the seventeenth century.

25. No doubt Empson sees *too* much: "[S]omebody in the Company thumbed over the texts in the ice-box and said 'This ["Kyd's" *Hamlet;* Empson is certain that the *Ur-Hamlet* is Kyd's] used to be a tremendous draw, and it's coming round again; look at Marston. All you have to do is just go over the words so it's *life-like* and they can't laugh at it'" (80). However fanciful in detail, this seems absolutely right in spirit. The revenge play was clearly vulnerable—see *The First Part of Hieronimo*—to spoof at the turn of the century; the vulnerability, the screaming implausibility of its deferrals, may well have contributed to its cachet. Even Empson's slightly flippant tone does little to undermine the shrewdness of his vision of Shakespeare's response to the challenge: he calls Shakespeare's solution "a bold decision, and [it] probably decided his subsequent career, but it was a purely technical one. He thought: 'The only way to shut this hole is to make it big. I shall make Hamlet walk up to the audience and tell them, again and again, "I don't know why I'm delaying any more than you do; the motivation of this play is just as blank to me as it is to you; but I can't help it." What is more I shall make it impossible for them to blame him. And *then* they daren't laugh.' It turned out, of course, that this method, instead of reducing the old play to farce, made it thrillingly life-like and profound" (84).

26. Neoclassicism is not its only Jonsonian feature. Hamlet recalls a coterie play, one that discriminates against the undiscriminating: "the play, I remember, pleased not the million, 'twas caviare to the general. But it was, as I received it—and others, whose judgments in such matters cried in the top of mine—an excellent play" (2.2.431–35).

27. Here is the place to return to a scholarly tangle in which the lower criticism again rises to the higher, the matter of the dating of *Hamlet.* I have accepted the argument that at least the F text of *Hamlet* refers to a War of the Theaters already underway, that it comes after *Cynthia's Revels,* perhaps after *Poetaster,* and perhaps after *Satiromastix* (which *Poetaster* anticipates). Though F *may* follow *Satiromastix,* Dekker may also have had access to versions of *Hamlet* before *Satiromastix* was drafted (see note 5 above). The higher criticism will do well to consider the relationship of the portrait scenes in the two plays. It has been argued that the comparison of the portraits of Claudius and Hamlet I is imitated in that particularly vicious moment in *Satiromastix* where two pictures of Horace-Jonson are juxtaposed; my argument would make it at least as appropriate to suppose Shakespeare's imitation of *Satiromastix.* Shakespeare's play is deeply interested in the appropriation of literary property, in assimilation and imitation. We now admire Spenser for boldly appropriating the tale of Sir Thopas as the visionary core of his epic, a redemption of vision from bathos. At a moment fascinated with vulgarizing mimesis, Shakespeare might well wish to recall the various images of the theorist of *poesis ut pictura* in *Satiromastix,* a redemption of imitative theory from a play that focuses its otherwise dissipated satiric energies on the issue of literary plagiarism. On the other hand—if *Satiromastix* follows *Hamlet,* then this scene is by no means casual. To compare Jonson with Claudius would be a palpable hit: it calls him vulgar, ignoble, a thief and not a Horatian imitator. Though we cannot be certain of the direction of influence here, we may be confident, I think, in the *seriousness* of influence.

28. Later in the same essay Weimann observes that, "although the players' scenes have more often than not been treated as merely marginal or topical in their interest, they in their own way provide a dramatized version of the problematic relationship between language and action" (281). This is, of course, to "reclaim" these portions of the play as thematically integral. I see these portions of the play as more fully performative, and as such, as momentary solvents of Weimann's, and Hamlet's, problematics.

29. There is news in this scene of other innovations, other institutionalizations. Not so momentously, the "Pyrrhus speech" translates recitations from classical epic from their secure and sanctioned place within Elizabethan educational practice and launches them within the unstable and irregular praxis of the urban theater. Hamlet the Dane may condescend to this praxis, but *Hamlet* the play thus accomplishes a key reification of stage *business.* The playhouse, complete with box office, is represented as a mature institutional transfiguration of the schoolroom.

30. The memory of Greene's insult is traced elsewhere and otherwise, when Polonius, with a pinched, Jonsonian censoriousness, observes that " 'Beautified' is a vile phrase" (2.2.111).

31. That *Ulysses* unfolds *Hamlet* is a commonplace of Joyce criticism, yet Shakespeare critics seem loath to welcome Joyce to their ranks; the center of Stephen Dedalus's musings on *Hamlet* (1: 401–61) may be found within the chapter known as "Scylla and Charybdis."

32. Jonson was apparently not alone in wishing to take Shakespeare down a peg. In 1602, Peter Brooke, the York Herald, accused William Dethick of elevating nobodies to

the status of gentleman. Shakespeare stands fourth in Brooke's list of twenty-three cases of abuse.

33. For a more detailed account of Jonson's response to competition, see my "Printing and the 'Multitudinous Presse': The Contentious Texts of Jonson's Masques," forthcoming in *Ben Jonson's 1616 Folio "Workes"*, ed. Jennifer Brady and Wyman Herendeen (Newark: U of Delaware P).

34. The players who arrive at Elsinore are of the old school, chary of popular patronage; no author travels with them, protecting his fictive investment or guarding his reputation; and they willingly sacrifice the integrity of their playtexts to the whims of their audience.

35. Goldberg's exploration of "the cultural graphology that locates the Shakespearean character" (309) distinguishes an important location of productive agency in *Hamlet*. It has been my purpose to explore the play's other locations, scenes of production other than the *tabula* of writing.

Works Cited

Albright, Evelyn May. *Dramatic Publication in England, 1580–1640*. New York: Heath, 1927.

Barton, Anne. *Ben Jonson, Dramatist*. Cambridge: Cambridge UP, 1984.

Blayney, Peter W. M. *Nicholas Okes and the First Quarto*. Vol. 1 of *The Texts of* King Lear *and Their Origins*. Cambridge: Cambridge UP, 1982.

Boas, F. S. *Shakespeare and the Universities*. Oxford: Blackwell, 1923.

Bowers, Fredson. *Essays in Bibliography, Text, and Editing*. Charlottesville: UP of Virginia, 1975.

———. "The Pictures in *Hamlet* III.iv: A Possible Contemporary Reference." *Shakespeare Quarterly* 3 (1952): 280–81.

———. Review of *Hamlet*, ed. Harold Jenkins. *Library* 6th ser. 5 (1983): 282–96.

———. "Seven or More Years?" *Shakespeare 1971: Proceedings of the World Shakespeare Congress, Vancouver, August 1971*. Ed. Clifford Leech and J. M. R. Margeson. Toronto: U of Toronto P, 1972.

Brown, John Russell. "The Compositors of *Hamlet* Q2 and *The Merchant of Venice*." *Studies in Bibliography* 7 (1955): 17–40.

Cairncross, Andrew S. "Shakespeare and the 'Staying Entries.' " *Shakespeare in the Southwest: Some New Directions*. Ed. T. J. Stafford. El Paso: Texas Western, 1969. 80–93.

Campbell, Oscar James. *Comicall Satyre and Shakespeare's* Troilus and Cressida. San Marino: Huntington Library, 1938.

Edwards, Philip, ed. *Hamlet*. The New Cambridge Shakespeare. Cambridge: Cambridge UP, 1985.

Empson, William. "*Hamlet*." *Essays on Shakespeare*. By William Empson. Ed. David B. Pirie. Cambridge: Cambridge UP, 1986. 79–136.

Ferguson, Margaret. "*Hamlet*: Letters and Spirits." Parker and Hartman 292–309.

Freedman, Jonathan. "Autocanonization: Tropes of Self-Legitimation in 'Popular Culture.' " *Yale Journal of Criticism* 1 (1987): 203–17.

Goldberg, Jonathan. "Hamlet's Hand." *Shakespeare Quarterly* 39 (1988): 307–27.

Greg. W. W. *The Shakespeare First Folio: Its Bibliographical and Textual History.* Oxford: Clarendon, 1955.

Harbage, Alfred. *Shakespeare and the Rival Traditions.* New York: Macmillan, 1952.

Hibbard, G. R., ed. *Hamlet.* The Oxford Shakespeare. Oxford: Clarendon, 1987.

Honigmann, E. A. J. "The Date of *Hamlet.*" *Shakespeare Survey* 9 (1956): 24–34.

———. "Shakespeare's Revised Plays: *King Lear* and *Othello.*" *Library* 6th ser. 4 (1982): 142–73.

———. *The Stability of Shakespeare's Text.* London: Arnold, 1965.

Jenkins, Harold, ed. *Hamlet.* The Arden Shakespeare. London: Methuen, 1982.

Johnson, Gerald D. "Nicholas Ling, Publisher 1580–1607." *Studies in Bibliography* 38 (1985): 203–14.

Jonson, Ben. *Ben Jonson.* Ed. C. H. Herford, Percy Simpson, and Evelyn Simpson. 11 vols. Oxford: Clarendon, 1925–52.

Jowett, John. "Ligature Shortage and Speech-Prefix Variation in *Julius Caesar.*" *Library* 6th ser. 6 (1984): 244–53.

Joyce, James. *Ulysses: A Critical and Synoptic Edition.* Ed. Hans Walter Gabler and Claus Melchior. 3 vols. New York: Garland, 1984.

Kirschbaum, Leo. "The Date of Shakespeare's *Hamlet.*" *Studies in Philology* 34 (1937): 168–75.

Kittredge, George Lyman, ed. *Hamlet.* By William Shakespeare. Boston: Ginn, 1939.

Nashe, Thomas. *The Unfortunate Traveller and Other Works.* Ed. J. B. Steane. London: Penguin, 1972.

Nosworthy, J. M. *Shakespeare's Occasional Plays.* New York: Barnes, 1965.

Omans, Stuart. "The War of the Theaters: An Approach to Its Origins, Development, and Meaning." Diss. Northwestern U, 1969.

Parker, Patricia, and Geoffrey Hartman, eds. *Shakespeare and the Question of Theory.* New York: Methuen, 1985.

Pollard, A. W. *Shakespeare's Folios and Quartos: A Study in the Bibliography of Shakespeare's Plays, 1594–1685.* Cambridge: Cambridge UP, 1909.

Reibetanz, John. "Hieronimo in Decimosexto: A Private-Theater Burlesque." *Renaissance Drama* ns 5 (1972): 89–121.

Shakespeare, William. *The First Folio of Shakespeare.* Ed. Charlton Hinman. The Norton Facsimile. New York: Norton, 1968.

———. Hamlet: *Second Quarto 1604–5.* Ed. W. W. Greg, reissued with a supplementary introduction by Charlton Hinman. Shakespeare Quarto Facsimiles 4. Oxford: Clarendon, 1964.

Small, Roscoe A. *The Stage-Quarrel between Ben Jonson and the So-Called Poetasters.* Breslau, 1899.

Smith, John Harrington, Lois D. Pizer, and Edward K. Kaufman. "*Hamlet, Antonio's Revenge* and the *Ur-Hamlet.*" *Shakespeare Quarterly* 9 (1958): 493–98.

Stirling, Brents. "*Julius Caesar* in Revision." *Shakespeare Quarterly* 13 (1962): 187–205.

Talbert, Ernest William. "The Purpose and Technique of Jonson's *Poetaster.*" *Studies in Philology* 42 (1945): 225–52.

Taylor, Gary, and Michael Warren, eds. *The Division of the Kingdoms: Shakespeare's Two Versions of* King Lear. Oxford: Clarendon, 1983.

Urkowitz, Steven. *Shakespeare's Revision of* King Lear. Princeton: Princeton UP, 1980.

———. " 'Well-sayd olde Mole': Burying Three *Hamlet*s in Modern Editions." *Shakespeare Study Today: The Horace Howard Furness Memorial Lectures [1982]*. Ed. Georgianna Ziegler. New York: AMS, 1986.

Warren, Michael J. "Quarto and Folio *King Lear* and the Interpretation of Albany and Edgar." *Shakespeare, Pattern of Excelling Nature*. Ed. David Bevington and Jay L. Halio. Newark: U of Delaware P, 1978. 95–107.

Weimann, Robert. "Mimesis in *Hamlet*." Parker and Hartman 275–91.

Werstine, Paul. "The Textual Mystery of *Hamlet*." *Shakespeare Quarterly* 39 (1988): 1–26.

Wilson, J. Dover. *The Manuscript of Shakespeare's* Hamlet *and the Problems of Its Transmission*. 2 vols. Cambridge: Cambridge UP, 1934.

The Form of
Hamlet's Fortunes

BARBARA MOWAT

FOR SHAKESPEAREANS, perhaps no recent critical move has had a more far-reaching effect than has the work of the scholars who are taking apart "our" texts. First came the de-construction of *Lear.* As the kingdom(s) divided, refusal to privilege "our" *Lear*—the *Lear* that we have now been taught to see as "conflated," as a combination of the quarto and Folio texts—gave way to a privileging sometimes of the quarto *Lear,* sometimes of the Folio, until, in the 1986 Oxford *William Shakespeare: The Complete Works,* we have been presented with edited versions of both early printed texts, but no version of the *Lear* that most readers, most theatergoers, most Shakespeareans know.[1] Now it is *Hamlet*'s turn—though here the pattern of deconstruction is, thus far, different. Instead of two (or three) *Hamlet*s, we have been given, by the Oxford editors and G. R. Hibbard in his single-volume edition of the play, *Hamlet* as it appears (more or less) in the Folio. Q2 *Hamlet,* accepted for so long as the privileged (copy-) text of the play, is found in spellings and other accidentals of the Oxford original-spelling edition, but otherwise has simply disappeared from these editions, echoes of it heard in words and phrases, shards and fragments of it printed in appendices.[2]

In this de-constructive time, my particular interest is in Q2/F *Hamlet,* a text that, as Paul Werstine has recently demonstrated, gives us a drama more complex, more mysterious, than that which can be read as inherent in either of the early printed texts. Werstine shows that, although we can never know, in an ultimate sense, how Q2 and F *Hamlet* came to be (we attach each of them to "Shakespeare," but we speak of "revision" or of "theatrical cuts or interpolations" at our peril), each can be read as giving us a hero, a set of relationships, a potential dramatic experience that belongs to that text alone, and that differs from the Hamlet/*Hamlet* of the combined Q2/F text, the play that lives in our minds—and in most twentieth-century editions. Since we cannot know what preceded Q2 and F *Hamlet,* we cannot determine whether the complex Q2/F text is an out-and-out creation of editorial combining or whether editors have, in fact, re-created a document that once existed as Shakespeare's "complete" *Hamlet* (an "original" of which both Q2 and F represent modifications). We cannot know, for instance, whether Shakespeare ever "meant" for Hamlet, in any given production, to liken himself both to Laertes (as he does in F's "by the image of my cause I see the portraiture of his") and to Fortinbras (as he does in Q2's "How all occasions" speech, with its "example" of "a delicate and tender prince, whose spirit ... makes mouths at the invisible event") (Werstine 22). We can, however, as I propose to do in these pages, trace in its printed manifestations the life of the Q2/F text in which this doubly imaged Hamlet has his existence.

The story of that life, I discovered, is a long—and, for me, a surprising—one. It begins with Nicholas Rowe and has not yet ended—will not end, I suspect, as long as Shakespeare is of interest to readers and theatergoers. Briefly, as I will try to show, the text of Q2/F *Hamlet,* except for a period of slightly more than one hundred years (1866–1980), has been radically unstable, multiform. Historically, that is, we do not have three (or four) *Hamlets* ([Q1], Q2, F, Q2/F), but numerous *Hamlets,* each with its own integrity—even, one might venture, its own Hamlet. The situation of the text in the 1980s, then, is more typical than unusual, as editors create their own *Hamlets,* breaking away from the editorial consensus that followed the publication of the Cambridge edition in 1866, the consensus that gave us texts of *Hamlet* that might differ occasionally in choice of variants, but that generally present a *Hamlet* that is full, familiar, seemingly stable, "natural"—apparently "reproducing, as near as may be, the work as it was originally written by Shakespeare," to quote the Cambridge editors (Clark and Wright 8: xi). As the post-1866 consensus breaks down, I will argue, we are in a position to recognize more clearly the impulses that have led—continue to lead—editors as they construct their versions of *Hamlet;* as Q2/F *Hamlet* comes increasingly under attack, we can, in analyzing just how it came into existence, begin to place it properly among *Hamlet*'s texts.

I

The example I mentioned above of three "imagings" of Hamlet—expressly mirrored in Laertes in F, in Fortinbras in Q2, in both young men in the combined text—is an attractive example in its clarity and in its significance (significance especially for teachers of the play), and it leads us to the beginning of Q/F's printed history, where the double image first appears. I say Q/F (instead of Q2/F) because the first conflation of quarto and Folio *Hamlet,* done by Nicholas Rowe in 1709, combined not F1 and Q2, but F4 and Q1676—a fact of some importance, but one that does not affect passages (or even lines) incorporated or omitted by Rowe: F4's variations from F1 are limited to individual words and to punctuation, and Q1676 (a "players' quarto" constructed by William Davenant for Thomas Betterton) follows Q2–Q6[3] except for emendations of words and additions of stage directions and surrounding materials—a dramatis personae list, act/scene divisions, etc. (The frequently made statement that Q1676 is a heavily cut text is misleading: many passages do contain inverted commas in the left margin indicating lines that the actors might choose to cut—or lines that were perhaps actually cut in eighteenth-century performance[4]—but all Q2–Q6 lines are present in Q1676.)

Until 1709, the quarto and Folio *Hamlet*s lived remarkably separate lives. F4, published in 1685, seems innocent of quarto influence, despite the fact that quarto *Hamlet* held the stage and was available in Q1676 (published again in 1683, only two years before F4's publication). More surprising, Davenant's 1676 quarto, except for F1/F2's minor impact on Q6 (see note 3), is equally innocent of Folio influence, following Q6

(1637) except (as mentioned above) for changes in words and in surrounding material, but without reference to the Folio.[5]

It is assumed—indeed, stated—by most who chronicle the history
of Shakespeare's texts that Nicholas Rowe, in his 1709 edition of Shakespeare's plays, simply reprinted F4. This charge goes back at least to
1768, with Edward Capell's "For this editor [Rowe] went no further
than the edition nearest to him in time, which was the folio of 1685,
the last and worst of these impressions; this he republished with great
exactness, correcting here and there some of its grossest mistakes"
(1:15–16).[6] As recently as 1985, J. Philip Brockbank, citing Rowe's claim
to have "compared 'the several editions' and given 'the true Reading as
well as I could from thence,' " wrote that "[i]n fact, Rowe followed the
usual practice of basing his text upon the most recent edition (Fourth
Folio), and his use of the earlier folios is casual and unsystematic. He
made some use of quarto readings in *Henry V* and *King Lear,* but for
the most part his interventions were, like those of earlier scribes and
press editors, modernizations and clarifications meant for the convenience of the modern reader" (718).[7]

It seems true that Rowe made little or no use of the folios that pre-
date F4. And it is certainly true that Rowe's text is primarily based on
Folio *Hamlet:* all of the F-only passages are included by Rowe, and
usually, when F and Q differ, he follows F. But Rowe's text is a genuine
Q/F conflation—not a complete one, in that he did not include 106 Q-
only lines. But he did include 7 Q-only passages (124 of the 230 lines
not present in F), and he used Q1676 frequently to provide variant
readings to F, or to correct garbled F4 words—a far more significant
incorporation of Q than is suggested by Alfred Jackson's study of Rowe's
edition, which claims that a prologue that Rowe took from quarto *Romeo and Juliet,* "together with Act IV, Scene ii [sic] of *Hamlet* which
he inserted from the 1676 prompt copy [sic], comprise the main differences from the Fourth Folio in regard to material" (466).[8]

Rowe's actual editorial procedures in constructing his *Hamlet* are
clearly illustrated in the first scene of the play. Briefly, Rowe uses F4 as
his copy-text, adds passages that he finds in Q1676 that are not in F,
and uses Q1676 to correct F4 readings. In 1.1, Rowe adds to F4 all of
the Q-only material, so that the scene is "complete," although at many
points it reads very differently from twentieth-century texts. Specifi-

cally, Rowe inserts from Q1676 eighteen lines of dialogue between Bernardo and Horatio (lines 108–25) immediately preceding the ghost's second entrance, retaining Davenant's alteration of Q6's "In the most high and *palmy* state of Rome" to "in the most high and *flourishing* state of Rome" (line 113; italics added).[9] Within this Q-only passage, Rowe introduces a major alteration (in only one other passage, a Q-only speech in 1.2, does Rowe take such a liberty), emending Q's[10] puzzling "As stars with trains of fire and dews of blood, / Disasters in the sun" (lines 117–18) to read "Stars shon with Trains of Fire, Dews of Blood fell, / Disasters veil'd the Sun" (lines that appeared in this altered form in Pope's and Theobald's editions as well). At several points in the scene, as throughout his text, Rowe uses Q1676 to correct F4: F4's "You come most *chearfully* upon your hour" becomes "you come most *carefully*" (line 6); F's "When th'Ambitious Norway combatted" is altered, from Q1676, to read "When *he* th'ambitious Norway combated" (61); F4's "Whose sore Task / *Dos't* not divide" becomes (following Q1676) "Whose sore task / *Does* not divide" (75–76). Marcellus's eight-line speech that begins "It faded on the crowing of the cock" is three times altered against Q1676, with F's "Some sayes" becoming "some say"; F4's "And (they say) no spirit" becoming "And *then,* they say, no spirit"; and F's "No fairy *talkes*" becoming "No fairy *takes*" (157–64). One phrase in Marcellus's speech, which appears in Rowe as "no Spirit dares walk abroad," is Rowe's own combination of F's "no spirit can walk abroad" and Q's "no spirit dares stir abroad" (161). Two stage directions found in Q1676 (and not in F): "*He* [i.e., the Ghost] *spreads his arms*" and "*the cock crows*" appear in Rowe as "*Spreading his Arms*" and "*Cock Crows.*"

Rowe's care in putting together the two texts shows itself most clearly in the textually complicated 4.7 (in Rowe, this "scene" is the concluding section of his 4.3), where five passages appear only in Q and three passages appear only in F. As throughout his *Hamlet,* Rowe includes all of the F-only passages; he includes as well two of the five Q-only passages. The first of the included quarto passages is a fourteen-line dialogue between Claudius and Laertes, which, in Q, comes immediately after Claudius's "even his mother shall uncharge the practice / And call it accident" (4.7.67). In Rowe, the passage reads:

LAER.
My Lord, I will be rul'd,
The rather if you could devise it so
That I might be the Instrument.
                              KING.
                              It falls right:
You have been talkt of since your travel much,
And that in *Hamlet*'s hearing, for a quality
Wherein they say you shine; your sum of parts
Did not together pluck such envy from him,
As did that one, and that in my regard
Of the unworthiest Siege.
                         LAER.
                         What part is that, my Lord?
                         KING.
A very Feather in the Cap of Youth,
Yet needful too, for Youth no less becomes
The light and careless Livery that it wears,
Than setled Age his Sables, and his Weeds,
Importing Health and Graveness. . . .

(The words "Instrument" and "Feather" are Davenant's changes from
Q6's "organ" and "riband.")

The combining of this passage with F4's text obviously required some
care on Rowe's part. The lines in F4 into which the above Q-only passage was to be inserted (between "call it accident" and "Some two
months hence") read:

But even his Mother shall uncharge the practice,
And call it accident: Some two Months hence
Here was a Gentleman of Normandy.

With the Q-only passage inserted, F's "Some two months hence" would
no longer work, metrically, in that Claudius's new line would read "Importing health and graveness. Some two months hence / . . . ." Rowe
therefore briefly abandons F4 to follow Q's "Importing health and
graveness: two months since / . . . ," in the process changing F's "hence"
to Q's "since."

The second Q-only passage included by Rowe in 4.7 is the ten-line
speech by Claudius that begins (as it appears in Rowe): "There lives

within the very flame of Love / A kind of wiek [following Q1676] or snuff." The inclusion of this passage created no metrical problems; Rowe simply took the passage from Q1676 and inserted it into Claudius's F4 speech. With Rowe's addition of these two Q-only passages, the scene is almost "complete," in that the three Q-only passages that Rowe omits are very brief, the longest being Claudius's "The scrimers of their nation / He swore had neither motion, guard, nor eye, / If you opposed them" (lines 100–02; the passage in Q1676 reads "The Fencers of their nation . . ."). The two other Q-only passages omitted from 4.7 are each less than a line in length, so brief that Rowe may have overlooked them—or, in one case, may have decided that F's "As by your safety, wisdom, all things else" is metrically sounder than Q's "As by your safety, greatness, wisdom, all things else," and thus chose not to add the extra word found in Q.

Rowe's exclusions of Q-only passages in other scenes are much more interesting, in that some of the passages are long and not easily overlooked. These omitted passages include Hamlet's twenty-four-line speech (1.4.23–38) on "the vicious mole of nature" (with its famous "so oft it chances in particular men," its "nature's livery or fortune's star"); Hamlet's "engiqer" speech in 3.4 ("there's letters sealed; and my two schoolfellows . . . marshall me to knavery" [209–17]); and a thirty-four-line passage of dialogue in 5.2 in which Hamlet and Osric "wrap" Laertes in their "rawer breaths" (106–41).

That Rowe's selective inclusion of Q-only passages involved conscious choice on his part seems probable when we look at his version of the final scene of the play. In a "complete" text of 5.2 one finds two F-only passages (including the important twelve-line speech [68–80] in which Hamlet asks "Is't not to be damn'd to let this canker . . . come in further evil" and in which he expresses regret at his graveside treatment of Laertes, whose favor he decides to court). One finds as well four Q-only passages—the thirty-two-line dialogue between Hamlet and Osric on the subject of Laertes (106ff., mentioned above); a twelve-line exchange between Hamlet and an anonymous lord, in which a message from Gertrude to Hamlet is delivered and received ("The Queen desires you use some gentle entertainment to Laertes before you fall to play." "She well instructs me" [193–206]); and two very brief passages (one of which [222] is Hamlet's "Let be"). Of these four Q-only passages, Rowe includes only the twelve-line dialogue with the anonymous lord; he does not include the long Hamlet-Osric dialogue that precedes it. Since throughout 5.2 Rowe used Q1676 to correct or alter F4 (e.g., F4's "my *tears* forgetting manners" is corrected to Q's [and, incidentally, F1's] "my *fears* forgetting manners" [17]; F's "There are no tongues else for's *tongue*" is altered to Q1676's "There are no tongues else for his *turn*" [183]; F's "He did comply with his Dug" [186] is changed to "He did so with his dug" [Q1676 reads: "He did so Sir with his dug"]), it seems highly unlikely that Rowe simply overlooked the lengthy and memorable exchange in which Laertes is divided inventorially, dozying the arithmetic of memory.

A further suggestion that Rowe consciously chose to omit this Q-only passage from the Osric dialogue appears (albeit indirectly) in Lewis Theobald's comment on the passage. Theobald, not finding the exchange about Laertes in Alexander Pope's edition, assumed that the omission was a conscious decision on Pope's part, and defended his own inclusion of the lines as follows: "I have restor'd here several speeches from the elder *Quarto*'s, which were omitted in the *Folio* Editions, and which Mr. *Pope* has likewise thought fit to sink upon us. They appear to me very well worthy not to be lost, as they thoroughly shew the Foppery and Affectation of *Osrick,* and the Humour and Address of *Hamlet* in accosting the other at once in his own Vein and Style" (7: 357n73). Since Pope followed Rowe closely in constructing his version of 5.2, it seems to have been Rowe (and not Pope) who "thought fit" to omit these "several speeches." The decision may have been affected by the fact that including the lines would have required adjustments to the F-text similar to (though much more complicated than) those Rowe encountered at 4.7.80. Or the motivation could have had more substantive grounds. We know that Rowe had thought seriously about the F-only passage in which Hamlet sees himself reflected in Laertes and resolves to "court his favours," in that the word "court" is Rowe's own emendation of F's "count"; it is possible that Rowe, a dramatist himself, recognized a possible contradiction between the attitude toward Laertes expressed by Hamlet in the F-only speech and that expressed in the mockery of Laertes that provides the substance of the Q-only Hamlet-Osric dialogue.

We can do no more than speculate on Rowe's reason for choosing to omit the Osric passage and to include the "anonymous lord" passage. We can, however, assert that Rowe has given us, in *his* 5.2, a version of *Hamlet* that differs from F, from Q, and from a Q2/F "complete" text. Rowe's version includes the double motivation for Hamlet's apology to Laertes (the empathetic decision reached in F, and the request from Gertrude found in Q)[11] but does not present Hamlet's wild swing of emotional reaction to Laertes (from empathy to angry mockery to courteous apology) found in the texts of 5.2 that include all of the Q/F material.

Rowe constructs a similarly unique text at other points of editorial decision. When he includes Q's "how all occasions" scene, he brings into the play attitudes not expressed by Hamlet in F—i.e., first, a determination on Hamlet's part to maintain his bloody thoughts as he is sent off to England, and, second, a sense of himself as mirrored/ contrasted in Fortinbras. When, as Werstine has shown (14ff.), the "how all occasions" soliloquy is backed up by the "enginer" speech, as it is in Q, we can read Hamlet as very aware, very alert, ready to act despite his current captive state. Rowe's Hamlet, who has no "enginer" speech, stands somewhere between F Hamlet (who leaves for England with no speech about his state of mind, who appropriately writes in his letter to Claudius that his "return" is "sudden, and more strange," and who is pleased to find that Providence has given him an "interim" that is his in which to act) and Q Hamlet (who sets out for England ready to hoist his captors on their own petar, who writes to Claudius only of a "sudden" return, and who says nothing about a providential interim).

Some of Rowe's exclusions/inclusions are, to me, puzzling—though some may well reflect the fact that Rowe was himself a dramatist. The "vicious mole of nature" speech (1.4.23–38) may, for example, have seemed to him to delay the entrance of the ghost unduly, and he may have decided that Shakespeare, realizing this himself, had cut it. This is speculation (Rowe does not address the issue in his preface to the edition). The fact is that Rowe does not add this speech to his basic F4 text, while he does add many others. He gives Polonius, for example, three lines from Q: "He hath, my lord, wrung from me my slow leave / By laboursome petition; and at last, / Upon his will I seal'd my hard consent" (1.2.58–60), transposing phrases so that the lines read: "by laboursome Petition / Wrung from me my slow Leave," an alteration that produces no particular improvement in meter or sense (though, since both Pope and Theobald chose to follow Rowe rather than Q in these lines, the new syntax may have sounded better to an eighteenth-century ear). Rowe does not include Horatio's "The very place puts toys of desperation, / Without more motive, into every brain / That looks so many fathoms to the sea / And hears it roar beneath" (1.4.76–80), nor does he include the line from 2.2 that reads: "as wholesome as sweet, and by very much more handsome than fine" (444), nor eight lines from Q's closet scene ("Sense sure you have"; "Eyes without feeling, feeling without sight ... Could not so mope" [3.4.72–77, 79–81]). Strangely, in the same scene, he *does* include Q's difficult ten-line passage beginning (as it appears in Rowe): "That Monster Custom, who all Sense doth eat / Of Habit's Devil" (168ff.) As noted above, Rowe does not include Hamlet's speech about his two schoolfellows, "adders fanged" whom he will "blow ... at the moon" (3.4.209–17), nor Claudius's Q-only lines "Whose whisper o'er the world's diameter / May ... hit the woundless air" (4.1.41–44).

The text of *Hamlet* that we find in Rowe, then, is his own specific conflation of Q and F, a *Hamlet* shaped primarily by Rowe's selective addition of Q passages to the F text, but affected as well by the fact that Rowe used Q1676 rather than Q6 (or any other of the pre-war quartos). From Q1676 Rowe picked up several "emendations"— "Feather" for "riband," "Instrument" for "organ," "flourishing" for "palmy"—some of which appear in Pope's edition and a few in Theobald's as well. More important, in Q1676 (as in the players' quarto that Rowe used in editing *Othello*[12]) Rowe found the kind of dramatis personae list that we associate with Rowe's edition, more consistent act/scene divisions than in the "elder quartos" (to use Theobald's phrase), and many stage directions that Rowe incorporated into his text. Many features that have entered the editorial tradition through Rowe, then, originated in the players' quartos. Thus the easy distinction that is made between literary texts and performance texts—made even by Alfred Jackson in his essay on Rowe's edition—seems perhaps too easy, and our tendency to ignore the players' quartos in our study of the history of Shakespeare texts may need to be rethought. Further, the idea that the Folio text represents the "acting version" of the play—an idea accepted by almost every current editor of *Hamlet* and a very important consideration for those who now elect to use the Folio as a control text—also seems less obvious in the light of the fact that the players' quartos continue the quarto tradition without reference to the Folio. This fact seems especially interesting in the case of Davenant's 1676 quarto of *Hamlet.* Davenant may, of course, simply have found Q6 an easier text to work with, physically, than the Folio. But Davenant may also have known that the quarto tradition was in fact the acted tradition.[13]

II

Pope's conflation of Q and F *Hamlet* is, like Rowe's, a specific combination of Q and F texts, one that at first seems to take us closer to a "complete"—if not altogether familiar—Q/F *Hamlet.* (The 1714 edition of Rowe's *Hamlet,* despite claims that John Hughes was responsible for major revisions of the 1709 edition, shows no changes to the strategies of combination of Q1676 and F4 that I have already detailed.[14]) Pope follows Rowe closely in his text of *Hamlet,* but adds four Q-only passages omitted by Rowe. He includes, first, Hamlet's "vicious mole of nature" speech (1.4.17–36), with the final problematic sentence (lines 36–38) silently omitted; Pope places the passage in a note at the bottom of the page rather than within the text, prefacing it with this comment: "These 21 lines following are in the first edition [i.e., Q2], but since left out, perhaps as being thought too verbose" (6: 365). Pope includes, within the text, Horatio's "the very place puts toys of desperation" (1.4.75–79), "added from the first edition," notes Pope, as well as a short passage in 4.3 ("a man may fish with a worm ..." [26–29]). Pope's fourth addition is the "enginer" speech (3.4.209–17), of which he notes: "The ten following verses are added out of the old edition" (6: 427).

Pope occasionally corrects Rowe against Q2 or Q4 (Pope lists, among his books collated, quartos of 1604 and 1611), with, for example, Rowe's "How *propos'd*" (the Q6–Q1676 reading) corrected to "How *purpos'd*" and Rowe's "*Nay,* 'tis already garrisoned" (as in Q6–Q1676) corrected to "*Yes,* 'tis already garrisoned" (4.4.11, 24). He adds Q2's *"now"* (after "hear") to F4/Rowe's "Wilt thou hear how I did proceed?" (5.2.27).

Pope's edition of *Hamlet,* then, adds thirty-six Q-only lines to the edition constructed by Rowe, and begins to correct Q1676 passages against Q2 or Q4. But, ironically, a new movement simultaneously sets in. Passages from F (all of which are included by Rowe) begin now to be silently dropped. The move toward a "complete" Q2/F *Hamlet* is thus no steady progress toward inclusion of all Q and F passages. Rather, as the Q-only passages are gradually included, small F-only passages disappear. Hamlet's letter to Claudius, which reads, in F and in Rowe, "my sudden, and more strange return," appears, in Pope (as in Q2+) as "my sudden return." This seems a minor deletion, except that "and more strange" can be seen as a part of the Folio characterization of Hamlet (Werstine 21). One wonders if Pope dropped the "and more strange" because he noticed that in the "enginer" speech, which Pope added from Q2, Hamlet makes clear that he feels very much in control of his future—a position that may be seen to conflict with F-Hamlet's letter about his "strange" return. Another removal of F-material—Pope's silent deletion of Hamlet's F-only "O, vengeance" (2.2.582)—may well result from Pope's suspicion (like Harold Jenkins's in the twentieth century) that the Folio includes actors' interpolations that should be removed. (Pope indicates such suspicion in his "Preface": "The folio edition ... is far worse than the Quarto's: First, because the additions of trifling and bombast passages are in this edition far more numerous. For whatever had been added, since those Quarto's, by the actors, or had stolen from their mouths into the written parts, were from thence conveyed into the printed text, and all stand charged upon the Author" [1: xvi]). Analogous critical decisions about conflicts introduced when Q and F are conflated, or wariness about the influence of the players on F, may in part govern Pope's other deletions of F-only lines, among which are: "tragical-historical, tragical-comical-historical-pastoral" (2.2.386), "lawful espials" (3.1.32), the word "all" from the end of the phrase "We are arrant knaves all" (3.1.129), "well, well" from Hamlet's "well, well, well" (3.1.92), and "Pox," from "Pox, leave thy damnable faces" (3.2.240); Pope also deletes the words "with him" from Polonius's "Pray you be round with him," as well as Hamlet's line that follows: "Mother, mother, mother" (3.4.4–5). He deletes "How now? What news?"

"Letters, my lord, from Hamlet" (4.7.36); and, in the final scene, Hamlet's "Why, man, they did make love to this employment" (5.2.55). Certainly Pope made many editorial decisions on the basis of "style" and of meter, and it may be that such considerations led him sometimes to delete F-only passages that displeased his sensibilities. It is also possible that his omissions of F-only passages show Pope as deliberately moving toward a Q2 text—i.e., the omissions may be not so much deletions as Pope's simple following of Q2 in preference to following Rowe. The evidence seems to indicate otherwise, in that more often than not Pope follows Rowe, and in a single scene Pope will follow Rowe's F4 or Q1676 readings while deleting F-only lines. In 4.7, for example, just after deleting "and more strange" and "Letters, my lord, from Hamlet," we find Pope scrupulously following Q1676/Rowe in reading "instrument" in place of Q2's "organ," and "feather" in place of Q2's "riband."

One can find tempting explanations for Pope's decision, at given points, for inclusion or exclusion of words and passages, but, finally, the more immediate and interesting point is that, in Pope as in Rowe, we find a very specific, partial conflation of Folio and quarto *Hamlet.*

III

With Theobald's *Hamlet,* almost all of the remaining Q-only lines are brought into the text. Theobald moves Hamlet's "so oft it chances in particular men" out of what he calls the "degraded" position given it by Pope (i.e., Theobald places it within the text rather than in a note at the bottom of the page), and he adds as its final sentence: "The dram of Base [sic] / Doth all the noble substance of worth out / To his own scandal"—his "slight Alteration" of the sentence as he found it in Q6 (*Shakespeare restored* 29): "The Dram of Ease [sic] / Doth all the noble substance of a Doubt / To his own Scandal." Theobald notes that this sentence "looks, indeed, to be desperate, and for that Reason, I conceive, [Mr. Pope] chose to drop it. I do not remember a Passage, throughout all our Poet's Works, more intricate and deprav'd in the Text, of less Meaning to outward Appearance, or more likely to baffle the Attempts of Criticism in its Aid. It is certain, there is neither Sense, nor Grammar, as it now stands" (*Works* 7: 248). Hence his "slight Alteration." (Theobald writes, in his *Shakespeare restored,* that he found

this passage in "a Quarto Edition ... printed ... in the year 1637" [29];
although he later claims to have collated the 1605 and 1611 quartos
[7: 499–500], he seems not to have noted Q2's reading, "dram of eale.")

Two couplets from Q's "Mousetrap" are added by Theobald, as are
eight lines from Hamlet's speech to Gertrude in Q's closet scene: "Sense
sure you have ... To serve in such a difference" and "Eyes without
feeling, feeling without sight ... Could not so mope" (3.4.72–76,
79–82). Theobald's comment on Pope's omission of these eight lines
from 3.4 is interesting both in its assumption about the Folio as a
playhouse document and in its comment on the "proper" editing of
Shakespeare's two-text plays:

> Mr. *Pope* has left out the Quantity of about eight Verses here, which I have
> taken care to replace. They are not, indeed, to be found in the two elder *Folio*'s
> but they carry the Style, Expression, and Cast of Thought, peculiar to our
> Author; and that they were not an Interpolation from another Hand needs no
> better Proof, than that they are in all the oldest *Quarto*'s. The first Motive of
> their being left out, I am perswaded, was to shorten *Hamlet*'s Speech, and
> consult the Ease of the Actor: and the Reason, why they find no Place in the
> *Folio* Impressions, is, that they were printed from the *Playhouse* castrated
> Copies. But, surely, this can be no Authority for a modern *Editor* to conspire
> in mutilating his Author: Such *Omissions,* rather, must betray a Want of *Dili-*
> *gence,* in *Collating;* or a Want of *Justice,* in the *voluntary Stifling.* (7: 313)

Theobald, in his version of 4.1, is the first to use the Q opening
entrance that brings in Rosencrantz and Guildenstern with the king
and queen, and that gives Gertrude (at line 4) a command to them to
exit: "Bestow this place on us a little while." In the same scene he adds
Q's "(Whose whisper o'er the world's diameter, / As level as the cannon
to his blank, / Transports its poyson'd shot;) may miss our Name, / And
hit the woundless air" (41–44; quoted as it appears in Theobald), giving us, for the first time, a conjectural phrase to fill the metrical and
syntactical lacuna following the previous line's "And what's untimely
done." Theobald fills the blank with "For, haply, Slander" (a phrase
altered by Capell to "So haply slander" and, recently, by Jenkins, to "So
envious slander").

In 4.7 (100–02) Theobald adds three Q-only lines to Claudius's speech
to Laertes: "The Scrimers of their nation, / He swore, had neither mo-

tion, guard, nor eye, / If you oppos'd 'em" (noting that "Some of the modern *Quarto*'s [i.e., Q1676+] have in the room of *Scrimers* substituted *Fencers*"); and, finally, in 5.2, the final major piece in this complex Q/F scene falls into place with Theobald's inclusion of the thirty-four-line Hamlet-Osric dialogue on Laertes.[15]

Some bits of Q are yet missing from Theobald's *Hamlet:* "Whether aught to us unknown afflicts him thus" (2.2.17); "as wholesome as sweet, and by very much more handsome than fine" (2.2.444–45); "One word more, good lady" (3.4.187); "Of him that brought them" (4.7.41); and occasional words and phrases, among them Hamlet's "Let be" (5.2.210). And, although Theobald does restore Hamlet's "Mother, mother, mother" to 3.4; "How now, what news?" "Letters, my lord, from Hamlet" to 4.7; and "Why, man, they did make love to this employment" to 5.2, most of Pope's F-only deletions are missing from Theobald as well.

Despite these small gaps, we have come, in Theobald's 1733 edition, very close to a "complete" Q/F *Hamlet,* though one still far different, in the actual words that appear on the page, from the Q2/F *Hamlet* that is familiar to twentieth-century readers, theatergoers, and scholars. Countless lines startle with a sudden omission or with an unfamiliar variant or long-forgotten reading that lingers from Q1676 or F4 or from a Pope or Theobald emendation. And such is the case with the texts of *Hamlet* for many years and through edition after edition.

Take, for example, Capell's text of 1768. I mention Capell in part because G. Blakemore Evans has called Capell "the first so-called modern editor" and his edition "an important landmark." Capell, says Evans, was "the first to put into practice ... the principle of copy-text," the first to recognize "the usual superiority of ... the 'good' quartos ... to those texts as they appeared in the First Folio," and thus the first to move away "from the eclecticism of the earlier editors" (i.e., Rowe, Pope, Theobald, Hanmer [1744], Warburton [1747], and Johnson [1765]). Capell's edition, according to Evans, is the "first 'pure' edited text," established not on the basis of earlier editions but "on his own thorough collation of all the obtainable sixteenth- and seventeenth-century editions (quarto and folio)" (33–34). Evans singles out Capell's edition of the "textually complex" *Hamlet* for particular praise: Capell was the first to base *Hamlet* "directly on Q2," Evans writes, and "no

later influential text comparably faithful to Q2 was produced until
Dover Wilson's edition in 1934" (33).

Yet a quick reading of Capell's *Hamlet* shows not only omissions—
primarily the exclusion of F-only passages also omitted by Pope and
Theobald (exclusions that, in the case of Capell's text, could be explained by what Evans points to as Capell's faithful adherence to Q2)—
but also readings that seem strange today where Capell has chosen to
follow F *rather* than Q2: e.g., "The lady protests too much" (the reading
of F and of the editors who preceded Capell; Q2 reads "The lady *doth
protest* too much" [3.2.228]), or where he follows earlier editors'
emendations. To select only two examples of the second practice:[16]

5.2.[6–8]
Q2:   ... rashly,
          And praysd be rashness for it: let us knowe,
          Our indiscretion sometime serves us well
          When our deepe plots doe fall [*uncorr.:* pall]
F1:   ... rashly,
          (And praise be rashness for it) let us know
          Our indiscretion sometimes serves us well
          When our deare plots do paule....
Pope: ... rashness
          (And prais'd be rashness for it) lets us know
          Our indiscretion sometime serves us well
          When our deep plots do fail....
Capell: ... Rashness
          (And prais'd be rashness for it!) lets us know
          Our indiscretion sometime serves us well
          When our deep plots do fail....

5.2.[195]
Q2:   A did sir [*corr.:* A did so sir] with his dugge before a suckt it,
F1:   He did complie with his dug before he sucked it.
Hanmer: He did complement with his dug before he sucked it.
Capell: He did compliment with his dug, before he suck'd it.

The sense of unfamiliarity that one experiences even in Capell when
one encounters a strange reading, or when one fails to find an expected
word or phrase that the editor has omitted, characterizes most eigh-

teenth- and nineteenth-century texts of *Hamlet*. Reading through these
texts sequentially, one has not only this sense of occasional dislocation
but also an awareness of a text that is quite unstable, shifting its terms
as each editor succeeds his predecessor, pulling in an F or Q line here,
dropping one there, choosing a new (or previously abandoned) variant,
reaching back for an editorial emendation or substituting an emendation of his own. One begins to believe that Q2/F *Hamlet* is a fantasy,
that a stable conflated text never existed, and that editors today are de-
constructing an illusion.

To demonstrate in the briefest form this shape-shifting quality of
Hamlet through the years, let me sketch out the editorial career of a
single line—or, rather, of ten words (they have been lineated in many
ways). The words appear, in Q2, as "who does me this, / Hah, s'wounds
I should take it," and, in F1, as "who does me this? / Ha? Why I should
take it" (2.2.56–57). Rowe's version, "Who does me this? / *Ha! Why
should I* take it" follows F4; Pope omits "Ha" altogether and emends
to read: "who does me this? / *Yet I should* take it—." Pope's version is
adopted by Theobald, Hanmer, Warburton, and Johnson. Capell (1768)
restores both "Ha" and F1's "*Why, I should* take it." In 1773, Jennens
adopts Q2's "Hah! *'Swounds I should* take it" (with an interesting and
accurate note tracing the history of the phrase from Q2 through Capell). In the same year, the Johnson and Steevens edition gives us Pope's
version; their 1778 edition then switches to Capell's F1 reading, a reading also followed by Malone (1790). In 1793, Steevens adopts but re-
lineates F1, placing "Ha!" on a separate line. Steevens's lineation of the
F1 reading is followed in 1803 by Reed, in 1821 by "Boswell's Malone,"
by Caldecott in 1832, and by Knight in 1841. Collier (1843) chooses
the Q2 reading, but places "ha?" at the end of the first line. Hudson
(1856) gives his own version of Q2: "Who does me this? / Ha! / *Zounds!
I should* take it"; in the same year, Chalmers follows F1, as does Singer.
The next year (1857), Dyce follows Collier in using Q2, lineating it as
did Collier, as "who does me this, *ha? / 'Swounds, I should* take it."
Staunton (in 1860) and White (in 1861) follow Collier and Dyce. In
1866, the Cambridge edition adopts the Q2 reading, but with Steevens's
lineation: "who does me this? / Ha! / 'Swounds, I should take it."

The instability of this tiny bit of text is multiplied throughout the
*Hamlet*s of the eighteenth and nineteenth centuries.[17] In the fifty-nine

lines that make up the final soliloquy in 2.2 there are (in addition to the variants that I have been tracing) eighteen substantive Q2/F variants; and the variants in each pair (*whole* conceit / *own* conceit; *the* visage / *his* visage; *scullion* / *stallyon,* etc.) replace each other in bewildering patterns and combinations as the soliloquy loses "O vengeance" but picks up "hum," reads "dear plots do fall," "deep plots do fail," or "dear plots do pall." The number of combinations, even in this one soliloquy, can be expressed mathematically (2^{19}) but is far too large for the mind fully to comprehend.

Yet, oddly, by 1866, with the Cambridge edition, the choices have largely been made. By this I mean that, if we look at standard modern Shakespeare texts: Kittredge, Alexander, Pelican (Harbage/Farnham), Riverside (Evans), Signet (Barnet/Hubler), Bevington—we find that *Hamlet* is remarkably consistent among them, and generally consistent with the Cambridge edition. This consistency is startling in light of the previous instability of the texts; and the correlation between modern, post–"New Bibliography" texts and the "unscientific" Cambridge is puzzling. But the consistency and the correlation are there. The Cambridge editors claim (as I noted earlier) to be "giving in [their] text all the passages from both Folio and Quarto" and, in doing so, to be "reproducing, as near as may be, the work as it was originally written by Shakespeare, or . . . as finally retouched by him after the spurious edition of 1603" (8: xi). One cannot judge the validity of their claim about faithful reproduction of Shakespeare's work, original or retouched, but one can say that their choices of variants and emendations, their inclusion of "all the [Q2/F] passages," produce a text that gave us, for many years, a stable Q2/F *Hamlet.* Occasionally an unexpected variant or emendation appears in its pages (e.g., at 1.1.93 they choose "covenant" [F] rather than today's preferred "comart" [Q2]; at 4.7.93 they choose Pope's "Lamond" over Q2's "Lamord"), but these differences are rare.

More common are the correlations we find between Cambridge and what I will call the "modern" editions (listed above). In the 2.2 soliloquy already discussed above, of the nineteen substantive variants Cambridge chooses the Q2 variant seven times (*own* / whole; *faculties* / faculty; *'Swounds* / why; *why* / who; *this* / I sure, this; *a dear* / the dear; *Hum* / —), the F1 variant nine times (*his* visage / the visage; *in's* / in his; *to Hecuba* / to her; *the cue for* / that for; *O, vengeance!* / —; *scullion* / stallyon; *brain* / braines; if *he but* / if a doe; may *be the devil* / may be a deale), and three times follows editorial emendations (Steevens's "wann'd" [Q2 *wand,* F1 *warm'd*], Rowe's *appall* [Q2 *appale,* F1 *apale*], and Pope's [or Q4's; Cambridge credits Capell with the emendation] "a dear father murder'd" [Q2 "a deere murthered," F "the deere murthered"]). In twelve of the nineteen cases, the "modern editions" agree with Cambridge; in the remainder, Riverside twice chooses the other variant ("all *the* visage," and omits "hum"); five times the modern editions differ (some choosing "scullion" and some "stallion"; some "the devil," others "a devil," etc.).

To take another passage of comparable length and textual complexity: in the opening sixty lines of 5.2 we find the following twenty-four substantive variants (in each case, the Cambridge choice is in italic):

Line	F1	Q2	
1	let me	*shall you*	
5	*methought*	my thought	
6	*bilboes*	bilbo	
7	praise	*praised*	
8	sometimes	*sometime*	
	dear	*deep*	
9	teach	*learn*	
17	*unseal*	unfold	
19	*Oh*	A	Delius: Ah
20	reason	*reasons*	
27	hear me	hear *now*	
29	villaines	villaines	Capell: *villainies*
30	ere	*or*	
36	*yeoman's*	yemans	
37	effects	*effect*	
40	as	*like*	
	should	*might*	
44	know	*knowing*	
48	*the*	those	
52	*subscribed*	subscribe	
54	sement	*sequent*	
57	*Why, man, they did make love to this employment*		
58	debate	*defeat*	
59	doth	*does*	

In twenty-one of the above twenty-four cases, the "modern editions" choose the same variant as Cambridge; in the three remaining cases, some prefer Delius's conjectural "Ah" to either the Folio "Oh" or the Q2 "A" (line 19), some prefer "ere" to "or" (line 30), some choose Q2's "those" over the Cambridge's choice of the F "the" (line 48); Riverside chooses "yeman's" over "yeoman's" and Kittredge selects "hear me" rather than "hear now"; but otherwise the texts are the same—a fact that would not have surprised me had I worked back from modern texts to Cambridge, but which seems astounding in the context of those earlier years of multiform variable *Hamlet*s. As I noted earlier, the correlation is also startling when we consider that, if Evans is correct in his history of the editing tradition, one should not expect much correlation between the Cambridge edition and editions published in the wake of the "New Bibliography." Evans writes (34) that "[w]ith Capell, Steevens, and Malone the text of Shakespeare had been brought about as far as the limited textual approach employed by these men could bring it, and the nineteenth century, although it produced many new editions under highly competent and learned editors . . . , brought very little advance in new theory or basic techniques. The culmination of the line initiated by Capell is the great Cambridge *Shakespeare* . . . which . . . was to remain . . . the standard for the next fifty years" (i.e., until the very early twentieth century). After describing the development of textual studies, Evans notes (35) that "[a]s a result of the impetus of the 'New Bibliography' a number of important editions of Shakespeare have appeared during the last fifty years"—and names in his list those that I have called "modern" texts. He implies that these texts differ importantly from the Cambridge edition. It is true that, in the case of some famous "cruxes" in *Hamlet*—"solid" / "sallied," "out of tune and harsh" / "out of time and harsh," etc.—one does find Cambridge sometimes choosing the F-variant, with the "modern editions" following Q2. But the basic text codified in the Cambridge Shakespeare is found in most editions of *Hamlet* until the 1980s.[18]

V

Those who are deeply committed to Q2/F *Hamlet* tend to speak of it as a living—an organic—entity. In the light of the text's traceable

history, it seems clear that its putting together (or putting *back* together) was, in fact, a very human activity, its existence thoroughly,
demonstrably, constructed.

And as it was constructed, so is it today being taken apart—and not
by Oxford alone. In Jenkins's Arden edition of *Hamlet* (1982), one
finds for the first time since Q2–Q1703 (so far as I can determine)
"What's Hecuba to him or he to her"; in Edwards's New Cambridge
Hamlet (1985), as in the two Oxford *Complete Works* (with spelling
and punctuation differences) one finds F's "That I, the son of the deere
murthered." And among all these recent major texts of *Hamlet* one
finds a general pulling away from a consensus text, as the Arden drops
F-only lines and favors unfamiliar quarto variants, and as Cambridge
and Oxford pull toward F (going so far, in the Oxford—as I noted
earlier—as to relegate most Q-only passages to appendices). As one
compares passages in these editions from the 1980s, one feels the text
being pulled from its point of momentary semi-stability, feels it once
again begin its textual shape-shifting, and realizes that those who com-
plain about the instability of Shakespeare's plays on the stage have
clearly never watched closely their metamorphoses on the page.

Yet, as I said at the outset, as the consensus breaks down, we can
now begin to see the text more clearly, and can see behind the pro-
cesses of constructing and de-constructing the text a powerful shared
impulse. Driven by a desire to recover the *Hamlet* that Shakespeare
wrote—to replace passages lost through actors' excisions or printers'
errors, to restore words garbled by interfering players or incompetent
printers, to take *Hamlet* out of the hands of previous editors and print
Shakespeare's own *Hamlet* (either his original text or his final text, but
in any event *his* text), editors from Rowe to Hibbard have searched for
Shakespeare's words,[19] and the result has been almost as many *Hamlet*s
as there have been editors. This yearning to recover Shakespeare's words
can be heard in editorial prefaces from every age, sometimes expressed
innocently and longingly (as in Rowe's "I must not pretend to have
restor'd this Work to the Exactness of the Author's Original Manuscripts. Those are lost, or, at least, are gone beyond any Inquiry I could
make; so that there was nothing left, but to compare the several Editions, and give the true Reading as well as I could from thence" [1:
A2–A2v]), sometimes composedly and confidently (as in the words of

the Cambridge editors, already quoted), sometimes learnedly and as-
sertively (as in Hibbard's "In keeping with the hypothesis that F *Hamlet*
is based on Shakespeare's fair copy and not, as many recent editors and
textual critics have argued, on an annotated copy of Q2 ..., F is used
as the control text for the present edition. The passages peculiar to
Q2, which were part of the play as originally drafted but then excised
from it before it came to performance, are therefore relegated to Appendix A" [131]). Acting sometimes under the pressures of subjective
belief about what "our Author" would surely have written, sometimes
under the influence of the felt rightness and familiarity of the accepted
consensus text, sometimes out of commitment to a theory of textual
origins, editors have searched for the words Shakespeare wrote, and
have, paradoxically, given us a plethora of *Hamlet*s.

Along with this common motivating impulse, *Hamlet* editors since
1709 have shared as well a seeming inability to be content with an F
or a Q text alone. From Rowe through Hibbard, it has not been enough
for an editor simply to give us F or Q2 *Hamlet;* each editor has needed
always to supplement one with the other, weaving the texts, in some
measure, together. The measure of Q2 found in the Hibbard and the
1986 Oxford texts is far less than in any text since the Folio itself (far
less than in Rowe), but Q2-only lines are, in fact, included, and echoes
from Q2 abound (in Hibbard, for example, Hamlet's 2.2 soliloquy, examined above, contains four Q2 variants; in the two Complete Oxfords,
the soliloquy contains *wand*/*wanned* rather than F's *warm'd;* Q's *why*
in place of F's *who*); in both Hibbard and the Complete Oxford texts,
we find Q2's "Ha? 'Swounds, I should take it").

If, as some argue, F *Hamlet* was printed from an annotated copy of
Q2, then F and Q2 *Hamlet* have been interconnected as printed documents almost from the beginning. If, as others believe, they were
printed from separate holograph manuscripts or their transcripts, the
connection was not through print but through a shared point of origin
in Shakespeare's mind and hand. Only if one believes that Q2 was
printed from Shakespeare's foul papers and F from the theater company's promptbook is there a felt distance between the two texts. It is
no wonder that editors, concerned as they have been since the early
eighteenth century with the origins of the early printed texts, have
found it impossible to break the connection and completely ignore one

version in favor of the other—and no wonder that a desire to recover the words (those Shakespeare first wrote, those he finally wrote, or those spoken on the stage) has provided so much editorial energy. Given the history of Q2/F *Hamlet,* a text that has changed and continues to change its shape, a text that has lived in its multiforms for more than two and one-half centuries and that promises always to affect any text of the play that is not a facsimile of the Folio or the quarto, the more dogmatic claims of present-day "revisionists" and determined "conflationists" seem a bit provincial—but understandable. The desire to recover "the text" is clearly a powerful drive—especially when the text is that of *Hamlet.*

Notes

1. On the two texts of *King Lear,* see, e.g., Taylor and Warren. Earlier studies of the two-text situation include Blayney and Urkowitz. One sees the privileging of one text over the other in such essays as David Richman's, and in the decision of Jay Halio, editor of the forthcoming New Cambridge *King Lear,* to produce a Folio *Lear* instead of either a "conflated" or a quarto text.

2. In the *Complete Works* (Wells and Taylor, 1986), in both the modern-spelling and the original-spelling editions, one finds most Q2-only passages at the end of the *Hamlet* text as "Additional Passages," pp. 775–77. The modern-spelling edition follows F1 for spelling and other accidentals; the original-spelling edition follows Q2 for such accidentals, but is otherwise the same text as the modern-spelling edition. In the Hibbard text, Q2-only passages are found in "Appendix A: Passages Peculiar to the Second Quarto" (pp. 355–69), accompanied by notes such as this introduction to the eighteen lines omitted from 1.1: "These eighteen lines were probably omitted from the text that lies behind F because they do not advance the action in any way. Moreover, if Horatio's speech was, as seems likely, intended to serve as an advertisement for *Julius Caesar,* there would be no point in including it when *Julius Caesar* was not being performed" (355).

3. Q2–Q6 are the traditional designations given the quartos of *Hamlet* that begin with the edition of 1604–05 (referred to as Q2 and Q3, even though, as the Cambridge editors point out, Q1605 "is not, properly speaking, a new edition, being printed from the same forms [sic] as Q2, and differing from it no more than one copy of the same edition may differ from another. The title-page differs only in the date, where 1605 is substituted for 1604" [Clark and Wright 8: x]). In this traditional numbering, the quarto printed in 1611 is known as Q4; an undated quarto, which seems to have been printed from Q4, is called Q5; the final pre–civil war quarto, Q6, was published in 1637, "printed from Q5 [with] the spelling ... modernized and the punctuation amended" [Clark and Wright 8: x). As J. K. Walton has shown, "for the printing of [Q6], a copy of the first or

second Folio was consulted" (113), but only to find "better" readings of particular, puzzling words. (I am grateful to Professor A. R. Braunmuller for calling this essay to my attention.)

4. An address "To the Reader" prefacing Q1676 ([Davenant], *The Tragedy of Hamlet Prince of Denmark, A2*) states that: "This Play being too long to be conveniently Acted, such places as might be least prejudicial to the Plot or Sense, are left out upon the Stage: but that we may no way wrong the incomparable Author, are here inserted according to the Original Copy, with this Mark' '."

James G. McManaway attributes the fact that these passages ("nearly 600 lines") are marked for omission in Q1676 to the fact that the publishers did unusually careful work: "[T]he publishers took the trouble," he writes, "to consult the prompter's book in the theater and to indicate differences between the literary and the stage texts" (94).

There is, by the way, no correlation between the passages marked for omission in Q1676 and the passages that Rowe chose to include or to omit. Most of the major Q-only passages that Rowe includes (among them Hamlet's "How all occasions" soliloquy) are marked, in Q1676, as "left out upon the Stage"; other major passages that Rowe does *not* include (e.g., the Hamlet/Osric dialogue about Laertes in the final scene) are *not* marked for omission in Q1676.

5. For a discussion of Davenant's 1676 quarto and its relationship to Q6, see Spencer (*"Hamlet* under the Restoration" and "D'Avenant's Adaptations" 174–84). The Cambridge editors (Clark and Wright) note that, besides the pre-war quartos, "several editions, usually known as Players' Quartos, were printed at the end of the seventeenth and beginning of the following century. Of these we have had before us during our collation, editions of 1676, 1685, 1695, and 1703.... It is ... worthy of notice that many emendations usually attributed to Rowe and Pope are really derived from one or other of these Players' Quartos" (8: x–xi). For a discussion of the Restoration players' quartos of another of Shakespeare's plays, see Velz.

Although there is extant a prompt copy of *Hamlet* from Restoration Dublin that is a marked-up F3 text (McManaway 95n2), the claim that quarto *Hamlet* held the stage in the Restoration is supported by the preponderance of evidence. McManaway felt confident, in fact, that Restoration and eighteenth-century performances of *Hamlet* (preserved in the eighteenth-century promptbooks based on Q1676) stand in a direct line with Elizabethan performances.

6. Capell gives Pope credit for the quarto additions, saying that, unlike Rowe, Pope inserted "many large passages, speeches, and single lines taken from the quarto's" (16).

7. Others who state that Rowe limited himself to the F4 text include D. Nichol Smith, who writes (xxviii): "[Rowe] was content to found his text on the fourth Folio, the last and worst; he had no idea of the superior claims of the first, though he professed to have compared the several editions. He corrected many errors and occasionally hit upon a happy emendation...." Irving Ribner, in his introduction to the Ribner/Kittredge *Complete Works* (1971), also writes that "Rowe did not consult either the First Folio or any of the quartos [though] he made a great many emendations so as to eliminate textual cruces" (57); and the entry under "Rowe, Nicholas" in *The Reader's Encyclopedia of*

Shakespeare states that "Rowe used the corrupt Fourth Folio for his text, and although he did not consult the quartos or First Folio, he made certain emendations which are the correct readings."

8. Jackson's reference to *Hamlet* 4.2 is, of course, to the scene containing Hamlet's "How all occasions" soliloquy, marked in modern editions as 4.4; it is marked as 4.2 in Rowe. Q1676 is not "a prompt copy," as Jackson calls it, though (as McManaway discovered) it was used in the eighteenth century as the basis for prompt copies.

9. Line numbers (and quotations, except where another source is specifically mentioned) will be from the Bevington edition (1980). When I am illustrating emendations and variants, I often (as here) add emphasis to point out the words changed.

10. I use the term Q when there is no substantive difference in the Q2–Q6, Q1676 reading. Similarly, I use F to indicate a reading that is substantively the same in F1–F4.

11. The fact of this "double motivation" for Hamlet's apology, recognized independently by Gary Taylor and Paul Werstine, is discussed by Werstine (3–4) and by Taylor in the Oxford *Textual Companion* (Wells and Taylor 400).

12. That Rowe used one of the Restoration "players' quartos" of *Othello* in constructing his text seems not to have been noticed. Horace Howard Furness collates Q1681 but does not list it among "texts collated" nor note its influence, through Rowe, on the editorial tradition of the play. Rowe bases his dramatis personae list for *Othello* on Q1681 (or, more likely, on one of its successors: 1687, 1695, 1705), following the players'-quarto order rather than that of F, and using modified players'-quarto descriptions of the characters (e.g., he follows Q1681+ in describing Montano as "The Moor's Predecessor in the Government of Cyprus" rather than F's "Governour of Cyprus," and he follows the players' quarto in identifying the hero not only as "the Moore" [as in F], but also as "General for the Venetians in Cyprus" [in Q1681+, this reads: "General of the Army in Cyprus"]). The players'-quarto dramatis personae list is essentially what we find in the influential Cambridge edition of 1866.

As in constructing his *Hamlet,* Rowe also uses one of the *Othello* players' quartos (spelling variations would suggest that he used Q1705) to correct F4 readings and to supply missing lines. In 1.3, for example, Rowe alters F4's "And portance in my Traveller's history. / Wherein of Antars vast, and desarts wild" to read (as it appears in Q1705): "And Portance in my Travels History; / Wherein of Antars vast, and Desarts idle"; he changes F4's "That I love the Moor" to Q's "That I did love the Moor"; and he alters F4's "Let her have your voice. / Vouch with me heaven" to Q1705's "Your Voices, Lords; beseech you, let her Will / Have a free Way. / Vouch with me, Heav'n [Q1705: Heaven]." (This third example, which, in Q1705, as in Rowe, is a conflation of Q1 and F, is found in this same conflated form in Q2 *Othello* [1630], suggesting that the players' quartos of *Othello* derive from Q2 [itself a conflation of Q1 and F].) It is possible that Rowe used *Othello* Q2 or Q3 (1630 or 1655) to "correct" F4, but the fact that his dramatis personae list is based on a players' quarto and that, in such deviations from F4 as mentioned above, spelling and other accidentals follow Q1705, makes it more likely that Rowe used Q1705.

13. One need not accept the stories, seemingly promulgated by Davenant himself, of Davenant's relationship (as godson or natural son) to Shakespeare to see Davenant as a link between the Jacobean/Caroline stage and the Restoration stage. Davenant's position as theater manager at the time of the closing of the theaters in 1642 and his central role in the opening and managing of theaters and acting companies after 1660 is enough to suggest that he would have brought to the Restoration theater some awareness of pre-war stage practices. (See entry under "Davenant, Sir William" in *The Reader's Encyclopedia of Shakespeare.*)

14. The mystery about John Hughes's own edition of *Hamlet* (an edition repeatedly praised by Theobald but unlocated by later editors, including Furness when he prepared his Variorum *Hamlet*) was finally solved in 1934 by Henry N. Paul; however, the alleged connection between John Hughes and Rowe's second edition is a mystery waiting to be solved. The self-confident assertions that, for Rowe's 1714 edition, Hughes "revised the text and compiled the index" and that he was "paid £ 28.7s. for his work on the 1714 edition of Rowe's *Shakespeare*" (Sherbo 2) are based on evidence that seems to me to fall apart upon close examination, leaving us with nothing but a single cryptic manuscript list. Sherbo quotes Harry M. Geduld (136), who gives no evidence for his statements about Hughes's work as Rowe's assistant, and Kathleen M. Lynch (132), who cites a manuscript in the Folger Shakespeare Library as her evidence that Hughes was paid £28 7s. "for what appears to have been substantial work by him on [the 1714 Rowe] edition." The manuscript that she cites is a short list written on a quarto sheet in "a hand circa 1740" (according to the Folger notation) with (in a second hand) a note that says, "This is the handwriting of Mr. Somerset Draper deceased who was servant to the late Mr. Tonson." The list itself is headed: "Paid the Editors of Shakespear" and reads: "Mr. Rowe—36.10 / Mr. Hughes—28.7 / Mr. Pope—Money 160, Do. Books 57.12 / ..." (Folger Shakespeare Library ms. S. a. 163). As far as I can determine, all of the claims about Hughes's connection with Rowe's second edition depend upon this cryptic list.

15. It is interesting to note that Theobald repeatedly states his indebtedness to the quarto edition of *Hamlet* edited by "the accurate Mr. Hughes." Henry N. Paul writes that this 1718 quarto, prepared by Hughes for the actor Robert Wilks when he took over the role of Hamlet from Betterton, is, in essence, the Davenant quarto (Q1676) corrected against Rowe, with F-only passages taken from Rowe's edition and inserted into the Q1676 text. In preparing his own rather carefully combined text, then, Theobald was drawing on both Rowe's Folio-based Q/F text and Hughes's quarto-based Q/F text (the first Q/F text of *Hamlet* to use the quarto as control text).

16. In passages quoted from Q2 where there are substantive press variants I use the terms *corr.* and *uncorr.* to refer to the second and the first states.

17. The "Notes" to the Cambridge *Hamlet* (8: 185–96) give "the readings of the different editions" for several passages, including 1.3.74 ("Are of a most select and generous chief in that"); 4.1.40–44 ("And what's untimely done / Whose whisper ..."); 4.5.14–16 (" 'Twere good she were spoken with"); and 5.2.205, 206 ("The readiness is all ..."). Each of these passages shows the same dizzying instability as in the words traced above.

18. To determine the reasons for the correlation between the Cambridge and the "modern" editions is another study. Fredson Bowers, in an important essay on Shakespeare's texts, stresses the central position of the Cambridge edition and suggests some reasons for its importance, but many questions remain unanswered. Richard Knowles (private correspondence) asks: "Is it due to [the Cambridge and the Globe's] authority, or to some other cause like inertia, or the fact that a great concordance was based on their text, or the diffferent fact that these editions happened along roughly contemporaneous with the *OED,* which so improved our understanding of Elizabethan idiom that thousands of previously contested readings now seemed obviously superior to their competitors and were chosen independently by very different editors; or what? It is remarkable, and seems to demand explanation." To this list of suggestions I would add the additional question of the impact on the text occasioned by the 1823 discovery of Q1, an impact that perhaps climaxed and stabilized with the 1866 Cambridge edition of *Hamlet* (Cambridge prints Q1 as an appendix to its *Hamlet*).

I owe considerable gratitude to Professor Knowles, as well as to Professors David Bevington, A. R. Braunmuller, and Taylor Littleton—and to the staff of the Folger Library Reading Room.

19. The editors of the Oxford *William Shakespeare: The Complete Works* point out that their concern is to recover instead the words spoken in performance in the London theaters in Shakespeare's time (both editions, xxxivff.). To that extent, then, their goal is different from that of the other editors.

Works Cited

Alexander, Peter, ed. *William Shakespeare: The Complete Works.* London: Collins, 1951.

Barnet, Sylvan, gen. ed. *The Complete Signet Classic Shakespeare.* New York: Harcourt, 1972.

Bevington, David, ed. *The Complete Works of Shakespeare.* 3rd ed. Glenview, Ill.: Scott, Foresman, 1980.

Blayney, Peter W. M. *Nicholas Okes and the First Quarto.* Vol. 1 of *The Texts of* King Lear *and Their Origins.* Cambridge: Cambridge UP, 1982.

Boswell, James, ed. *Plays and Poems.* By William Shakespeare. "Boswell-Malone Edition." 21 vols. London, 1821.

Bowers, Fredson. "Today's Shakespeare Texts, and Tomorrow's." *Studies in Bibliography* 19 (1966): 39–65.

Brockbank, J. Philip. "Shakespearean Scholarship: From Rowe to the Present." *William Shakespeare: His World, His Work, His Influence.* Ed. John F. Andrews. 3 vols. New York: Scribner's, 1985. 3: 717–32.

Caldecott, Thomas, ed. Hamlet, *and* As You Like It. By William Shakespeare. London, 1832.

Capell, Edward, ed. *Mr William Shakespeare His Comedies, Histories, and Tragedies.* 10 vols. London: J. and R. Tonson, 1768.

Chalmers, Alexander, ed. *Plays of William Shakespeare*. 8 vols. London: Longman, 1856.

Clark, William George, and William Aldis Wright, eds. *The Works of William Shakespeare*. The Cambridge Shakespeare. 9 vols. London: Macmillan, 1863–66.

Collier, John Payne, ed. *The Works of William Shakespeare*. 8 vols. London, 1842–44.

[Davenant, William], ed. *The Tragedy of Hamlet Prince of Denmark*. By William Shakespeare. London: J. Martyn and H. Herringman, 1676.

Delius, Nikolaus. *Shakespeare Lexicon*. 2nd ed. Bonn, 1852.

Dyce, Alexander, ed. *The Works of William Shakespeare*. 6 vols. London, 1857.

Edwards, Philip, ed. *Hamlet*. The New Cambridge Shakespeare. Cambridge: Cambridge UP, 1985.

Evans, G. Blakemore. "Shakespeare's Text." *The Riverside Shakespeare*. G. Blakemore Evans, textual ed. Boston: Houghton, 1974. 27–41.

Farnham, Willard, ed. *Hamlet Prince of Denmark*. By William Shakespeare. Harbage 930–76.

Furness, Horace Howard, ed. *Hamlet*. The New Variorum Shakespeare. 2 vols. London: Lippincott, 1877.

———, ed. *Othello*. The New Variorum Shakespeare. London: Lippincott, 1886.

Geduld, Harry M. *Prince of Publishers: A Study of the Work and Career of Jacob Tonson*. Bloomington: Indiana UP, 1969.

Hanmer, Thomas, ed. *The Works of William Shakespear*. 6 vols. Oxford, 1743–44.

Harbage, Alfred, gen. ed. *William Shakespeare: The Complete Works*. The Pelican Text Revised. New York: Penguin, 1969. New York: Viking, 1977.

Hibbard, G. R., ed. *Hamlet*. The Oxford Shakespeare. Oxford: Clarendon, 1987.

Hudson, Henry N., ed. The *Works of Shakespeare*. 11 vols. Boston, 1851–56.

Hubler, Edward, ed. *The Tragedy of Hamlet Prince of Denmark*. By William Shakespeare. Barnet 910–61.

Jackson, Alfred. "Rowe's Edition of Shakespeare." *Library* 4th ser. 10 (1929–30): 455–73.

Jenkins, Harold, ed. *Hamlet*. The Arden Shakespeare. London: Methuen, 1982.

Jennens, Charles, ed. *Hamlet*. By William Shakespeare. London: N. Bowyer and J. Nichols, 1773.

Johnson, Samuel, ed. *The Plays of William Shakespeare*. 8 vols. London: Tonson-Corbet, 1765.

Johnson, Samuel, and George Steevens, eds. *The Plays of William Shakespeare*. 10 vols. London, 1773. 2nd ed., London, 1778.

Kittredge, George Lyman, ed. *The Complete Works of Shakespeare*. Boston: Ginn, 1936.

Knight, Charles, ed. *Works*. By William Shakespeare. Pictorial ed. 7 vols. London, [1838–43].

Lynch, Kathleen M. *Jacob Tonson, Kit-Cat Publisher*. Knoxville: U of Tennessee P, 1971.

McManaway, James G. "The Two Earliest Prompt Books of *Hamlet*." *PBSA* 43 (1949): 288–320. Rpt. in *Studies in Shakespeare, Bibliography, and Theater*. By James G. McManaway. Ed. Richard Hosley, Arthur C. Kirsch, and John W. Velz. New York: Shakespeare Assoc., 1969. 93–120.

Malone, Edmond, ed. *The Plays and Poems of William Shakespeare.* 10 vols. London, 1790.

Paul, Henry N. "Mr. Hughs' Edition of *Hamlet.*" *Modern Language Notes* 49 (1934): 438–43.

Pope, Alexander, ed. *The Works of Shakespear.* 6 vols. London: Jacob Tonson, 1725, 1723.

The Reader's Encyclopedia of Shakespeare. Ed. Oscar James Campbell and Edward G. Quinn. New York: Crowell, 1966.

Reed, Isaac, ed. *The Plays of William Shakespeare.* 21 vols. London, 1803.

Ribner, Irving. Introduction. *The Complete Works of Shakespeare.* Ed. Irving Ribner and George Lyman Kittredge. Waltham, Mass.: Ginn, 1971. 3–83.

Richman, David. "The *King Lear* Quarto in Rehearsal and Performance." *Shakespeare Quarterly* 37 (1986): 374–82.

Rowe, Nicholas, ed. *The Works of Mr. William Shakespear.* 6 vols. London: J. Tonson, 1709.

Sherbo, Arthur. *The Birth of Shakespeare Studies: Commentators from Rowe (1709) to Boswell-Malone (1821).* East Lansing, Mich.: Colleagues, 1986.

Singer, Samuel W. *The Dramatic Works of Shakespeare.* 10 vols. Chiswick, 1826.

Smith, D. Nichol. "Shakespearean Criticism in the Eighteenth Century." *Eighteenth Century Essays on Shakespeare.* Ed. D. Nichol Smith. 2nd ed., rev. Oxford: Clarendon, 1963. xi–xxxvii.

Spencer, Hazelton. "D'Avenant's Adaptations." *Shakespeare Improved: The Restoration Versions in Quarto and on the Stage.* Cambridge: Harvard UP, 1927. 137–91.

———. "*Hamlet* under the Restoration." *PMLA* 38 (1923): 770–91.

Staunton, Howard, ed. *The Plays of William Shakespeare.* 3 vols. London, 1858–60.

Steevens, George, and Isaac Reed, eds. *The Plays of William Shakespeare.* 15 vols. London, 1793.

Taylor, Gary, and Michael Warren, eds. *The Division of the Kingdoms: Shakespeare's Two Versions of* King Lear. Oxford: Clarendon, 1983.

Theobald, Lewis. *Shakespeare restored.* . . . London, 1726.

———, ed. *The Works of Shakespeare.* 7 vols. London: J. Tonson, 1733.

Urkowitz, Steven. *Shakespeare's Revision of* King Lear. Princeton: Princeton UP, 1980.

Velz, John W. " 'Pirate Hills' and the Quartos of *Julius Caesar.*" *PBSA* 63 (1969): 177–93.

Walton, J. K. *The Quarto Copy for the First Folio of Shakespeare.* Dublin: Dublin UP, 1971.

Warburton, William, ed. *The Works of William Shakespeare.* 8 vols. London, 1747.

Wells, Stanley, and Gary Taylor, et al. *William Shakespeare: A Textual Companion.* Oxford: Clarendon, 1987.

Wells, Stanley, and Gary Taylor, gen. eds. *William Shakespeare: The Complete Works.* The Oxford Shakespeare. Oxford: Clarendon, 1986.

———. *William Shakespeare: The Complete Works: Original-Spelling Edition.* The Oxford Shakespeare. Oxford: Clarendon, 1986.

Werstine, Paul. "The Textual Mystery of *Hamlet.*" *Shakespeare Quarterly* 39 (1988):
    1–26.
White, Richard Grant, ed. *The Works of William Shakespeare.* 12 vols. Boston, 1857–66.

Editing Renaissance Drama in Paperback

DAVID BEVINGTON

Act 1, Scene 1 *The battlements of a castle.*

Enter Bernardo and Francisco, two sentinels, meeting.

BERNARDO

Who's there?

FRANCISCO

Nay, answer me. Stand and unfold yourself.

BERNARDO

Long live the King!

FRANCISCO

Bernardo.

BERNARDO

He.

FRANCISCO

You come most carefully upon your hour.

BERNARDO

'Tis now strook twelf. Get...

FRANCISCO

"'Tis now strook twelf"! Do you mean "'Tis now *struck twelve*"?

127

BERNARDO

Huh?

FRANCISCO

Where did this *strook twelf* stuff come from?

BERNARDO

It's right here in my script. Look.

[They huddle around a torch, consulting Bernardo's script.]

FRANCISCO

Well, I'll be damned. Strook twelf. There it is, big as life. Who gave you this?

BERNARDO

Wait a minute, I think I hear Horatio and Marcellus.

—Stand ho! Who is there?

HORATIO

Friends to this ground.

MARCELLUS

And liegemen to the Dane.

HORATIO

What, hath this thing appeared again tonight?

FRANCISCO

Yes. I asked Bernardo what time it was, and he answered, "'Tis now strook twelf."

HORATIO

Strook twelf?

BERNARDO

Let me show you.   *[They all gather around his script.]*

HORATIO

I think it be no other but e'en so.

Well may it sort that . . .

MARCELLUS

Wait. Wait a minute. I can't find a word of what you're saying in my script.

HORATIO

You can't? It's right here in mine.   *[They compare scripts.]*

FRANCISCO

Something's rotten in the state of Denmark, I tell you.

HORATIO

A mote it is to trouble the mind's eye.

BERNARDO

Do you mean "moth"?

HORATIO *[Ignoring Bernardo's remark]*

In the most high and palmy state of Rome,

A little ere the mightiest Julius fell . . .

MARCELLUS

Stop. Stop! Not a word of what you're saying is set down in my part.

BERNARDO

Mine either.

FRANCISCO

Say, isn't your name Bernardo? It's spelled "Barnardo" in my script.

BERNARDO

I can't believe this.

HORATIO

... The graves stood tenantless, and the sheeted dead
Did squeak and gibber in the Roman streets
At stars with trains of fire ...

MARCELLUS

Horatio, I'm not going to let you go on like this. Not only are you brazenly reciting a passage cut from the F text, you've changed it to "At" when everybody knows it reads "As" in Q. Q2 I should say. We used to play that speech before Q2 got put in the dustbin and F took over.

HORATIO

What in the world are you talking about? F? Q2?

MARCELLUS

My God, you an actor, and you mean to tell me you don't know your F from your Q?

HORATIO

Now look, if you're going to start getting nasty—

MARCELLUS

I'm beginning to think you don't know your F from a hole in the ground.

BERNARDO [*Intervening*]

What the F is going on here?   [*A spotlight comes up on Hamlet,
                                                who has been watching the scene.*]

HAMLET

This heavy-headed revel east and west
Makes us traduced and taxed of other nations.
So oft it chances in particular men ...

MARCELLUS

There's another one. This place is becoming a regular den of surreptitious Q2 loyalists.

FRANCISCO

I'm partial to Q1 myself.   [*He adopts a thrasonical stance.*]
          O, what a whoreson dunghill slave am I!
Now there's poetry for you.

MARCELLUS

Now look, are we going to agree to stick to F or not?

HAMLET

You're a fine one to talk, Marcellus. Everybody fingers you as the guy who sold that junky copy of Q1 to the printer in the first place. Most of it was just stuff you made up.

MARCELLUS

It wasn't me, it was the guy who played Lucianus.

HAMLET

You played Lucianus too.

MARCELLUS

And besides, my name isn't Marcellus or Lucianus. Those are my parts.

[*He nurses a hurt pride.*]

HORATIO

Wait a minute, wait a minute. I still don't understand a word of all this talk about Q and F. Who is 't that can inform me?

MARCELLUS

Wait a minute, you've stolen my line. I say "Who is 't that can inform me?" and you answer, "That can I."

HORATIO

But I can't. I don't understand this F and Q thing from nothing. I repeat, who is 't that can inform me?

SHAKESPEARE [*Coming onstage*]

Gentlemen, gentlemen! Please. It's quite simple, really. And wonderfully unimportant.

MARCELLUS

Shakespeare, please don't try to claim that Q2 represents anything more than your foul papers.

SHAKESPEARE

Foul papers! Are you trying to get personal with me? What do you mean, foul papers? I know my handwriting is shaky, especially hand D, but...

MARCELLUS

I mean your author's holograph.

SHAKESPEARE

Hollow what?

HAMLET [*Intervening*]

Perhaps we could agree to call them your manuscript.

SHAKESPEARE

Anyway, I wrote out the play, of course, and changed it some (Ben Jonson says I never blotted a line, but he's just blotto), and then later I added some things I rather like. Hamlet (I mean, Richard), you must remember that piece we worked out together about occasions spurring revenge. Come, give us a taste of your quality. Come, a passionate speech. If it live in your memory, begin at this line—let me see, let me see:

How all occasions do inform against me
And spur my dull revenge!

[*He is joined by Burbage in a joint recital.*]
SHAKESPEARE AND BURBAGE
What is a man
If his chief good and market of his time
Be but to sleep and feed? A beast, no more.
[*They have their arms around one another's shoulders
and are doing a soft-shoe routine to stage left.*]
SHAKESPEARE
Now, that really is rather good. We ought to try that again some time. I never
was happy about cutting that.
MARCELLUS
How can we? The damned play is much too long as it is.
HORATIO
We could cut out the parts of Marcellus and Lucianus.
MARCELLUS
Now listen, we can't have authors telling us how to play their plays. Cuts are
cuts and I say we stick with F or I'm going to Equity about this.
SHOUTS FROM THE AUDIENCE
Down with the author! There ain't no author!
[*Marcellus starts shoving Shakespeare toward the wings.*]
SHAKESPEARE [*As he is disappearing*]
O, vengeance!
MARCELLUS
Now, that really is the last straw. Adding an actor's interpolation! Nobody has
any respect for textual theory these days.
SHAKESPEARE [*Sticking his head out from the
wings*]
It is not an actor's interpolation. It's my interpolation. I also said I didn't want
you to mouth your lines or tear a passion to tatters to split the ears of the
groundlings . . .
FROM THE AUDIENCE
Who are you calling groundlings?
[*A ripe tomato lands in Shakespeare's face. Exit.*]
HAMLET
Now look here . . . [*By now, the actors are all at one another's throats. The
Q2 team, consisting of Hamlet and Francisco, seems to be having the better
of the F team, consisting of Marcellus and Bernardo. Horatio, still uncom-
prehending, is being pummeled in the middle.*]
CLAUDIUS [*Who has been watching from the
gallery*]
Give me some light. Away!
HAMLET
What, frighted with false fire?

GERTRUDE

Hamlet, really! Everyone knows that line is from F and is not in Q2 and is the same as that awful Q1 except Q1 reads "fires." Stop saying these things!

[*The boy actor playing Gertrude starts to bite Hamlet's shin.*]

HAMLET

Why, let the strooken deer go weep.

GERTRUDE

Strucken, dammit, not strooken! Who taught you English?

COURTIERS

Lights, lights, lights!

POLONIUS

Hey, I'm supposed to say "Lights, lights, lights." It's assigned to "Cor." in Q1, meaning Corambis, thus supporting Q2, "Pol."

FRANCISCO

Who's Corambis?

A COURTIER

The F assignment of "Lights, lights, lights" is to "All," and I'm going to be allowed to say this line or I quit.

[*General fighting ensues. The lights come up. Enter the stage manager.*]

STAGE MANAGER [*Looking bleakly and imploringly out to the audience*]

Is there an editor in the house?

*   *   *

MY RECENT experience in editing Renaissance drama in paperback centers on Shakespeare, but I hope that what I have to say about the Bantam Shakespeare (in twenty-nine volumes, published February 1988) will apply to other Renaissance dramatists as well. The opportunity of providing an inexpensive text designed for wide use in college and high school, as well as for more general reading, is exciting. One can hope to reach large numbers of readers, some of them new to Shakespeare or Renaissance drama. How can one make the texts as available as possible to such readers without loss of essential accuracy? Most editors will recoil from the recent example of A. L. Rowse (1984–86), not because the notion of dispelling the mystery of Shakespeare's language is a bad idea in itself but because Rowse's practice of modernizing "thou" to "you" and "hath" to "has," along with modernizing grammatical agreements that E. A. Abbott regards as standard Elizabethan usage ("My old bones aches," *Tmp.* 3.3.2) and providing some more startling substitutions of modern "equivalents" for archaic words, is arbitrarily and inconsistently done in such a way as to leave untouched the metaphoric density of many difficult passages in Shakespeare. Other more recent editing attempts, acknowledging that the language difficulty in Shakespeare cannot be resolved by occasional word substitutions, have deployed the ultimate solution of a facing-page translation,[1] but such editions require twice as much paper as another text and seem to reduce the Shakespearean original to the status of an artifact, as in the Loeb Classical Library, to be consulted on occasion rather than read for itself. Students are likely to read the "trot."

If we veer away from these extremes of modernizing, we confront in the other direction a series of more conservative choices. The New Penguin Shakespeare gives us the text on a page unencumbered with glosses (though some of the stage directions are editorially provided). The commentary notes, in the back, are unusually full and informative, but they are not easy to use. The editors' desire to have the reader experience the play on his or her own is admirable in intention, and no doubt works well for the experienced reader, or for actors (who for their own reasons often prefer not to be distracted by notes), but for most of us the help is too unavailable when it is needed. The very fullness of the notes attests to the difficulties we encounter at every turn in attempting to understand Shakespeare's language. (And the same is true of Lyly, Marlowe, and their contemporaries.) Surely the notes ought to be on the page.

The way the notes are keyed to the text is no less important. Bubbles (as in the Signet Classic Shakespeare) or footnote numbers (as in Fraser and Rabkin's *Drama of the English Renaissance,* 1976) tend to interrupt the reader and insist that the note be consulted, whether needed or not; and such devices do not work well when many notes are necessary, since the text will then be continually disfigured by superscript numbers or other markers. Numbering notes by line number only, on the other hand, gives insufficient notice to the reader as to whether a word or passage is glossed or not, unless (as in the Pelican Shakespeare and the new Bantam) the line of text is also numbered in the column. A numbered line signals the reader that a gloss is available, but leaves it up to the reader to decide if something remains unexplained for that reader; a passage in which most of the lines are numbered points to a passage of particular density, while longish gaps in the numbering signal clear sailing for a time.

Such a system leaves the paperback editor free to concentrate on as many glosses as are really necessary to let the reader capture something of the range of possible meanings in the text. Wordplay must be explained, even though glosses can never fully exhaust the possible range of meanings; sexual double entendre, though it should not be luridly proclaimed, needs to be pointed out. Single-word glosses are often inadequate. The pursuit of a well-worded, concise, and illuminating commentary is an unending search, one that requires incessant testing for accuracy and clarity. What will the intellectually curious but linguistically underinformed reader fail to grasp in an unfamiliar grammatical construction, an inverted word order, a complex metaphor? Glosses in our older editions, designed for learned readers, concentrated on textual cruxes, on rare Elizabethan usages, on historical sources. The task for a paperback editor is to identify and address potential sources of misreading.

One of the readiest ways to make a new paperback edition of a Renaissance dramatist as available as possible for a wide readership is to modernize punctuation thoroughly and consistently. Michael Warren has awakened us to the manifold dangers of such modernizing, and indeed punctuation can distort as well as clarify meaning. Warren uses this danger as an argument that modern-spelling editions necessarily "continue to erect invisible barriers between us and the plays" (169), but to my mind it is an argument chiefly for more scrupulous reconsideration of what we do. Sometimes a line is genuinely ambiguous in the original text, as in *Antony and Cleopatra* 1.5.53, when Cleopatra, responding to Alexis's description of Antony's sending of greetings to Egypt, asks (in the Folio reading), "What was he sad, or merry?" The modern editor is under constraint to choose between "What, was he sad, or merry?" or "What was he, sad or merry?" (I have chosen the first.) Presumably Shakespeare meant one or the other, not both; any edited text that preserves the Folio punctuation avoids the risk of error but at the expense of allowing the reader to remain uncertain and to experience the line, given the modern reader's understanding of punctuation conventions, as a puzzle. Informed choosing is what editors regularly do as a service to readers, and, when editors make mistakes, as they invariably do, the solution is not to give up the enterprise but to correct those errors in subsequent editions as thoughtfully as possible, based on textual and linguistic information about Elizabethan punctuation, and to provide in a note the degree of uncertainty remaining.

So too with Caesar's response to the news of Antony's death, "Looke you sad Friends" (5.1.26), which can be punctuated as "Look you sad, friends?" or "Look you, sad friends. . . ." The first seems more likely in context, though both are possible. Similarly, in the response of an Egyptian to Caesar's asking where he has come from—"A poore Egyptian yet, the Queen my mistris," etc. (5.1.52)—the phrase "A poore Egyptian yet" can be read in apposition to "the Queen my mistris," or can, with a semicolon or period after "yet," either refer to the speaker's having come from Cleopatra (the "poore Egyptian") or describe the speaker himself as one who concedes he will soon owe allegiance to Rome or else proudly declares his Egyptian identity still. Or, with a comma after "Egyptian," the "yet" can imply that Cleopatra is still very much a queen, however poor she may be in power and wealth. These manifold possibilities enrich the text and should be noted to the extent that space provides, but they are not all available in the Folio punctuation in any case. A modern-spelling edition will direct the reader to what the editor regards as the most plausible choice (in this instance I have chosen the period after "yet"), while allowing for alternatives. We should not shrink from this role of interpreter for today's reader, but we should choose on the basis of all information available and learn from our (and others') mistakes so that editions become progressively closer to some kind of informed accuracy.

The hard choices I have cited are not uncommon, but they are vastly outnumbered in any case by instances where modern punctuation can indeed clarify and bring a text up to date without appreciable distortion. Punctuation conventions change rapidly, and the texts prepared even thirty years ago are, to our ears, laden with semicolons and commas that are no longer necessary. Instead of introducing the conventional comma splices, why not print simply "Well, get thee gone. Farewell" or "Give me my robe. Put on my crown. I have immortal longings on me" (5.2.276–78)? Lighter punctuation can move both verse and prose more clearly and swiftly. The editor who repunctuates is interfering, if you like, but the attempt should be to interpret as clearly as possible in modern terms the seeming intent of the original.

One must be continually aware that "intent" is a complex issue, that "meaning" is often diverse or even illusory, and above all that understanding is subject to the subjective points of view of the times in which editors and readers live. This is only to say, however, that editing is an organic process, ever changing, subject to reversals of all its judgments. No better explanation is needed for the frequently asked question "Why another edition?" than that editors must continually and conscientiously readdress the problems of textual interpretation in terms of contemporary values and language without losing sight of what past editors can richly provide. In editing the Bantam Shakespeare I found myself spending a great deal of time on punctuation, and addressed literally thousands of queries to the associate editors and textual consultants of this edition, David Kastan, Robert Keane Turner, and James Hammersmith. Even though I had edited all of Shakespeare for Scott, Foresman less than ten years earlier (Bevington 1980), the number of changes introduced into the Bantam text was large, astonishingly large. Some of this must have been the result of previous indecisiveness or inexperience on my part, but I think that in part too it is a sign of how much work is continually required to bring a Renaissance dramatic text accurately up to date.

The question of modernized spelling, ably addressed by Stanley Wells and Gary Taylor (1979, 1984), deals with a similar problem in that the editor must continually choose when to intervene, when to interpret, by offering the modern form of a Renaissance word. The modern form may seem roughly equivalent in meaning, or equivalent in some meanings but not others; at the same time it may well alter values of resonance, sound, meter. The Riverside Shakespeare stands as the most extensive recent attempt (short of old-spelling editing) to preserve the flavor of many Elizabethan words, but it does so at the expense of creating a language no one ever spoke or wrote, somewhat like the consciously archaic style of Edmund Spenser. The Riverside strategy is devoted to the conservative proposition that the reader is best able to sort out the resonances and linguistic flavor of certain words if they are given in their original form, but the idea of leaving matters to the reader is unavoidably complicated by the intrusiveness with which the editor must constantly decide which words to modernize and which not. Thus we are given *fift* instead of *fifth,* *strook* instead of *struck,* *th'art* instead of *thou'rt,* etc., along with *Antony* for *Anthonie, dislimns* for *dislimes, lock'd* for *lockt, midst* for *middest,* and the like. Since spellings are to a significant extent standardized in the Riverside, an old spelling may in fact represent a range of Elizabethan spellings; *moe,* for example, is used to represent both *moe* and *mo* in the originals. When the Riverside preserves a form like *egall* along with *equal* (the latter being more numerous), it may be preserving compositorial spellings. The original texts do not show much consistency in distinguishing the usages of *moe* and *more* (the latter being more common); why then should we preserve variations of this sort that are essentially arbitrary and subject to changing fashion in the Renaissance, especially since the choice in some cases may be compositorial? I am encouraged to see that no edition of Renaissance drama since the Riverside Shakespeare has followed the solution it proposed in 1974.

Surely, a rigorous modernization of spelling offers not only a potentially more consistent formulation but one that is in keeping with the aim of providing a text that is as available and contemporary as possible. But at what cost in accuracy? If the new Penguin and the Oxford Shakespeares have set an admirable standard in modernizing, the debate goes on endlessly about individual cases. Some seem easy: *kindred* for *kinred, o'clock* for *a clocke, bairn* for *barne, compromise* for *compremise, lief* for *leve* or *lieve, joust* for *just, mongrel* for *mungrel, osprey* for *asprey.* Others seem more difficult, as though some important flavor is being lost, though this may well be the result of our familiarity with the older form in the editions we used to read. Should it be *i' God's name* or *a' God's name, account* or *accompt, afraid* or *aferd* (or follow the choice of the original texts), *angrily* or *angerly, apricots* or *apricocks, bankrupt* or *bankrout, beholden* or *beholding, handkerchief* or *handkercher, howsome'er* or *howsoe'er, momentary* or *momentany, mushrooms* or *mushrumps, random* or *randon, ribbon* or *riband, venture* or *venter?* The linguistic issues are not identical in these cases and blanket rules will not apply. The changes from *porpentine* to *porcupine* and *pomgarnet* to *pomegranate* strike me as particularly wrenching, especially since both words are often used as the names of inns rather than of the animal or fruit, though the *OED* sees no reason to regard

the older forms as anything other than variant spellings, and I concede
in principle that these words ought to be modernized like most of the
previous ones cited. (I have kept *beholding* and *momentany,* since the
OED lists them as separate words with histories of their own.)

Consistency is difficult to achieve. *Account* provides a satisfactory
modernization of *accompt,* but *count* for *compt* usually has the wrong
resonance; to our ears, it is not idiomatic to say that "we shall meet at
count" (*Oth.* 5.2.273) or that scores will be struck away "from the
great count" (*AWW* 5.3.57). Scansion creates problems in our attempts
to modernize *persever,* with its accent on the second syllable, or *cons-
ter,* with its accent on the first syllable, as opposed to *construe. Swounded*
is a problem for modernization in verse, though *swoonèd* will perhaps
do.

Strong forms of verbs can pose difficult questions. Does one retain
arose where we would say *arisen, begun* for *began* ("A great while ago
the world begun," *TN* 5.1.405), *broke* as a past participle ("I have broke
your hest to say so," *Tmp.* 3.1.7), *catched* for *caught, drave* for *drove,
forbid* for *forbade, forsook* for *forsaken?* Some of these choices have
metrical implications, while in others a substitution would be easy.
Even if we decide to keep strong verbal forms throughout (as the Bantam edition has done), since the consequences are often metrical, is
such a decision consistent with the broader policy of modernization?
What is a spelling variant and what is not? Does one print *dreamt* or
dreamed, or whichever occurs in the copy-text? *Learned* or *learnt?* Is
egal a form of *equal* or another word? What about *enow* and *enough?
Ev'n* and *e'en?* Is it going too far to regard *fashion's sake* as a modernization of *fashion sake, God's sake* for *God sake?* Are *hoised* and *hoisted*
two different words? (They certainly are metrically different.) Is the
quaint and familiar *God buy you* anything other than an Elizabethan
form of *God b' wi' you,* and *god-den* anything more than a variant of
good e'en? (Bantam has opted for *equal, enough, fashion's sake, God
b' wi' you,* and *good e'en,* but retains *hoised* on metrical grounds and
because the *OED* regards it as a separate word of which *hoisted* was
originally a corruption.)

Words beginning in *in-* and *un-* often appear in unfamiliar form in
Elizabethan drama and could be altered to the modern "equivalent"
without substantial damage—*unauspicious, uncapable, incertain, in-*

charitable, incivil, uncurable, indistinguished, undiscernible, individ-able, etc.—though surely these can be regarded as "strong" forms as differentiated by the *OED* as to meaning as well as form. (Bantam retains the older forms of these words.) But what of more indifferent pairs, like *toward/towards* and *afterward/afterwards*? They could be standardized according to American usage, especially since there is no assurance that the spellings in the original texts are consistently Shakespeare's, but I decided to leave them as they inconsistently appear, since no difficulty in comprehension is posed for the modern reader and since American and British usage vary. In that case, should one close up *be gone* where American usage calls for one word in the imperative mood? And what about *forever* (American usage) or *for ever* (British and Elizabethan usage)? Here I chose to modernize and Americanize, since the connotations are changed (as they are not really by *toward/towards*), and one can make useful distinctions between an imperative *Begone!* and a declarative or interrogative "I know you'd fain be gone" (*MM* 5.1.120). Some closed-up words in American usage like *anymore* and *goodwill,* on the other hand, strike me as too recently coined (even barbaric), and I have resisted them, though I freely confess that this is a matter of personal view. *Farther* and *further* is an instance where a modern distinction theoretically exists, though it is not widely understood or agreed upon, and where meanings overlap in any case, and I have found it easier to follow the original copy (with its own inconsistencies) rather than split hairs.

A number of potential choices raise questions of historical complexity. Is the *hoboy* enough like the *oboe* to be called an oboe, or does *hautboy* better express a sense (to be explained in a note, as I have done) that it is an ancestor of the oboe, an archaic instrument of the same family? Can *huswife* be modernized to *housewife,* or are there instances where that choice obliterates too flatly the sense of *hussy*? I would argue that it does, as in "Doth Fortune play the huswife with me now" (*H5* 5.1.80), and that the original word is needed to alert the reader to a multiple meaning that, since Elizabethan times, has evolved into two different words. *Ancient/ensign* is perhaps a similar case requiring the retention of an archaic form (treated under a separate entry in the *OED*) to signal the reader that the word embodies a confused linguistic tradition of "standard-bearer" (*ensign*) and ancient, former (*ancienne*), as in *Lear* 5.1.32, "Let's then determine / With th' ancient of war [i.e., experienced officers] on our proceeding."

Is *berrord* a *bear-herd* or a *bear-ward*, or should one opt for the variety, found in the Riverside, of *berrord*, *bearard*, and *bear-herd*? Does one attempt to adjudicate between the multiple and overlapping meanings of *trauaile* by variously converting it to *travel* and *travail*, depending on what appears to be the primary meaning in the particular passage (as I have done, with a word of explanation about the other possibilities)? Does *corse* convert easily into *corpse* (generally I would say yes), or is the modern sense of a lifeless body too jarring in tone when a living body may be in question?

Characterization can be a factor in spelling choice. If one modernizes *pumpion* or *pompion* to *pumpkin*, is one losing the speaker's voice, or is one discarding a perfectly standard Elizabethan spelling that only looks quaint to our modern sensibilities? "Pompion the Great" in *Love's Labor's Lost* sounds in character, and probably should be retained, but Mrs. Ford's description of Falstaff as a "great watery pumpion" (*Wiv.* 3.3.41) probably is best rendered by *pumpkin* lest we attribute too much flavor to what she probably regards as a normative spelling. *Lanthorn* is irresistibly attractive in act 5 of *A Midsummer Night's Dream* ("This lanthorn doth the hornèd moon present"), especially with its visual play on *horn*, but elsewhere the spelling is quite neutral. A modernizing editor would be most hesitant to retain the old spelling in Romeo's "A Lanthorne slaughtred youth" (Q2 text of *Rom.* 5.3.84), but one must then consider whether one is playing fast and loose by retaining the old spelling in *Midsummer*. Similarly, one is tempted to think that Bottom's repeated use of *Mounsieur* as he addresses the fairies in act 4, scene 1 of *Midsummer* is part of his ineffable way of speaking, but the evidence suggests that it is an entirely normal way of spelling for Elizabethans and not a "humorous" effect; hence, it should be modernized. In such cases the editor should judge what appears to be the primary effect intended and provide the modern form that best expresses that effect. The process is interpretive and hence subject to the bias of personal judgment, and another generation may learn to do it better or at least differently, but that is what editing is about: well-informed choices.

Proper names can present the thorniest problems of all. I find the Oxford policy of modernizing in foreign languages—*Biron, Longueville, Chatillon, Rousillon, Lavache, René (Reignier), Petruccio, Glyndwr*—jarring at times because the English have always anglicized foreign names, and it is clear that at times Shakespeare did so too. Place names modernize well; forms like *Roan (Rouen), Burgonie (Burgundy),* or *Cotsole (Cotswold),* unless spoken in situations that clearly bespeak "humorous" character, seem archaic. Metrical considerations can complicate this issue. In general, the geographical form recognizable today offers the best choice. *Ardenne* for *Arden* (proposed by Stanley Wells) is another issue, having to do with primary associations of meaning; to me giving up *Arden* in favor of a presumed French location involves too great a sacrifice in terms of the Golden World and the Stratford countryside of Shakespeare's boyhood.

Family proper names, on the other hand, need at times to be accorded the tolerance for inconsistency and archaic quality we usually allow to family preference and personal idiosyncrasy. We should keep *Mordake,* for example, in place of *Murdoch,* while eschewing at the same time spellings that are simply Elizabethan variants, like *Bullingbrook (Bolingbroke), Woodvile (Woodville),* and *Brakenbury (Brackenbury).* The *Dictionary of National Biography* is a generally reliable guide to standard spelling of British family names. The occasional benefits of clarifying a rhyme, as with *Bullingbrook,* are outweighed, in my view, by problems of inconsistency; if one hopes to preserve Elizabethan pronunciation, there is no end of older spellings that should be preserved, and an old-spelling edition is presumably the best answer. *Bullingbrook* is made to rhyme with *look* (*R2* 3.4.99–100), but that fact doesn't solve the problem of how *look* was pronounced (often ambiguously with a long *u* as in Scottish dialect, according to Cercignani, 124, 134).

Common first names can usually be given their most recognizable modern form, like *Phoebe (Phebe), Sylvia (Silvia),* and *Thisbe (Thisby).* The choice of *Mote* for *Moth* is not easy, in *Love's Labor's Lost* and especially in *Midsummer,* where the suggested meaning may well include both a speck of dust and a flittering insect, but historical dictionaries certainly support *moth* as a variant of *mote,* and *moth* is used in Shakespeare's text, even elsewhere in *Midsummer* ("A moth will turne the ballance," Q1, 5.1.318), to mean a speck of dust, so that the editor should probably choose *Mote* as the primary meaning. First names that reveal humorous traits, such as *Lance (Launce)* and *Moldy* (the British would say *Mouldy*), invite a spelling that makes clear the play on words. (*Nim* for *Nym,* on the other hand, seems to me less compelling because we are dealing with an anglicization of German.)

Paperback editing of Elizabethan plays does certainly pull the editor away from "purism" and toward the effective presentation of Elizabethan language in as contemporary terms as possible. My point, however, is that such an emphasis does not lessen the complexity of the task or the potential integrity of the editorial solution if pursued with sufficient care. In the Bantam Shakespeare, the associate editors and I decided after lengthy debate to preserve strong verbal forms and other features of Elizabethan grammar (including unfamiliar prefixes as in *incivil*) while modernizing what can historically be regarded as an Elizabethan spelling variant. This decision was by no means a foregone conclusion, since at least one member of the editorial board, Robert Turner, had been led by his extensive editing experience to vote in favor of providing modern equivalents for strong verbal forms and unfamiliar prefixes. We sorted all this out, arrived at a series of positions, and then proceeded to consult on individual cases.

Hyphenation alone took months of consideration. Hyphens are generally on the way out in American English, though not without some purist resistance, and the issues are particularly vexed when one deals with an author from an earlier literature who uses compounds no longer in the vocabulary. Our Bantam decision was most often for closed-up words (*dovelike, lukewarm, Moorditch, nonperformance, o'erpicturing, springtime*) or for separate words (*Ascension Day, acorn cups, cuckold maker, dumb show*) while recognizing that some prefixes still take hyphens (*ill-left*), that two nouns following an adjective can be ambiguous if left unhyphenated ("*the old church-window,*" where *old* might seem to modify *church* or *window* if no hyphen is provided), and that the closing up of some older forms may seem unfamiliar (*prologue-like, vizard-like, basilisco-like*). The avoiding of ambiguity should be an editor's first consideration. Paperback editing does not reduce the number of problems to be addressed, or lessen the need for as much sensitivity as editors can muster. The results are virtually invisible to most readers, and should remain so, but the cumulative effect can be one of increased clarity.

By the same token, paperback editing does not relieve the editor of responsibility for reviewing carefully every possible textual problem and all recent textual analyses on the subject. One main justification for newly edited texts in every generation is that we have seen an explosion in textual studies—"explosion" in the sense of an increase in volume and also in controversy. The challenge of the two-text theorists, focusing at first on *Lear* as their most compelling case but extending inevitably to *Hamlet, Troilus,* and a number of multi-text plays, while sometimes overstated, has forced a rethinking of the entire editorial process.[2] The connection between this movement and theories of indeterminacy gives added timeliness to newly discovered uncertainties as to what we mean by a text, an author, an intention. Editing is by its nature intentionalist; that is, editing must choose a version of a text, and must argue that it represents what the author meant to say at a certain point. Even a decision to edit two texts of *Lear* is intentionalist, if also allowing for indeterminacy: it posits a series of states of the text, one perhaps closer to the author's manuscript, one in which theatrical production has had some influence. Should theatrical changes be included in a dramatic text, especially when the dramatist is, like Shakespeare, closely in touch with the acting company?

The choices we have made in the Bantam Shakespeare will appear conservative in this context, but I hope they are defensible on two grounds. First, although I fervently believe that all serious students of Renaissance drama need to study texts in their evolving state, in order to understand more and more fully how complex the process of writing and rewriting must have been, thus forcing us to acknowledge how approximate any printed text must be in representing what we mean by *"King Lear,"* I also feel that most readers need to start with *a* text, not two or more. Two texts of *Lear* throw a burden of comparison onto readers who are apt to feel baffled and impatient. Readers need more assistance, and have a right to expect it from an editor. Two texts are also more expensive, heavier to carry around. If *Lear* requires two texts, why not *Hamlet,* and then how many more?

Some revisionist textual critics I know and admire consider editing to be, in itself, a contradiction in terms. I see the point of their argument. To what other conclusion can post-structuralism logically come? How can one write even one commentary note when paraphrasing is necessarily seen as reductive and too approximate, too apt to obscure the resonance and infinite suggestiveness of the original, whatever that may have been? I don't deny that "fixing" a text and a gloss runs this reductive risk. But I favor a pragmatic approach to clarification of meaning or meanings, even if the approach is illusory and even oxymoronic. As to adjudicating between quarto and Folio texts of *Lear* and similar plays, I also believe it is easier to argue for Shakespeare's having wished to add the newly included material in either text than to prove that Shakespeare initiated the process of cutting we find in the Folio *Lear* or *Hamlet*. Many of the cuts in these instances are not rewritings but major excisions, and they may have been forced upon Shakespeare by practical restraints of performance length or other possible factors. One cannot prove this, but one cannot prove the reverse, either. Conflated texts do sometimes create contradictions, and may well produce plays that were too long to have been acted; they probably bring together materials that Shakespeare wrote at different times. But they do give the reader most of what Shakespeare wrote, and, if we edit with an awareness of what textual studies have taught us lately, we can eliminate duplicate passages, look at bibliographical evidence for determining how the plays were put together, and otherwise minimize the costs of bringing together such varied material under a single title like "*King Lear*" or "*Hamlet.*" The commentary can alert the inquisitive reader to the problems and point out where to go for further study. Since the paperback editor has the task of giving the reader one play to start with, however, that editor should embrace the responsibility of making choices rather than putting too many things off onto the reader.

If space permitted, I would like to discuss much more. Editing sources, for example (an important feature of the Bantam Shakespeare), has opened my eyes in disillusionment to the carelessness with which sources are edited almost everywhere, in hardcover as in paperback. I have found significant errors and inconsistencies, often on every page, in Walter Skeat's editing of Plutarch, in the Signet Classic Shakespeare's sources, and in Joseph Satin's *Shakespeare and His Sources.*[3] Geoffrey Bullough's *Narrative and Dramatic Sources of Shakespeare,* so seemingly authentic in its old-spelling format, is, alas, not to be trusted;

serious errors occur in every source I have collated against original texts. Richard Hosley's *Shakespeare's Holinshed* and T. J. B. Spencer's *Elizabethan Love Stories* are considerably better, though not free of occasional error. It is as though we exercise a double standard, and do not demand the sort of care in editing sources that we take for granted (though we do not always get) in the editing of dramatic texts.

Another editing issue is that of lineation, concerning which I feel that all modern editions, paperback or otherwise, have been far too complacent in accepting as authorial the supposed iambic pentameter verses editorial tradition has fabricated out of half lines by two or more speakers. Many verse lines thus created by the editor (virtually never in the original quartos and Folio) are justified by the convincing result, but many others can vary from three to six or seven feet and can introduce other irregularities that we would find extraordinary if found in a regular verse line in the original. Such fabrications are simply the result of our not being sufficiently skeptical about received editorial tradition, as I have argued at greater length in a recent review of the new Oxford Shakespeare ("Determining the Indeterminate").

Act-scene division is no less problematic. The Bantam position is that we are better off accepting conventional act-scene divisions, since so many works of reference are keyed to them by now, than attempting to impose new act-scene divisions throughout; given the current state of uncertainty as to how such divisions are to be adjudicated, any new system (like Oxford's) is apt to create one new diversity and confusion without successfully making its claim for definitiveness. At the same time, since the conventional markings are at times arbitrary and based on outmoded nineteenth-century notions of staging, we need to minimize their impact on the page in terms of moving the reader from scene to scene; the effect should be fluid, as it was in the Elizabethan theater.

Other issues remain that could be discussed, including editorially added stage directions and speech prefixes, but perhaps enough has been said to make the point that paperback editing can and must be as rigorous and scrupulous in its pursuit of editorial consistency as any "critical" edition, even while it necessarily pursues a vigorous course of modernization and making Elizabethan drama available to today's reader.[4]

146 DAVID BEVINGTON

Notes

1. See, for example, Charney, Betken, and Durband.

2. See, for example, Taylor and Warren.

3. The Signet version of North's translation of Plutarch's Life of Coriolanus, for example, changes "like as a fat soile bringeth forth herbes & weedes that lieth unmanured" (*Lives,* trans. North, 237) into "as a fat soil that lieth unmanured bringeth forth both herbs and weeds" (*Coriolanus,* ed. Reuben Brower, 210). In Satin's selected edition of sources, in the Life of Marcus Antonius, "For he denied not that he kept *Cleopatra,* but so did he not confesse that he had her as his wife" (*Lives,* trans. North, 984) becomes "For he denied not that he kept Cleopatra, neither did he confess that he had her as his wife" (Satin 581). Skeat's liberties are constant and no less astonishing. These examples could be multiplied hundreds or probably thousands of times.

4. One problem with a paperback edition is to know how to make sufficient acknowledgment of the sources of one's ideas. The Bantam edition provides a brief annotated list of recommended reading, but the critical works listed there do not begin to exhaust my indebtedness to friends, colleagues, and predecessors. The introductions and the commentary notes contain no citations and yet are heavily indebted to others. I think particularly of how much I have learned from Barbara Mowat about the late romances, from John Wallace about *Timon of Athens,* and from Peter Lindenbaum about *The Winter's Tale.* These and many others deserve a recognition that I have ungenerously failed to give.

Works Cited

Abbott, E. A. *A Shakespearian Grammar.* New ed. London: Macmillan, 1886.

The Bantam Shakespeare. Ed. David Bevington. 29 vols. New York: Bantam, 1988.

Betken, William T., ed. *Romeo and Juliet.* The Other Shakespeare: Unexpurgated Edition. Rhinebeck, N.Y.: Bardavon, 1985. [Also available: *The Two Gentlemen of Verona.*]

Bevington, David, ed. *The Complete Works of Shakespeare.* 3rd ed. Glenview, Ill.: Scott, Foresman, 1980. [An earlier second edition appeared in 1973 under the same title, ed. Hardin Craig and David Bevington.]

Bevington, David. "Determining the Indeterminate: The Oxford Shakespeare." *Shakespeare Quarterly* 38 (1987): 501–19.

Bullough, Geoffrey, ed. *Narrative and Dramatic Sources of Shakespeare.* 8 vols. London: Routledge; New York: Columbia UP, 1966–75.

Cercignani, Fausto. *Shakespeare's Works and Elizabethan Pronunciation.* Oxford: Clarendon, 1981.

Charney, Maurice, ed. *Julius Caesar.* The Shakespeare Parallel Text Series. Maurice Charney, sen. ed. New York: Simon & Schuster, 1975.

Durband, Alan, ed. *Hamlet.* Shakespeare Made Easy Series. New York: Barron's, 1985. [Also available: *King Lear, Macbeth, The Merchant of Venice, A Midsummer Night's Dream, The Tempest,* and *Twelfth Night.*]

Fraser, Russell A., and Norman Rabkin, eds. *Drama of the English Renaissance.* 2 vols. New York: Macmillan; London: Collier Macmillan, 1976.

Hosley, Richard, ed. *Shakespeare's Holinshed.* New York: Putnam's, 1968.

North, Thomas, trans. *The Lives of the Noble Grecians and Romanes Compared Together by That Grave Learned Philosopher and Historiographer, Plutarke of Chaeronea.* London: Vautroullier, 1579.

The Oxford Shakespeare. *William Shakespeare: The Complete Works.* Stanley Wells and Gary Taylor, gen. eds. Oxford: Clarendon, 1986.

The Complete Pelican Shakespeare. *William Shakespeare: The Complete Works.* Alfred Harbage, gen. ed. The Pelican Text Revised. Baltimore: Penguin, 1969.

The New Penguin Shakespeare. T. J. B. Spencer and Stanley Wells, gen. eds. Harmondsworth: Penguin, 1968– .

The Riverside Shakespeare. G. Blakemore Evans, textual ed. Boston: Houghton, 1974.

Rowse, A. L., ed. The Contemporary Shakespeare Series. Lanham, Md.: UP of America, 1984–86.

Satin, Joseph, ed. *Shakespeare and His Sources.* Boston: Houghton, 1966.

The Signet Classic Shakespeare. Sylvan Barnet, gen. ed. *Coriolanus,* ed. Reuben Brower. New York: Signet-NAL, 1966.

Skeat, Walter, ed. *Shakespeare's Plutarch.* London: Macmillan, 1892.

Spencer, T. J. B., ed. *Elizabethan Love Stories.* Harmondsworth: Penguin, 1968.

Taylor, Gary, and Michael Warren, eds. *The Division of the Kingdoms: Shakespeare's Two Versions of* King Lear. Oxford: Clarendon, 1983.

Warren, Michael J. "Repunctuation as Interpretation in Editions of Shakespeare." *English Literary Renaissance* 7 (1977): 155–69.

Wells, Stanley. *Re-editing Shakespeare for the Modern Reader.* Oxford: Clarendon, 1984.

Wells, Stanley, and Gary Taylor. *Modernizing Shakespeare's Spelling, with Three Studies in the Text of* Henry V. Oxford: Clarendon, 1979.

McKerrow's "Suggestion" and Twentieth-Century Shakespeare Textual Criticism

PAUL WERSTINE

N OW THAT the Oxford Shakespeare has finally been published, over
fifty years after R. B. McKerrow first began to edit Shakespeare for
the same press, it may be appropriate to review an array of the editorial
theory on which the published edition rests. In its original form, that
theory was first articulated in 1935 in McKerrow's "Suggestion Regarding Shakespeare's Manuscripts," which, in spite of its modest title, may,
without exaggeration, be termed the foundation of twentieth-century
Shakespeare textual criticism as well as the ultimate basis for the recently published Oxford Shakespeare, no matter how different this
edition may be from the one that McKerrow projected. In his "Suggestion," McKerrow purported to have found a way to force the printed
texts of Shakespeare's plays to yield up the secrets of their origins.
What's more, McKerrow asserted that some of the printed texts preserved signs of what his age most valued—the "creative process" itself,
the moment of Shakespeare's initial composition of a play. These precious printed versions, McKerrow said, were set into type from Shake-

149

speare's "foul papers." Sadly, according to McKerrow, other early printed texts were based upon nothing more than theatrical manuscripts in the hands of nameless scribes—upon so-called "promptbooks." Still others, the "bad quartos," were judged to have no transcriptional link whatsoever with Shakespeare, and McKerrow paid scant attention to these. Since McKerrow's time, scholars have come to value theatrical manuscripts more highly than he did, but, throughout this century, they have still insisted upon maintaining the terms of his distinction between "foul papers" and "promptbooks" and have extended the criteria for the "detection" of the origins of a printed text in one or the other kind of manuscript. The general editors of the recently published Oxford Shakespeare, Stanley Wells and Gary Taylor, differ from their predecessors chiefly in the boldness and daring with which they have wielded McKerrow's categories—particularly with regard to plays that survive in more than one early printed version.[1]

I

The historical context of the 1935 "Suggestion" may be of some interest. In 1931 W. W. Greg, who later became chiefly responsible for the wide influence that the "Suggestion" has enjoyed, had published his two-volume survey of extant dramatic manuscripts from the period c. 1590 to c. 1650. Greg there had asked, "What treatment did the book-keeper mete out to the author's stage-directions?" and had answered "that as a rule he left them alone" (1: 213). The same is true of speech prefixes. "[T]he whole question," Greg went on, "badly needs studying in relation, not to *a priori* expectation, but to the actual evidence of the Books [dramatic manuscripts] themselves, and meanwhile the more we are able to suspend judgement perhaps the better" (1: 209).

But McKerrow, busy generating editorial theory to serve as a basis for his projected Oxford Shakespeare, neither suspended judgment nor studied the extant manuscripts when he made his two-fold "Suggestion" that variable naming of characters in the stage directions and speech prefixes of printed texts indicated that such texts had been set into type from Shakespeare's "original MS."; and that "a copy intended for use in the theatre would surely, of necessity, be accurate and unambiguous in the matter of the character-names" (464). McKerrow's attention was focused exclusively upon Shakespeare the individual and upon "present[ing] Shakespeare's work as nearly in the form in which he left it as the evidence which we have permits, clearing it indeed as far as possible of the numerous errors with which the ignorance and carelessness of copyists and printers have disfigured it, but without superfluous comment or any attempt to improve upon the text as the author left it" (*Prolegomena* 1). He needed a principle according to which he could categorize the early printings of the plays in relation to their author and select as the basis of his edition the versions that represent, as nearly as possible, "the author's original wording" (*Prolegomena* 2).

And so McKerrow imagined the principle that he needed and articulated it by constructing a concept of Shakespeare the author through "projection, in more or less psychologizing terms, of . . . the traits" that McKerrow determined to be pertinent in some of the early printings (Foucault 150). He simply asserted that variations in the naming of characters in some of these printings emanated intelligibly from the operation of Shakespeare's "creative" powers:

Is it not natural that, in his first draft at any rate, [Shakespeare] should at times follow the practice of the novelist rather than of the person writing a play for the Press, distinguishing his characters just as and when they needed to be distinguished . . . , calling them by their functions (Goldsmith, not Angelo [in *The Comedy of Errors*]; Father, not Capulet [in *Romeo and Juliet*]) or their peculiarities (Braggart or Pedant, not Armado or Holophernes [in *Love's Labor's Lost*]) just when those functions or peculiarities happened to be uppermost in his mind, knowing perfectly well that the most cursory indications were quite sufficient for his purpose and not troubling himself about any formal consistency? I cannot help thinking that even nowadays in the heat of composition a writer might easily do the like; and it must be remembered that we have cause to suspect that Shakespeare was not any too careful of minor details. ("Suggestion" 464–65)

If Shakespeare varied his naming of the characters according to function or peculiarity, then one would assume that Armado, for example, should be designated *Braggart* when he is bragging and *Armado* when he is not. Such, of course, is not the case, since he is always called *Armado* in 1.2, even though he brags a good deal, referring to himself as "a man of great spirite," "a compleat man," and claiming that he

Valour gives thee place" (C4v; 3.1.68). Such facts, however, are irrele-
excels Samson with a rapier just as Samson did him in "carying gates"
(B1v–2v; 1.2.1, 44, 75). Then in the first part of 3.1 (before the entrance of Costard) he is called *Braggart*; yet he brags little except
perhaps in the last speech prefixed *"Brag."*: "Most rude melancholie,
Valour gives thee place" (C4v;3.1.68). Such facts, however, are irrele-
vant to McKerrow's position, for he never argued that Shakespeare
varied the naming of characters according to peculiarities evident in
their speeches but, instead, according to the functions or peculiarities
"uppermost in [Shakespeare's] mind" at the time that the dramatist was
inscribing a name. Therefore the first part of McKerrow's "Suggestion"
cannot be falsified by reference to playtexts; but it cannot be verified
either.

The second part of the "Suggestion" concerns the treatment allegedly
handed out to Shakespeare's variations in naming by theatrical personnel. According to McKerrow's *a priori* expectation,

A prompter of a repertory theatre could hardly be expected to remember that
Bertram was the same person as Rossillion [in *All's Well*], or Armado the same
as Braggart. Such variations would be an intolerable nuisance to him when he
suddenly needed to know what actors were on the stage in a particular scene,
or to follow the action and be ready to prompt while thinking about something
quite different, as one familiar with his job would probably do! It is difficult to
imagine a theatrical scribe, at any rate, not attending to a point of this kind.
("Suggestion" 464)

Had McKerrow bothered to look, for example, at the manuscript of
Henry Glapthorne's *The Lady Mother* (1635)—one of those that Greg
had listed as "Elizabethan prompt-books" (*Documents* 1: 305–08)—
then he could have repaired the failure of his imagination. According
to Arthur Brown, editor of the Malone Society reprint, *The Lady Mother*
is a scribal copy; the scribe was employed in the theater, for he consistently supplied warnings for actors to be ready some twelve to twenty
lines before their actual entrances—a purely theatrical concern (viii).
Did this scribe render character-names unambiguously, as McKerrow
was sure a scribe must? No. One of Glapthorne's characters is the steward Alexander Lovell. The scribe usually designated him "Alexander"
in stage directions but "Lov:", "Lo:", or simply "L:" in speech prefixes
(with only one exception—"Ale:", lines 1276–77) until line 1919,

after which the scribe used "Alex:", "Ale:", or "Al:" as the speech prefix. We cannot know if the scribe introduced such ambiguity or merely transcribed what he found in the no longer extant authorial copy. Yet we know that other ambiguities in character names were *introduced* in the process of the preparation of the scribal copy for the stage. As originally transcribed, the first scene of act 5 called for the entrance of a character called the "Recorder," whose speech prefix was always "Re:" ("Rec:", "Reco:", or "Recor:"). In censoring the play, Sir William Blagrave, Deputy to the Master of the Revels, altered "Recorder" to "Iudg" or to "Sr" in the stage direction and text, but left the "Re:" speech prefixes untouched. Then the theatrical scribe changed the first half-dozen "Re:" speech prefixes to "Sr Hu:" or to "He:" (for "Sir Hugh," the proper name provided by the scribe or the author to the Iudg-Recorder at this late stage) but left well over a dozen "Re:" speech prefixes standing. As a result this transcript by a theatrical scribe represents a character entering under the generic name "Iudg," but designated in the speech prefixes first by his proper name "Sr Hu:" and later by the official title "Re:". According to McKerrow's expectations, such variation in naming would have been intolerable in a theatrical manuscript like *The Lady Mother*; had the play ever seen print in such a form, McKerrow would have been forced by his theory to conclude that it had been printed directly from Glapthorne's own papers; in fact, such variation was produced collectively by theatrical censor and theatrical scribe—perhaps with the aid of the author, too, but long after original composition.

Although contradicted by historical documents, McKerrow's speculations were not rejected; instead they have been accepted by many, including Greg, the scholar of this century most familiar with dramatic manuscripts—but also McKerrow's close friend. Greg, at first, was cautious, but the further in time his writing became distanced from his study of the manuscripts, the more enthusiastic he became about McKerrow's hypothesis. The change can be seen in Greg's comments about *The Comedy of Errors,* the play that McKerrow discussed in greatest detail in the "Suggestion" and the one he was most convinced was set from Shakespeare's own papers. In 1942, in *The Editorial Problem in Shakespeare,* Greg refused to commit himself entirely to McKerrow's guess:

The erratic speech prefixes point on McKerrow's theory direct to the act of
composition, . . . and in a carefully prepared prompt-book the abnormalities of
the prefixes would presumably have been cleared away. . . . But the text is
generally clean, and at this early date it is particularly dangerous to dogmatize.
Perhaps a tolerably careful author's copy may have been made to serve on the
stage with a minimum of editing. (140)

However, by the time Greg wrote *The Shakespeare First Folio* in 1955,
he had come to embrace McKerrow's "Suggestion" much more fervently:

In the case of an early play that must have come to the Chamberlain's men
from some other company it is, of course, particularly dangerous to dogmatize,
but the manuscript behind F [the First Folio of 1623] *was clearly the author's,*
and since it is difficult to believe that the confusion in the character names
and prefixes would have been tolerated in a prompt-book, it would seem that
the manuscript was *most likely foul papers.* (201–02; italics added)

Since Greg's *Shakespeare First Folio* has enjoyed almost scriptural status
among Shakespearean editors and textual critics in the latter half of
this century, McKerrow's "Suggestion" has lived on long after the editorial concerns from which it issued have changed.

II

The measure of the change in editorial fashion since McKerrow's
time can be gauged from Stanley Wells and Gary Taylor's General Introduction to their Oxford Shakespeare. Gone is McKerrow's preoc-
cupation with the author alone and with the recovery of the plays in
the form in which Shakespeare left them. Instead the creation of drama
is regarded as a communal process and the goal of the editor has become the performing text—the fruits of Shakespeare's collaboration
with the other members of his theatrical company in bringing the
authorial version of a play into production:

We have ample testimony from the theatre at all periods, including our own,
that play scripts undergo a process of, often, considerable modification on their
way from the writing table to the stage. Occasionally, dramatists resent this
process; we know that some of Shakespeare's contemporaries resented cuts
made in some of their plays. But we know too that plays may be much improved
by intelligent cutting, and that dramatists of great literary talent may benefit

from the discipline of the theatre. It is, of course, possible that Shakespeare's colleagues occasionally overruled him, forcing him to omit cherished lines, or that practical circumstances—such as the incapacity of a particular actor to do justice to every aspect of his role—necessitated adjustments that Shakespeare would have preferred not to make. But he was himself, supremely, a man of the theatre. (xxxiv)

Such an emphasis upon the plurality of agents in the formation of a playtext seems far more consistent with what we find in historical documents—such as the manuscript of Glapthorne's *The Lady Mother* already noticed—than McKerrow's single-minded concern with the author. We might expect then that the Oxford editors would have abandoned the categories of McKerrow's generation: authorial manuscripts ("foul papers" in the jargon of textual criticism), "promptbooks," and "bad quartos" (a class of playtext that McKerrow largely ignored in the belief that, as mere "reports," "bad quartos" had no transcriptional links to his prized author ["Suggestion" 462n]). Once the plays are no longer valued as the products of an individual "creative" mind, but as the labor of a community—the "cry of players"—there is no cause to follow McKerrow in imagining that such anomalies as the variable naming of the characters must be projected only upon an authorial persona.

However, the Oxford editors have not abandoned McKerrow's categories or his way of generating them; if anything they have insisted upon the stability and the integrity of these categories and upon their own ability as editors to distinguish among these kinds of texts and to arrange them in relation to each other and to an author. Rather than rejecting the author-centered textual theory of McKerrow and Greg, the Oxford editors have tried to ground an edition of the communally achieved performing text upon it.

This contradiction between editorial theory and editorial goal left unresolved, they have proposed, in some cases, merely to invert the traditional hierarchy in which these kinds of texts have been ranked.[2] As long as the editorial goal was final authorial intention, "foul papers" texts enjoyed pride of place because they were believed to stand in closest relation to Shakespeare; beneath them came the so-called "promptbook" texts and, far behind, the "bad quartos." Now that the brass ring has become the performing text, "foul papers" texts are held less in esteem; in their purest state, a state beyond recovery according

to Stephen Orgel ("What Is a Text?" 3), they contain no "book-keeper" 's
notes and, it is thought, offer no help in reconstructing the performance text. "Prompt-copy" texts are preferable, although they may
offer very little in the way of production notes, but best of all, at least
for such plays as *Henry V* and *Richard III*, are the "bad quartos," now
regarded as useful records of performances even if they were, allegedly,
put together only from memory.

   Gary Taylor has developed a most ingenious strategy for recovering
from "bad quartos" alleged revisions made to plays during rehearsals
by Shakespeare's own company (Wells and Taylor, *Modernizing*
72–123). Depending upon the stage directions and speech prefixes of
these texts as reliable and accepting the long and wholly unsubstan-
tiated tradition that the "bad quartos" are abridged versions for provincial performance, Taylor has reconstructed doubling patterns for
two of them, *Henry V* and *Richard III*; then he has gone on to identify
what changes to the Folio versions (the alleged "foul papers" texts)
were necessary in order to make performance possible for reduced
casts; and finally he has claimed that some of the other differences
between the "bad quarto" and the Folio texts' stage directions and
speech prefixes are evidence of revision during rehearsal of the plays
by Shakespeare's own company at the Theatre or the Globe—features
of the performing text as opposed to the authorial one.

   The naming of characters in the speech prefixes and stage directions
remains *the* pertinent feature of printed plays according to current
Shakespearean editorial theory—in part because of the preservation of
McKerrow's speculations long after the assumptions on which they
were first erected have shifted and in part because of the reliance by
Taylor upon this feature in the Shakespeare "bad quartos" as the basis
for his analysis of them as the quintessential performing texts. If there
is anything to this complex theory, we should expect to find that confusion and ambiguity in the character-naming is concentrated in the
playtexts believed to have been set from "foul papers"; that such ambiguity is largely absent both from printings of the plays that benefited
from consultation of "promptbooks" and from the non-Shakespearean
manuscript "promptbooks" themselves; and finally that variability in
the naming of characters approaches zero in the "bad quartos"—otherwise it would be impossible to construct precise accounts of how the

actors who, allegedly, used these as the basis of performance divided roles among themselves. I propose to examine a small selection of texts as a test of these expectations—the quarto of *Much Ado about Nothing* (allegedly a "foul papers" text) and its Folio counterpart (said to have been printed from a copy of the quarto that had been annotated with reference to a "promptbook"); the "bad quartos" of *Henry V, Richard III* (which, although not at all bad, is still regarded by Taylor and many others as a memorially reconstructed text ["Copy-Text"]), *The Merry Wives of Windsor,* and *Romeo and Juliet*; and the manuscript "prompt-book" of Anthony Munday's *John a Kent and John a Cumber,* which, like most of the printed plays to be examined, dates from the 1590s. This scatter of plays is selected according to no *a priori* principle. Emphasis will fall most heavily upon the "bad quartos," because so much has been made of their recent "rediscovery." The reader should be warned in advance that the correlations between current theory and the texts are negligible.

III

Quarto *Ado* (1600) was not among the printed plays that McKerrow used to exemplify his "Suggestion," but it has long been regarded as a classic example of the "foul papers" text, even though Greg (*Folio* 277–78) and E. K. Chambers (1: 385–86) were both prepared to acknowledge the possibility that it also contained some playhouse annotation. An argument that it is strictly a "foul papers" text was recently advanced by Wells, who used quarto *Ado* as an example of the problems encountered by an editor of performing texts when confronted by one based on "foul papers." In view of the long tradition of uncritical acceptance of McKerrow's "Suggestion," Wells regarded it as an established fact—"It has long been recognized that one of the surest marks of the author in process of composition is the presence in directions and prefixes of variable designations for a single character" (*"Ado"* 7)— and concentrated instead upon extensions of the original theory. If, as McKerrow had suggested, inconsistency in the naming of characters in printed prefixes indicates "foul papers" as printer's copy, then, reasoned Wells (following Greg [*Folio* 112]), the *absence* of prefixes for characters named in entrance directions similarly indicates the *presence* of

Shakespeare's hand in printer's copy. (In the jargon of textual criticism characters who are named in entrance directions but who have no speech prefixes, who are addressed by no one, and who seem to have been granted no function at all are called "ghosts.") Just as McKerrow had projected the anomalies that he noticed in speech prefixes upon a purely imaginary construction of Shakespeare's authorial persona, so did Wells with these ghosts: "Occasionally, it seems, Shakespeare wrote a name in a stage direction, then abandoned his intention of writing the character into the scene, but omitted to amend the direction" (*"Ado"* 3). Continuing to follow Greg (*Folio* 112), Wells assumed that theatrical personnel would have exorcised these ghosts, just as McKerrow believed (wrongly) that the same agents would have regularized ambiguous speech prefixes.

Whoever raised these ghosts, the quarto of *Ado* is the haven of many. Innogen, who is to enter at the beginning of each of the first two acts with Leonato as "his wife," is regarded as such a character, as is the "kinsman" of Leonato's who is also listed in the entrance direction that initiates the second act (A2, B3; 1.1.0, 2.1.0). It appears that neither of these characters has anything to do or say from one end of the play to the other. Not so with the remaining four ghosts: each of these has a role at some point in the play, yet each is listed in the quarto in a scene where he is evidently not wanted. Balthasar is conjured up needlessly part way through 1.1 (A3; 1.1.95), and so are *"Iohn and Borachio, and Conrade"* part way through 2.1 (C1v; 2.1.210). The pair of Iohn and Borachio are particularly visible ghosts in 2.1: since they are supposed to enter at the beginning of 2.2, their ghostly presence in the latter half of 2.1 leads to violation of the law of reentry.

How serious an impediment are these ghosts to acceptance of quarto *Ado* as a performing text compared to what we find in, say, the "bad quartos," now regarded as thoroughly dependable records of performance? Quarto *Henry V* is full of ghosts, beginning with Bardolfe, who enters with Nim, Pistoll, and the Boy but who fails to say anything or interest anyone until Flewellen beats them all in a half-page later (C2v; 3.2). A number of ghosts appear just before Henry begins his soliloquy "O God of battels": *"Enter the King* [already on stage], *Gloster, Epingam, and Attendants"* (E1; 4.1). Gloster, having never exited, enters again after the soliloquy is over (E1v) and yet again at the beginning of the following quarto scene (E1v; 4.3 [4.2 does not intervene in the quarto]), thereby breaking the law of reentry. Both Clarence and Warwick are ghosts when they encounter Williams and Flewellen fighting (F2v; 4.8); and both nobles have appeared out of nowhere, since according to Taylor's casting chart for the play, only Exeter is with Henry when the King sets off to catch up to Flewellen at the end of the previous scene (F2v). Gebon almost becomes a ghost as well in 3.7 since he is silent and unaddressed for about thirty lines after his entrance and then for almost another thirty after his only speech (D2v –3). In 4.6, Pistoll too threatens to turn into a ghost when he enters at the beginning of the scene but has nothing to do but utter the last of the scene's more than thirty lines, "Couple gorge" (E3v –4). In quarto *Richard III* Dorset is a ghost in 3.1, since he is listed in an exit direction but has taken no part in the scene (as a member of the Queen's party, he scarcely belongs here with Gloucester, Buckingham, Catesby, and Hastings; E4v –F2v). As listed in 3.1, his appearance violates the law of reentry, for he appears at the end of the previous scene as well (2.4), but exactly the same is true of the Cardinal, who is a ghost in neither scene. Gerald Johnson identified several more ghosts in his study of the *Merry Wives of Windsor* quarto: Bardolfe in the first scene, Shallow and/or Slender in scenes 8, 10, 13, and 15 (157–62). With so many ghosts in the "bad quartos," some of them appearing contrary to the law of reentry, we must conclude, it would seem, that these quartos will give us little help in arriving at performing texts. *If* we accept the "bad quartos" as records of performance, we can easily swallow the possibility that quarto *Ado* may also be a performing text.

There is no need, however, to defend the possibility that it is one only by analogy with the "bad quartos." A contemporary "promptbook," namely *John a Kent and John a Cumber,* may be just as much haunted by ghosts as is quarto *Ado.*[3] The opening direction for its second scene reads in part as follows:

Enter at one doore *Ranulphe* Earle of Chester, *Oswen* his son <n> young *Amery* Lord *Mortaigue,* wth them the Countesse, her daught<> Marian, and fayre *Sidanen.* (lines 137–39)

"Lord *Mortaigue*" says and does nothing here or anywhere else in the play and is never addressed. For this reason, Muriel St. Clare Byrne, editor of the play for the Malone Society, suggested that "Lord *Mor-taigue*" must simply be another name for "young *Amery*" and so he may be, but there is not a scrap of evidence to support the association of *Amery* with *Mortaigue*: it is just as likely that *Mortaigue* is a ghost (xi). The reader of the direction should not be misled by the absence of a comma between "*Amery*" and "Lord *Mortaigue*" into supposing that the two must be the same. Commas are omitted between the names of different characters on several occasions in this manuscript (918–920, 1031–32). And "Lord *Mortaigue*" is not the only possible ghost. Oswen and Amery may well be ghosts after their entrance at lines 581–83 and again after they are said to come on at line 920.[4] Their entrance at lines 581–83 is duplicated at lines 595–96, after which Oswen ceases to be a ghost but Amery does not.[5] Then lines 604–05 provide an entrance for "seruaunts"; Munday wrote a speech for one of these but later cut it (608–10), reducing the servants to ghosts. Such they continue to be in the "promptbook." Therefore Wells's (and Greg's) theory that the absence, in a printed play, of speech prefixes for characters named in entrance directions must indicate that "foul papers" stood behind the printed version is contradicted by the repeated appearance of the same phenomenon in a manuscript "promptbook" of the period, just as the evidence from such "promptbooks" defies McKerrow's "Suggestion."

IV

But ghosts are raised as only one of the obstacles in the way of the possibility that quarto *Ado* and other printed playtexts that are like it were based on performing texts. What about the opposites of ghosts— characters who take part in a scene, as indicated by speech prefixes, but whose names are missing from stage directions? Again Wells would project such anomalies upon Shakespeare in the throes of creation: "But sometimes Shakespeare involves characters in action without mentioning them in directions, and, it would seem, without having considered at what point they should enter" ("*Ado*" 6). As often in "*Ado*," Wells's hypothesis is derived from Greg, who wrote, "[T]he au-

thor may, of course, write a speech for a character for whose presence
he has not provided, in which case the book-keeper will certainly need
to add the name to the initial direction" (*Folio* 112).

Examples of this allegedly authorial practice are rife in quarto *Ado*.
Margaret and Ursula, who participate in 2.1, are provided with no entrance when Leonato and the rest of the family arrive to begin the
scene: *"Enter Leonato, his brother, his wife, Hero his daughter, and
Beatrice his neece, and a kinsman"* (B3). There may be the same problem with Borachio in the same scene, but the blame for his omission
is harder to fix upon Shakespeare. The entrance for the visitors contains,
among its obvious errors, the word *or* instead of the customary *and:*
*"Enter prince, Pedro, Claudio, and Benedicke, and Balthaser, or dumb
Iohn"* (B4). Perhaps, as has often been suggested, *"or"* was the compositor's misreading of *Bor* for Borachio. No such excuse is available,
however, for the omission of Conrade and the Watch from 4.2 (*"Enter
the Constables, Borachio, and the Towne clearke in gownes"* [G3v]).
And perhaps the Watch is also left out in 5.1—*"Enter Constables, Conrade, and Borachio"* (H3v)—although this time it is hard to demonstrate a need for their presence (*"Ado"* 7). When we want to make the
case for "foul papers" as printer's copy for quarto *Ado*, we concentrate
on this handful of errors and suppress the fact that of its forty-one
directions for entrance, only six demonstrably omit the names of necessary characters; the directions are therefore accurate in this respect
eighty-five percent of the time.[6]

Quarto *Ado* compares very favorably with the "bad quartos," those
records of performance, in the accuracy and completeness of its stage
directions, as the following table shows:

Quarto	No. of entrance directions	Indefinite or erroneous directions	Accuracy
MWW Q1	53	6	89%
Rom. Q1	65	11	83%
Ado Q1	41	9	78%
H5 Q1	45	12	73%
R3 Q1	86	24	72%

From this analysis of a scatter of playtexts, only the "bad quartos" of *The Merry Wives of Windsor* and *Romeo and Juliet* seem superior to quarto *Ado* in accuracy. Even *Wives* Q1 is far from perfect: it omits Falstaffe's attendant boy from the direction on sig. C2v, in spite of the reference to his presence on sig. C3; it leaves out both Iohn Rugby and Bardolfe from the entrance on sig. D3, although both are addressed later in the scene; on sig. E1v appears the marvelously indefinite *"Enter all,"* but it should probably have reference to *"Foord"* and *"all the rest,"* a phrase carefully defined at the top of sig. E1v as referring to *"Page, Doctor, Priest, Slender, Shallow"*; then sig. E2 has an entrance for Falstaffe alone, but the second line in the scene is Bardolfe's; on sig. E4 Mistresse Anne Page enters as *"Page,"* and on sig. G2 she is not distinguished from the rest of the *"boyes drest like Fayries."*

If we want to follow Taylor in seeing the "bad quartos" as exact records of performance and apply his principles to them in order to determine the minimum cast that could stage them so that we can go on to discover which alterations in their casts were necessitated by alleged abridgment and which were changes made in rehearsal by the full company, then the figures for *Romeo and Juliet* Q1 in the chart above are dangerously deceptive. All but twenty-two of the sixty-five entrance directions in that quarto are for scenes that require only five or fewer actors to be on stage at the same time, the scenes that would have taxed the resources of a small company to the least extent. Only two of these forty-three are indefinite (C1, I2v), only two more demonstrably wrong (H2v, I4) as revealed by study of the speech prefixes in the scenes in which they appear. But the stage directions for the more crowded scenes in the *Romeo* quarto tell quite another story; while those that call for the entrance of only one or two characters into one of these crowded scenes are in the main accurate, every one of the directions that mark the entrance of three or more characters into such scenes proves either indefinite or wrong, when we check the speech heads. In these cases, the very ones in which we most need to depend upon the quarto in reconstructing the cast of this performing text, the text always disappoints us: it calls for an indefinite number of *"Citizens"* on sig. A4v; it calls only for *"old* Capulet *with the Ladies"* to enter for the banquet scene (C2v), omitting the *"Cos."* to whom Capulet is speaking and Tybalt, leaving us wondering when the Nurse will come in, whether or not the invited Paris has arrived, and how many actors (if any) in the roles of servingmen Capulet may be addressing when he orders lights and the tables turned up; it confronts us again with an indefinite number of *"Citizens"* in the second brawl scene (F2), an indefinite number of *"Watch"* in the final scene (K2v), and the *"others"* with whom the Prince enters in that last scene (K3). How does one compile a cast list from this information?

In this respect, the *Merry Wives of Windsor* quarto is much the superior, not only to the *Romeo* quarto but also to any of the rest. Nineteen times *Wives* calls for the entrance of more than two characters into one of its more crowded scenes; only two of these directions are wrong or indefinite, the two that I have already identified on sigs. E4 and G2. There are thirteen comparable directions in the *Henry V* quarto, ten of them wrong or indefinite. The series begins on the first page of the quarto with the entrance of *"other Attendants"* (A2), continues with an indefinite number of *"Thambassadors from France"* (A4); the "others" who enter with the *"King of* France, Bourbon, Dolphin" (C1); Henry's *"Lords"* (C3); *"others"* (D1v); the omission of Warwick, Yorke, and Bedford from the entrance on sig. E1v; Henry's *"Nobles"* (E3v); *"the Lords"* (F1); Henry's *"Lords,"* France's *"others,"* and the *"Duke of* Burbon," who is addressed as *"Burgondie"* (F4v); concluding on the penultimate page (G2v) with *"the Lordes"* again, not to mention the thoroughly wrong entrance of *"Gloster, Epingam, and Attendants"* (E1) already discussed. Quarto *Richard III,* the other "performing" text for which Taylor has compiled a doubling pattern, is still worse: seventeen of its twenty comparable directions are wrong or indefinite (85%).[7] In comparison, the "foul papers" text in quarto *Ado* would provide far more reliable information: twelve of its stage directions require the entrance of more than a pair of characters into the more populous scenes in the play, but only six of these directions are either wrong or indefinite.

We need not consider the problem of drawing up a cast list for a "bad quarto" only in such general terms; Gary Taylor has published an actual doubling chart compiled from the 1600 quarto of *Henry V* (Wells and Taylor, *Modernizing* 72–119). He begins from the long-standing hypothesis that the quarto represents a version of the play abridged for performance by a reduced cast. There is, of course, no external evidence for this hypothesis, but the internal evidence can supposedly be found in the omission of scenes (the Choruses, 1.1, 3.1, 4.2), in the transposition of scenes (4.5 and 4.4), in the omission of roles from scenes (for example, the Messenger from 2.4, Makmorrice and Iamy from 3.2, and several more), in the substitution of one role for another (Burbon for the Dolphin in the Agincourt scenes). But do these features in themselves demonstrate abridgment for a reduced cast? Gerald Johnson's analysis of the *Wives* quarto suggests otherwise. In that quarto, too, scenes are omitted (4.1, 5.1–4) and transposed (3.4 and 3.5), roles are omitted from scenes (Simple from the first, Fenton from the fourth, Caius from the thirteenth), and sometimes one role is substituted for another (Shallow for Pistoll in the last scene). Nevertheless, Johnson's doubling chart indicates that no fewer than fourteen actors would be required to stage the play as it appears in the quarto, which is therefore hardly an abridged version for a reduced cast. I am not claiming that Johnson's skill at analysis exceeds Taylor's or that his method differs; both proceed from the same assumptions—that roles were not split between actors, that actors did not double roles back-to-back, exiting in one role at the end of a scene and entering in another at the beginning of the next. The point is that the evidence traditionally cited in support of the hypothesis that quarto *Henry V* is a playtext abridged for a smaller cast does not necessarily support such a hypothesis. The same evidence appears in quarto *Wives,* but quarto *Wives* proves, upon finer analysis, not to be a text prepared for a reduced cast. And the stage directions of quarto *Wives* make it a far more reliable text from which to compile a doubling chart.

In addition to these doubts about Taylor's initial premise, there are some specific problems with his doubling chart (Wells and Taylor, *Modernizing* 114–15). I have mentioned one already, namely his assumption that the King exits at the end of 4.7 in pursuit of Flewellen accompanied only by Exeter, but enters shortly after the beginning of 4.8 accompanied by Warwick and Clarence as well. The direction for entrance at the beginning of 4.7 is so indefinite that we cannot say that Taylor is wrong, but once we notice the discrepancy between the scenes, we may wonder if more actors are not required. The actor to whom Taylor ordinarily assigns the role of Warwick may be busy playing Burbon in 4.7, according to Taylor's doubling pattern, and so we may need to postulate one more actor than Taylor allows—twelve, rather than eleven. There is another problem with Orleance in 2.4 (C1–2v). The scene opens with the direction: *"Enter King of* France, Bourbon, Dolphin, *and others."* When the King speaks, he directly addresses "you Lords of *Orleance,* / Of *Bourbon,* and of *Berry"*; later the Constable speaks. Altogether six actors seem to be required—King, Dolphin, Constable, Berry, Burbon, Orleance—or five at least, given the possibility raised by Taylor that the Constable may be the same as Berry—one individual with two titles (112–13). But the Constable cannot be Orleance, for the two appear later as independent roles. Yet, for this scene, Taylor lists in his doubling chart (114–15) only the King, Dolphin, Constable, Burbon, and Berry; when we realize that Orleance also needs to be listed, we also realize that, according to Taylor's own rules of the game, Orleance cannot be doubled by the actor to whom Taylor ordinarily assigns the role (that actor has just left the stage as Bardolfe), and, furthermore, we find that no other actor in Taylor's doubling pattern is available to assume the role of Orleance without having to split it. Another actor is required—this company of eleven actors has swelled to thirteen. Then the entrance direction on sig. D1v calls for the *"King,* Clarence, Gloster *and others"*; here Taylor admits that he has available only one actor to play *"others"* and so concludes that *"others"* must be Exeter alone (86–87). On sig. F4v, the text calls for *"the King of* England *and his Lords"*; again Taylor has only one actor to play *"his Lords,"* and so they, too, become Exeter. Finally, Taylor breaks his own prohibitions against back-to-back doubling and role-splitting by requiring one hypothetical actor to double both Warwick and Burbon back-to-back twice and by splitting Burbon's role between two actors. I submit that Taylor's analysis of quarto *Henry V* fails to establish that the quarto is a dependable report of an abridgment of the play—a performing text for eleven—and, further, that given the imperfections in the quarto's stage directions, precise reconstruction of the performance on which it may have been based is beyond recovery. There is little justification then for promoting a "bad quarto" to the top of the hierarchy of texts in our quest for the performing text of a play.

Identification in "bad quartos" of a feature supposed to indicate the use of "foul papers" as printer's copy does not, of course, establish that "bad quartos" (*pace* Steven Urkowitz) were set into type from authorial manuscripts, especially since the feature that allegedly marks only "foul papers" is also to be found in extant theatrical manuscripts. I return to the manuscript of *John a Kent and John a Cumber.* At lines 1295–96, the author Munday originally wrote the stage direction "Enter Sr Gosselen denvyle, Griffin, Powesse, Euan, the Countesse | *Sydanen* and Marian"; there follow speeches for all the characters listed. In the course of preparing this manuscript for the theater, the book-keeper, using his distinctive grayish ink, struck the name "Euan" from the direction, apparently not noticing the speech for this character some thirty-five lines later, which was left untouched. Here we have an example of an author correctly listing characters in a stage direction, only to have a book-keeper introduce error. Thus the absence of speakers' names from entrance directions in printed plays certainly cannot be assumed to indicate that such plays were printed from "foul papers," whatever Greg and Wells may assert. These omissions may just as likely be the marks of a manuscript that was used in the theater.

V

So far I have left unchallenged Wells's assumption that Folio *Ado* was annotated with reference to a "promptbook." By "promptbook" here I do not mean a historical document—such as *John a Kent* with all its imperfections; instead I mean what McKerrow, Greg, and Wells mean, that is, a metaphysical entity, an ideal "promptbook," one in which all irregularities have been regularized, all ghosts exorcised, all characters scrupulously listed in the stage directions for the scenes in which they appear. Since both the quarto and the Folio texts of *Ado* are themselves historical documents, neither resembles an ideal "promptbook" much at all. In support of the belief that the Folio text was influenced by an ideal "promptbook," Wells can cite the expulsion of the ghosts *"Iohn and Borachio, and Conrade"* (Hinman, Norton Facsimile through-line-number [TLN] 615), the addition of sound cues such as an ideal "promptbook" is supposed to include—*"Maskers with a drum."* (TLN 494)—and the substitution of an actor's name for a character's—Iacke Wilson's for Balthaser's (TLN 868). Against possible annotation from an ideal "promptbook" is the omission of the names of at least one and possibly two characters from the stage direction at TLN 2341, Leonato's brother and the Sexton—names found here in the quarto. We know that the brother's name should have been included since he speaks in the scene that follows at TLN 2416–17. It would be convenient to blame this omission on the Folio compositor at work on this page— Compositor D, it turns out—and Wells, by implication, does so (*"Ado"* 4: "accidental omission (common in F)"). Now Compositor D set twenty-six pages of Folio *LLL, MND, MV,* and *Ado,* all from quarto copy; nowhere in these pages can he be convicted of omitting even one necessary name from a stage direction. It seems unlikely then that he should be the one responsible here for the double omission; instead we might suppose that the annotator made the deletion and made it for the same reasons that he made other changes in the Folio text. Either he followed the ideal "promptbook" here, which was (in contradiction to its very nature) in error for this stage direction (although it is not all that unlikely, from what I have noted above, that such an error might be found in an actual historical document used in the theater), or he used his own authority as he may also have done elsewhere. The evidence for annotation from an ideal "promptbook" (if such a thing ever existed) of Folio copy for *Ado* is hardly as secure as Wells implies in his reconstruction of the transmission of the text.

The evidence for "foul papers" behind the quarto is no better. Of course, the quarto provides us with the three ghosts exorcised from the Folio, but the quarto also contains actors' names among its speech prefixes—Kemp and Cowley—such as are found in "promptbooks." Ordinarily when such names are found in texts that we want to derive from "foul papers," we say that Shakespeare inscribed the names during original composition to instruct his company about who he wanted to play a role; when we find such names in texts we want to derive from "promptbooks," we use the names as evidence of such copy— "Iacke Wilson" in Folio *Ado.*

As Greg pointed out in his *Dramatic Documents,* "It has been lately argued, and not without some show of reason, that in certain instances the actors' names that appear in stage-directions and as speech prefixes in printed texts were written not by the prompter but by the author himself. While I should not venture to deny that this is possible, I think it is at least pertinent to point out, what I believe to be the fact, that in every instance in which an actor's name appears in a manuscript play it is written in a different hand from the text, or at any rate in a different ink and style, showing it to be a later addition and not part of the original composition" (1: 215–16).[8] Only after Greg had accepted McKerrow's "Suggestion" did Greg extend it in an effort to overturn his own argument and the evidence of the extant manuscripts themselves as regards the appearance of actors' names. In *The Editorial Problem* Greg wrote: "It is true that [the theory that actors' names may have been inscribed by playwrights in their original manuscripts] is unsupported by any evidence in the extant manuscripts, in which actors' names are added by the book-keeper: but to this it may be replied that it is in the foul papers that the author's use of actors' names would appear, and that they would probably be eliminated in the course of preparing the promptbook" (40). This tortured logic becomes available only after one has accepted McKerrow's notion that theatrical personnel were scrupulous in erasing all irregularities from authorial manuscripts, a notion flatly contradicted by extant manuscripts. The distinction between quarto *Ado* as a "foul papers" text and Folio *Ado* as one influenced by a "promptbook," in this respect, rests upon imaginary evidence that has been imagined to have disappeared. It is ironic that McKerrow's "Suggestion," so much a product of his imagination, should continue to be supported as editorial theory by imagined evidence.

I submit that quarto *Ado* is as likely to derive from a theatrical manuscript as the Folio is. Both contain ghosts, both omit necessary characters from stage directions but include them through speech prefixes, both offer the same variety in the naming of characters in speech prefixes and stage directions, and both print actors' names—this last feature to be found only among manuscripts used in the theater. The evidence is nicely divided for both quarto and Folio.

VI

Our legacy from McKerrow and Greg is a convenient set of textual categories—"foul papers," "promptbooks," and "bad quartos" (only the first of these terms deriving from usage by Shakespeare's contemporaries [compare Long 93])—the belief in our ability to classify texts in terms of these categories and so to arrange texts in series in relation to their authors and the stage, and the need to believe that there exists an orderly text that we can recover or create. As soon as we begin to test the categories against texts, however, every time we seize upon a feature in the hope that it will distinguish only one category, it shows up in a text that we would like to socket into another category. "Bad quartos," "foul papers," and "prompt-copy" tend to coalesce. The quest for a stable entity called a "performing text" thus becomes as quixotic as the abandoned quest for authorial intention. At least for the former, we could assume that authorial intentions once were available in Shakespeare's manuscripts, now lost; the performing text is so unstable that it never existed in any written form. It was realized only in the voices and gestures of the actors, which probably—we cannot *know*—varied from afternoon to afternoon and night to night in the manner suggested by the marvelously indefinite stage direction often quoted from Heywood's *The Captives: "Eather strykes him wth a staffe or Casts a stone"* (lines 2432–34).

Notes

An earlier version of this paper was presented at the Seminar on Textual Studies at the annual meeting of the Shakespeare Association of America in Montreal, March 29, 1986. A section from it is to appear in the collection of essays deriving from that seminar: *Speech Prefixes and the Editor* (New York: AMS).

1. In a table entitled "Summary of Control-Texts," the Oxford editors list the seventy or so manuscripts that they infer once lay, at one or more removes, behind the printed versions of Shakespeare's plays. In characterizing these manuscripts, the editors refer to McKerrow's categories—"foul papers," "promptbook," and "report" (a neutral term for "bad quarto")—no fewer than forty-five times. In ten more cases, the editors avoid McKerrow's terminology but still employ his fundamental distinction between "authorial" and "theatrical" manuscripts with such terms as "holograph," "authorial papers," "Shakespeare's revised manuscript," or "theatre manuscript." Only in a minority of cases do the editors express any doubt about their categorization of these hypothetical manuscripts (*Textual Companion* 145–47).

2. In this paragraph, I generalize from Wells and Taylor's decision to privilege Folio readings in their (modern-spelling and original-spelling) texts of plays originally published in quartos that they believe were printed from Shakespeare's "foul papers" when they believe that copy for the Folio was annotated with reference to a "promptbook"; an example of this textual situation is *Titus Andronicus,* which Wells discusses in *Re-editing Shakespeare for the Modern Reader* (79–113). Hence I write of Wells and

Taylor's inversion of McKerrow's preference for "foul papers" over "promptbook" texts. Wells and Taylor also incorporate into their texts of plays published both in "good quarto" and/or Folio texts and in "bad quartos" an unusually large number of "bad quarto" readings—especially in *Henry V*—and in this way promote "bad quartos" to the top of the hierarchy of classes of texts—but only for substantive readings, and only for some of the plays that appeared in "bad quartos." In this connection, it should be noted that Wells and Taylor follow traditional theory and practice in using as copy-texts for accidentals in their original-spelling edition only "good quarto" or Folio texts of plays also printed in "bad quartos." The single exception to such traditional practice is the use of the 1597 quarto of *Richard III* as copy-text, even though they believe it is a memorially reconstructed text (Taylor, "Copy-Text").

When my essay was first written, the *Textual Companion* had not yet appeared. Therefore my essay necessarily concentrates on earlier textual criticism written and (except in the case of Taylor's work on *Richard III,* which has yet to be published) published before the *Textual Companion.* In my view, however, the *Textual Companion* has not superseded this earlier work but merely incorporated it. Just as in the early days of the Oxford project, Wells employed *Ado* as the "test case" for plays first printed in quarto from "foul papers" and later printed in the Folio from quarto copy annotated with reference to a "promptbook," so the General Introduction to the *Textual Companion* uses *Ado* as its leading example of such a paradigm, which, according to the *Companion,* is "exactly the same" for five other plays (14). Wells's brief note on *Ado* in the *Companion* refers the reader to his earlier article on the play for his editorial policy (371).

At the beginning of the Oxford project, Taylor anticipated that his investigation of *Henry V* (interrogated here in my essay) would be extended to every Shakespeare "bad quarto" and that every one would yield up a trove of authorial revision: "[G]iven an appropriately thorough investigation of the imperfect text, it should be—and in *Henry V* has been—possible to identify several classes of variant which could represent authorial revision" (Wells and Taylor, *Modernizing* 164). Taylor extended his investigation to *Richard III* in his seminar paper; William Montgomery took it to *2 Henry VI* in an edition of *The First Part of the Contention, 1594* (1985). But it is hard to tell from the *Textual Companion* how much further such investigations progressed. While Taylor's General Introduction to the *Textual Companion* speaks of "bad quartos" as a class in laudatory terms ("the 'unreliable' text might preserve the authorial intention—especially if the line in question was spoken by an actor who helped to reconstruct the text"; "a memorial reconstruction may represent a more finished, dramatic, socialized phase of the text than that preserved in an edition printed from Shakespeare's foul papers" [28]), it does so with specific reference only to *Henry V* and *Richard III.* Practice with "bad quartos" varies widely in the edition itself. For example, John Jowett, editor of *Romeo and Juliet,* does not altogether abandon Taylor's theory about "bad quartos" and "authorial revision" but expresses some caution about it: "This edition allows for the potential presence in the Q1 text of Shakespeare, as possible reviser of details of the final theatrical text, but recognizes the presence of another hand . . . contributing material that might be difficult to distinguish from the authorial" (289). (I might substitute "impossible" for "difficult.") Jowett is openly pessimistic about the "bad quarto" of *Wives*: "Q is of particularly limited value, even compared with other bad quarto texts" (341); strangely he makes no reference to Johnson's study, which was originally presented to the same seminar as Taylor's study of *Richard III*. My critique of Taylor's methods with "bad quartos" remains highly relevant, however, because these methods continue to inform the Oxford editions of *Henry V* and *Richard III* (by Taylor) and because his theory of reconstructing casting for "bad quartos" is the basis for the most daring of Oxford's editorial interventions, *"Pericles, Prince of Tyre* (A Reconstructed Text)" (Taylor, "Transmission").

3. Although I cite only *John a Kent* as a "promptbook" with ghosts in it, it should not be understood that this manuscript is at all exceptional in this regard. For ghosts in *Edmond Ironside*, see my " '*Enter a Sheriffe*'."

4. Much later in the scene that follows the entrance at line 920, it is indicated that Oswen and Amery are conducting Marian and Sydanen to Chester. Whether they were represented as leading off Marian and Sydanen in the scene containing line 920 is impossible to determine. This kind of problem always arises in dealing with the staging of Renaissance plays because the playtexts, printed or manuscript, radically underrepresent the action that took place on stage. Perhaps Innogen and the kinsman of *Ado* had mute parts to carry out that never were recorded in any manuscript.

5. Perhaps Amery appears in this scene simply because he is always paired with Oswen, just as Leonato is paired in public with Innogen in acts 1 and 2 of *Ado*.

6. There is no entrance on sig. B2 for the cousins and friend that Leonato may be addressing there; on sig. C4v we have *"Enter Benedicke alone,"* but the second line is the Boy's.

7. *"Enter Executioners"* (C4); *"&c."* (D3v); *"Clarence Children"* (E1v); *"others"* (E2v); *"&c."* (E4v); *"Enter the Lords in Councell"* (G1); *"other Nobles"* (H4v); *"Enter K. Richard marching with Drummes and Trumpets"* (I4v); *"others"* (L2); *"&c."* (L2v); *"Enter the Lordes to Richmond"* (M1); *"&c."* (M2); *"other Lords,&c."* (M3); stage direction omits the "neece" referred to in the first line of 4.1 (H3); stage direction omits the other "lordsc" (sic) addressed by Richmond on L3v (L3); Dorset omitted from stage direction (B3v); Boy omitted from stage direction (H4v).

8. The suggestion about the appearance of actors' names in "foul papers" was originally made by Allison Gaw and then by McKerrow in "The Elizabethan Printer."

Works Cited

Chambers, E. K. *William Shakespeare: A Study of Facts and Problems*. 2 vols. Oxford: Clarendon, 1930.

A . . . Comedie, of Syr Iohn Falstaffe, and the merrie Wiues of Windsor. . . . By William Shakespeare. London, 1602.

The Cronicle History of Henry the fift. London, 1600.

Edmond Ironside: Or, War Hath Made All Friends. Ed. Eleanore Boswell. Malone Soc.
   Reprints. Oxford: Malone Soc., 1927 [1928].
An Excellent conceited Tragedie of Romeo and Iuliet. London, 1597.
Evans, G. Blakemore, textual ed. *The Riverside Shakespeare.* Boston: Houghton, 1974.
The First Part of the Contention, 1594. Ed. William Montgomery. Malone Soc. Reprints.
   Oxford: Malone Soc., 1985.
Foucault, Michel. "What Is an Author?" *Textual Strategies: Perspectives in Post-Struc-
   turalist Criticism.* Ed. Josué Harari. Ithaca: Cornell UP, 1979. 141–60.
Gaw, Allison. "Actors' Names in Basic Shakespearean Texts, with Special Reference to
   Romeo and Juliet and *Much Ado.*" *PMLA* 40 (1925): 530–50.
Glapthorne, Henry. *The Lady Mother.* Ed. Arthur Brown. Malone Soc. Reprints, 1958.
   Oxford: Malone Soc., 1959.
Greg, W. W. *Dramatic Documents from the Elizabethan Playhouses.* 2 vols. Oxford:
   Clarendon, 1931.
———. *The Editorial Problem in Shakespeare: A Survey of the Foundations of the Text.*
   Oxford: Clarendon, 1942.
———. *The Shakespeare First Folio: Its Bibliographical and Textual History.* Oxford:
   Clarendon, 1955.
Johnson, Gerald D. "*The Merry Wives of Windsor,* Q1: Provincial Touring and Adapted
   Texts." *Shakespeare Quarterly* 38 (1987): 154–65.
Heywood, Thomas. *The Captives.* Ed. Arthur Brown. Malone Soc. Reprints. London: Ma-
   lone Soc., 1953.
Hinman, Charlton, ed. *The First Folio of Shakespeare.* The Norton Facsimile. New York:
   Norton, 1968.
Long, William B. " 'A bed / for woodstock': A Warning for the Unwary." *Medieval and
   Renaissance Drama in England* 2 (1985): 91–118.
Loues labors lost . . . by W. Shakespere. London, 1598.
McKerrow, R. B. "The Elizabethan Printer and Dramatic Manuscripts." *Library* 4th ser.
   12 (1931–32): 253–75.
———. *Prolegomena for the Oxford Shakespeare: A Study in Editorial Method.* Oxford:
   Clarendon, 1939.
———. "A Suggestion Regarding Shakespeare's Manuscripts." *Review of English Studies*
   11 (1935): 459–65.
Much adoe about Nothing . . . by William Shakespeare. London, 1600.
Munday, Anthony. *John a Kent and John a Cumber.* Ed. Muriel St. Clare Byrne. Malone
   Soc. Reprints. Oxford: Malone Soc., 1923.
Orgel, Stephen. "The Authentic Shakespeare." *Representations* 21 (1988): 1–25.
———. "What Is a Text?" *Research Opportunities in Renaissance Drama* 24 (1981):
   3–6.
Taylor, Gary. "The Casting of Q *Richard III.*" Seminar paper for "The 'Bad Quartos' as
   Documents of the Theatre," International Shakespeare Congress, Stratford-upon-Avon,
   1981.

———. "Copy-Text and Collation (with Special Reference to *Richard III*)." *Library* 6th ser. 3 (1981): 33–42.

———, ed. *Henry V.* The Oxford Shakespeare. Oxford: Clarendon, 1982.

———. "The Transmission of *Pericles*." *PBSA* 80 (1986): 193–217.

The Tragedy of King Richard the third. London, 1597.

Urkowitz, Steven. "'Well-sayd olde Mole': Burying Three *Hamlet*s in Modern Editions." *Shakespeare Study Today: The Horace Howard Furness Memorial Lectures [1982].* Ed. Georgianna Ziegler. New York: AMS, 1986. 37–70.

Wells, Stanley. "Editorial Treatment of Foul-Paper Texts: *Much Ado about Nothing* as a Test Case." *Review of English Studies* ns 31 (1980): 1–16.

———. *Re-editing Shakespeare for the Modern Reader.* Oxford: Clarendon, 1984.

Wells, Stanley, and Gary Taylor. *Modernizing Shakespeare's Spelling, with Three Studies in the Text of* Henry V. Oxford: Clarendon, 1979.

Wells, Stanley, and Gary Taylor et al. *William Shakespeare: A Textual Companion.* Oxford: Clarendon, 1987.

Wells, Stanley, and Gary Taylor, gen. eds. *William Shakespeare: The Complete Works.* The Oxford Shakespeare. Oxford: Clarendon, 1986.

———. *William Shakespeare: The Complete Works: Original-Spelling Edition.* The Oxford Shakespeare. Oxford: Clarendon, 1986.

Werstine, Paul. "'*Enter a Sheriffe*' and the Conjuring Up of Ghosts." *Shakespeare Quarterly* 38 (1987): 126–30.

Broken Brackets and 'Mended Texts: Stage Directions in the Oxford Shakespeare

LESLIE THOMSON

I

IT IS CURIOUS that, whereas modern editors of Shakespeare and other Renaissance dramatists expend considerable effort—and ink—developing and justifying theories for modernizing and emending dialogue, relatively little attention is given to stage directions. On the one hand, this is understandable since little is known for certain about the interior architecture of the theaters, and stage directions in the original texts are usually inadequate. On the other hand, however, these editors are dealing with drama, a visual medium, and the descriptions of the action are an integral part of the whole text. Indeed, for the reader all stage directions—both original and added—are crucial since they will determine what the mind's eye sees. A glance at the textual introductions to the Arden, Pelican, Riverside, Penguin, Signet, Revels, New Mermaid, and Regents editions of Shakespeare and his contemporaries suggests that in the matter of stage directions editors are in remarkable accord: square brackets are used to indicate additions to directions and unless the nature of the directions is important in determining textual provenance, they are not a concern.[1] However, the inadequacy of original directions and the ease with which square brackets and emendations can be added have invited editors to be far freer with the content and treatment of stage directions than with dialogue. While all the editions listed above use the same editorial signals of emendation for directions, there is often a considerable difference in the degree of information provided as well as in the information itself. Although the rationale behind these decisions is rarely given, it is worth considering whether the editor has a particular reader in mind as he or she works and if this affects the treatment of stage directions. The problem is that in reality Renaissance playtexts must serve not only the person with a general interest but also the student and the academic—not to mention the actor and director. Thus an editor must or should take this into account when emending both dialogue and directions, despite the fact that it is questionable whether it is possible to prepare an edition that will satisfy the different needs of all these potential users. The recent publication of the Oxford *William Shakespeare: The Complete Works* provides a particularly good opportunity to explore these related issues.

Certainly, for one who has become used to the conventional signals of editorial emendations to stage directions, reading a play in the *Complete Works* can be a disconcerting experience. Not only have the square brackets indicating additions to directions in the original text(s) disappeared, but to discover when such changes have been made, the reader must consult a separate volume, the Oxford *Textual Companion* (Wells and Taylor et al.). As well, one must become accustomed to new "broken brackets"[2] used for stage directions that are in some way conjectural. When expected signals are absent and new ones with new meanings appear, it is difficult not to react negatively to the whole enterprise. But this would be a mistake: when the initial frustration has abated it becomes apparent that this new edition offers a very readable and easily visualized version of Shakespeare's plays well suited to the needs of the general reader—if that is for whom it is intended.

Probably the general reader will be happy merely to be told what to visualize, but surely students should either be learning to pick up the verbal signals for themselves, or at least be prompted by the text to evaluate editorial decisions about them. And if the system developed for the *Complete Works* makes it difficult for the student to do this, the scholar will find him- or herself continually frustrated by having to search through several sections of the *Textual Companion,* sometimes in vain, for even indications, let alone explanations of emendations to directions.

What follows is intended not so much as criticism as an exploration of the issues and problems related to stage directions in Renaissance plays and an examination of an innovative attempt to solve them. Certainly it is always easier to find fault with others' proposals than to offer alternatives, but it seems to me that this edition creates problems that, because of the physical separation of emendation and explanation, can easily go unnoticed, even by a reader familiar with the plays. But that reader will also find many extremely perceptive and satisfying staging proposals that should be acknowledged. And, whether criticism or praise is the result, this evaluation would not have been possible without the *Textual Companion,* which was not yet available when this study was being researched and written. Stanley Wells, one of the general editors of the whole Oxford Shakespeare project, provided me with proof copies of the General Introduction, the Textual Introductions to several plays, and the Editorial Procedures, enabling me to proceed with my analysis.

As I have suggested, it seems important that an editor of Renaissance plays consider the needs of readers when deciding how to treat stage directions. But it is curiously difficult to discover at what readership the *Complete Works* is aimed: is it the "common man," the student, the academic—or all three? And if the unannotated volume of the plays is intended for general reading, is it compatible with the scholarly orientation of the *Textual Companion*? Before evaluating what the Oxford editors have done, I felt I should try to discover for whom they were doing it.

In the General Introduction to the *Textual Companion,* Gary Taylor introduces the issue of the intended reader several times, but seems never to face it head on. The "editing of works of literature," he says, "is an attempt to understand the past, and to make that past more accessible to our own contemporaries" (7). The closest Taylor comes to addressing the issue of readership is when he quotes R. B. McKerrow's *Prolegomena for the Oxford Shakespeare:* " 'There can be no edition of the work of a writer of former times which is satisfactory to all readers, though there might, I suppose, be at least half a dozen editions of the works of Shakespeare executed on quite different lines, each of which, to one group of readers, would be the best edition possible' " (3). Taylor agrees, adding that "[n]o edition of Shakespeare can or should be definitive. Of the variety of possible and desirable undefinitive editions, one asks only that they define their own aims and limitations: that they be self-conscious, coherent, and explicit about the ways in which they mediate between writer and reader" (3–4). True enough, but surely the mediation should be different depending on the intended reader, as McKerrow's words seem to imply. In this part of his introduction Taylor is discussing both the Oxford original- and modern-spelling editions, which, of course, are intended for two very different readerships, the one strictly scholarly—but the other?

At the end of the General Introduction Taylor refers specifically to the "readers of the *Oxford Complete Works*" when he discusses the editors' decision to put the playtexts in one volume and the textual commentaries in another. His consideration of the advantages and disadvantages of this decision ignores problems of which he seems unaware: "[The] *Textual Companion* . . . enables us to record and explain our editorial decisions in greater detail than would be possible if collation and text cohabited in a single volume; moreover, by opening both books it should be possible to make text and collations simultaneously available (which cannot be done when collations are placed at the back of a text and can only be reached by flipping back and forth)" (61). Certainly this is true, but the cumbersomeness and cost of two substantial books seem virtually to eliminate most general readers and students as users and make it likely that only the scholar will want both.

The intended reader of the *Complete Works* is more clearly defined by Stanley Wells in *Re-editing Shakespeare for the Modern Reader,* a collection of four lectures in which he sets out his editorial principles and the reasons for them. In the third chapter, "The Editor and the Theatre: Editorial Treatment of Stage Directions," Wells addresses the subject that will be the focus of the analysis to follow here, and I shall return to his discussion later. We can infer the nature of the *Complete Works* and its readers when Wells says that "few, if any, of the new directions in the *Complete Oxford Shakespeare* will be different in kind from those to which readers of scholarly editions are accustomed" (76–77). Later Wells says, "I think that non-Shakespearian additions in a scholarly edition should be in language which does not jar with what surrounds it, but which is, so far as possible, intelligible to the modern reader" (77). In the penultimate paragraph he comes more directly to the point concerning both readership and the treatment of stage directions, which for Wells are related issues:

> I qualified what I just said with the phrase "in a scholarly edition". Again we need to recognize that plays may properly be edited in different ways to suit different readers. I am assuming that our editions [*Complete Works* and Oxford English Texts] will be used mainly by students and scholars with a concern for authenticity. We shall not print square brackets to signal alterations or additions to directions when we believe that they are indisputable: when they merely regularize names, for instance, or when they indicate action which is indisputably required by the text. I find square brackets an irritating distraction, and I think that their use inhibits editors from providing necessary information. (78)

Wells cites McKerrow to defend the omission of square brackets: "Even McKerrow, in his plans for a designedly conservative edition, clearly had reservations about their use: 'I do not defend them in the stage directions on any logical grounds. They are simply a matter of convenience. If it is understood that a bracketed name or direction is not in the copy-texts, this will in practice often save much space in the collation notes' (pp. 50–1)." Wells adds that in the Oxford English Texts editions same-page collation notes will make alterations and additions "readily identifiable" (78). But not as identifiable, it seems to me, as when they are signaled by square brackets in the text of the play itself, as is done in the Arden editions, which also collate them below. Concerning the *Complete Works* Wells says, "[W]e shall rely more on the reader's confidence, but the *Textual Companion* will print all the directions of the relevant early edition or editions, so again it will be possible for the interested reader to see where changes have been made" (78). This seems to me to miss the point: as a teacher and student of the plays, I want to know as I am reading where emendations have been made to the original text, whatever its authority. And, as I hope to show, for a user of this edition whose research focuses on staging and therefore stage directions, the methods adopted by the Oxford editors create special difficulties.

Wells's detailed consideration of stage directions apart from other aspects of the text is a welcome and thorough review of the peculiar problems posed by absent or inadequate stage directions in Renaissance plays. Since the plays were written to be rehearsed and then performed, the particulars of staging were developed during that process and rarely survive in written form—if they were ever committed to paper. As Wells notes, this problem is especially acute in Shakespeare's plays, since as a member of the company he was present to tell his fellow players what to do as they spoke his words, if the dialogue did not make the actions obvious. The players, in turn, probably suggested pieces of business to him. As well, changes from Shakespeare's proposed staging were surely made by himself or others as practical consider- ations made them necessary. In other words, the provenance of even those stage directions present in the extant texts is uncertain. Fur- thermore, inaccuracies in foul papers suggest that just because it was written down does not mean it was done, and directions in scribal transcripts may not be authorial.[3]

What all this means is that an editor is probably justified in claiming and taking an extra degree of freedom when emending or adding stage directions. And every Shakespeare play requires the addition of some basic stage directions and the correction of others to bring them into conformity with implications in the dialogue. Most modern editors go much further, following a standard set down by McKerrow and quoted by Wells: "[F]or 'The great majority of those adults [the general reader] who now read Shakespeare', the ' "best" text ... is likely to be one completely modernized both in spelling and punctuation, with full stage directions aiding them to visualize the action as it would be if staged by a reasonably conservative producer.' " Wells concurs, but adds his view that, "once the decision has been made to pass beyond 'diplomatic' editing and to alter and add directions, there is no reason to make any distinction between the needs of a general reader and those of a specialist" (*Re-editing* 66). Certainly Wells is right that the textual critic, among others, is probably "no less lacking in the visual imagination required to infer action from dialogue" than any "general reader" (66), but this premise, it seems to me, fails to consider that while the general reader reads Shakespeare out of general interest and to get a general sense of the play in a modern performance, the specialist, particularly one interested in staging, often studies the play for relationships between what was said and done in an original performance.[4] Thus, while it is helpful to know how an editor believes it might be or have been done, one also wants some indication both that a stage direction is an alteration or addition to the original and what the reasons for the emendation are. One of Wells's editorial principles is to "be rather bolder than most of us have been about acting on our own judgement, without requiring editorial precedent" (*Re-editing* 76). And while it must be agreed that past practice should be more open to question and revision than has been the case, surely when such changes are made, or totally new directions added—conjecturally or not—some discussion of the matter is required. But there are occasions when the curious specialist refers to the *Textual Companion* to check what seems to be a new direction and finds only the cryptic, "This edition; *not in* QF."

II

In what follows close attention will be given to *King Lear*, and then reference will be made to particular staging suggestions in *Richard II*, *1 Henry IV, The Tempest, Othello, Troilus and Cressida,* and *Richard III*. This procedure is not intended to suggest that these are the only plays offering material for analysis, nor that *King Lear* presents the most problems; neither do I want to imply that these plays are necessarily representative of the Oxford *Complete Works* as a whole. The choice of *King Lear* has been determined partly because Stanley Wells has provided me with the textual notes for the play, and partly because it happens that the play offers an opportunity to discuss many of the problems with stage directions alluded to above that recur through the edition, as my discussion of specific aspects of the other plays in section three should indicate. My aim is to note such matters as where the Oxford version differs from others, how the stage direction in question is treated, what support there is for it, and how it affects our sense of the action or character, or our overall interpretation. For purposes of comparison I have used the Arden, Riverside, and Pelican editions, and, in the cases of *1 Henry IV, Troilus and Cressida,* and *The Tempest,* the Oxford English Texts single-volume editions as well. While the *Complete Works* prints both the first quarto and the Folio versions of *King Lear* in full, for reasons to be discussed below a consideration of the stage directions need not be concerned with both. The Folio text is the one referred to here.[5]

When one is looking specifically for differences between the Oxford and other editions, interesting new possibilities concerning never-before-questioned actions can become apparent. Such is the case with the first exit in *King Lear,* when, after the opening conversation between Kent, Gloucester, and Edmund, Lear enters and tells Gloucester to "Attend the lords of France and Burgundy" and Gloucester responds, "I shall, my lord" (1.1.34–35). The Folio and the *Complete Works* have *"Exit"*; in this they are alone. To my knowledge all editors since Edward Capell (1768) have Edmund exit with his father. While I have suggested above that a problem in the Oxford is that emendations to original texts are added without explanation, here a long-accepted exit is omitted. Surely the difference between Edmund staying or leaving is significant enough to warrant discussion, but the textual notes to the quarto version merely acknowledge Capell's emendation. If Edmund stays he is a mute, observing presence on stage until all but France and the three sisters exit (line 266.1). This presents interesting problems and possibilities: on the one hand any actor and director must decide what Edmund does, how he reacts during Lear's love-contest; but on the other, Edmund's commentary on the "excellent foppery of the world" has even more bite if he has just seen it in action. So I want to know why the Oxford editor departs from accepted practice.

During Edmund's commentary on superstition an example of a "conjectural emendation" occurs. "—O, these eclipses do portend these divisions" is preceded by *"[He reads a book]"* (1.2.134, 133.1). Presumably the support for this is to be found when Edmund tells Edgar "of a prediction I read this other day..." (lines 138–39). But why should this even raise the possibility that he is reading it again now? Are we to look for a connection between the contents of the letter Edmund gives Gloucester and those of the book, inferring that the one is as specious as the other? The textual notes are silent on the matter.

In the scene when Edmund sets up his fight with Edgar the Oxford edition adds business that, it seems to me, would have created unnecessary problems, at least on the Renaissance stage as we believe it to have been. On one of several occasions through the *Complete Works* when a new use of the gallery is suggested we find, "[*Enter Edgar at a window above*]," as Edmund is unfolding his plot to us. At "Brother, a word, descend. Brother, I say," we read, "[*Edgar climbs down*]," while Edmund continues speaking to him (2.1.15.1–19.1). The quarto textual notes provide an interesting insight into how the Oxford editors have taken dialogue literally when adding stage directions, creating problems where none would otherwise exist.

That Edgar *is* 'above' seems evident from Edmund's call to him to 'descend'; but no time is allotted (as usually happens) for Edgar to descend by the tiring-house steps. If Shakespeare had wanted the usual staging, he could easily have provided it by having Edmund call Edgar ... before addressing the audience for three lines ('My father ... fortune helpe'). It thus appears that Shakespeare deliberately forwent the usual technical expedient, and this implies that he did not want the usual staging. It would be natural—and dramatically effective—for Edgar in these circumstances simply to climb over the upper stage railing and jump or climb down to the main stage, with or without Edmund's help.

If so, this staging would be very rare; but Edgar need not be seen above at all since he does not speak until he joins Edmund on the main stage. Surely there are enough staging problems without creating new ones based on dialogue that could as easily have been intended to establish Edgar's whereabouts without the necessity of having him appear above.

The next major piece of stage business is with the stocks, and here too the *Complete Works* offers a conjectural staging that differs from previous versions and subtly alters the dynamics of the scene. Cornwall twice says "Fetch forth the stocks" (2.2.122, 129). After the first time the Oxford editor adds the direction "[*Exeunt some servants*]"; the second time "[*calling*]" is added, suggesting that Cornwall's impatience to punish Kent is what causes him to repeat the command. The textual notes provide no discussion of this conjecture, and to my knowledge no previous editor has offered it. Neither, however, do other editors speculate on why Cornwall gives the same order twice; the lines are usually left without stage directions or comment. By making the staging more specific, the Oxford conjecture calls attention to the repetition and prompts a consideration of what else it might imply. The absence of information in other editions prompts the inference that Cornwall calls off stage both times and servants within finally enter with the stocks shortly after the second command. But the Oxford direction for servants on stage to go off raises an interesting possibility. According to the Folio—but not the quarto—servants enter with Cornwall and the others (2.2.41.1 –3); thus he could well be giving them the order. The question is whether they obey him the first time he speaks or are hesitant and must be commanded again—perhaps in anticipation of the servant's actual refusal to obey Cornwall in the blinding scene. Since all three interpretations of the evidence, and therefore all three versions of the staging, seem equally possible, when an editorial decision is made to add to the original text some explanation seems necessary. After all, the "[s]pecially designed brackets [to] identify conjectural stage directions"[6] do not indicate exactly what is conjectural, the actual direction or merely its location, and without a textual note a reader—general or otherwise—has no way of knowing without checking this version against others.

At the end of Kent's soliloquy in the stocks the Oxford editor makes another departure from usual practice; one that prompts a new awareness of the visual element and its implications. It is customary to treat Edgar's speech as a new scene, separate from what comes before and after, but, as the Folio and Oxford texts indicate, it is not.[7] The stage is not cleared when Edgar enters nor when he exits, since Kent is on stage asleep in the stocks throughout Edgar's self-pitying speech, providing a silent but eloquent commentary. Thus whereas act 2 usually has four scenes, the Oxford version has only two; this raises difficulties for cross-referencing between editions, but such problems are more than compensated for by the reminder to the reader of the visual facts.

Since I have several times complained about the absence of textual notes to explain emendations, it is ironic that on one of the few occasions when one is given, there is reason to take issue with it. At the beginning of Lear's "Take physic, pomp" soliloquy he sends the Fool off with the words: "Nay, get thee in. I'll pray, and then I'll sleep" (3.4.27). In the previous line the *Complete Works* adds the conjectural direction

"⌐*Kneeling*⌐" and a textual note that this "is suggested by F's description of the following speech as a prayer." But is it a prayer?—to the "poor naked wretches"? It is difficult to accept that the self-dramatizing "Take physic, pomp" would be spoken from a kneeling position—but perhaps Lear rises here; the Oxford editor does not indicate when he does so. If we go by the Oxford text he is on his knees for the next hundred and thirty lines, something the editor surely does not intend, here or elsewhere in the *Complete Works* when an action such as kneeling is begun but not ended.

The blinding of Gloucester offers a new interpretation of Cornwall's descriptive dialogue. The stage direction for "Upon these eyes of thine I'll set my foot" is "⌐*Cornwall pulls out one of Gloucester's eyes and stamps on it*⌐" (3.7.66, 68.1). Thus when Cornwall, referring to the remaining eye, says, "Lest it see more, prevent it. Out, vile jelly!" we are told, *"He [pulls out] Gloucester's other eye"* (81, 81.1). All of this is absent from the original text(s) but the "Oxford brackets" are around only "pulls out," presumably because this, like the previous direction wholly within the brackets, is conjectural and the rest is not. Such a staging would certainly make the action more horrific, although one would not have thought it possible—or necessary.

The stage directions at the end of this scene and the next provide one example of a virtue of this edition and one of a vice. Whenever there is a dead body to be got off stage we find the sort of direction that ends 3.7: *"Exeunt [with the body]."* The reader probably would not remember the dead servant lying there, and this is a good reminder of how the exit would look. (Although one wonders why the body's removal is conjectural in the Oxford sense.) The next scene, in which Edgar meets his blind father, ends with Edgar saying "Give me thy arm. / Poor Tom shall lead thee." This is followed by, *"Exit Edgar guiding Gloucester"* (4.1.73–74, 74.1). If the first example is a helpful reminder, this redundancy is surely its antithesis. As well, the latter is one of many unconjectural emendations with no textual authority, but nowhere is this acknowledged. One must refer to the listing of Folio stage directions found at the end of the textual notes to discover their absence from the original. The problem is exacerbated because on the page of the playtext such stage directions in the *Complete Works* have the same visual status, being unbracketed, as a direction present in a Folio or quarto.

In another departure from tradition that makes a subtle difference to the sense of a scene, the Oxford editor follows the Folio and does not have Oswald exit as he announces Albany's entrance and Goneril says "I have been worth the whistling" (4.2.29–30). There is an explanatory textual note: "Editors follow Q in having Oswald exit after his speech; this is, however, not strictly necessary, and his presence increases the indecorum of the quarrel, and (perhaps) confirms his inseparability from his mistress." (A similar explanation for having Edmund remain on stage in the play's first scene would be welcome.) The view expressed in the note is furthered by having Goneril "[*Exit with Oswald*]" when she says she will "read and answer" Regan's letter (4.2.55, 55.1). Curiously, while the editor does not follow the quarto in having Oswald exit earlier, he does follow it in having Goneril exit at this point. Again there is a textual note: "This edition; *not in* F; *Exit.* Q. If Oswald does not leave earlier . . . and if Goneril exits here, then Oswald must go with her. However, the absence of an exit direction in F may be correct: her presence, and her reaction to the Messenger's next revelation, could be dramatically effective."

The editors have made the controversial decision to print both the quarto and Folio versions of the play, with the result that neither is the conflation of the two given in other editions. At least this is generally the case with the dialogue; but, as the last examples suggest, it seems that stage directions from the one have been shifted silently into the other. Presumably the underlying premise is that stage directions are less likely to be authorial than dialogue—although if a direction can be changed or added in the theater surely dialogue is equally open to theatrical alteration. Another example of this kind of quarto/Folio conflation of stage directions occurs in the Dover cliff scene when we read: "GLOUCESTER (*kneeling*) O you mighty gods" (4.5.34). The direction "*He kneels*" is found only in the quarto. The round brackets used throughout the Oxford edition are merely a way of separating speaker's name, direction, and dialogue; they do not signal an editorial decision. This addition of quarto stage directions continues with, "*Gloucester falls forward,*" an expansion of the quarto's "*He fals*" (4.5.41.1). The problem is not that these directions are incorrect or should not be added but that their absence from the Folio is not indicated in the textual notes; one must go hunting through the list of original quarto directions to discover their source.

After Lear's entrance in the cliff scene there are two conjectural directions that, because they are without specific dialogue support, verge on editorializing by subtly changing the visual effect. When Gloucester asks, "Is't not the King?" and Lear responds, "Ay, every inch a king," the Oxford adds, "[*Gloucester kneels*]" (4.5.107, 107.1). Perhaps this is implied by Lear's next words, "When I do stare, see how the subject quakes!"—but not necessarily. With even less reason the reader is told that Lear speaks "When we are born, we cry that we are come / To this great stage of fools" after "[*removing his crown of weeds*]" (lines 177.1, 178). This suggests an improvement in Lear's mental state that is belied by his exit running and crying "Sa, sa, sa, sa!" (line 199). Finally, at the end of the scene, after Edgar has killed Oswald and addressed the body: "Here in the sands / Thee I'll rake up," the Oxford editor has Edgar "[*Exit with the body*]," then return to lead his father off, after Gloucester's comparison of himself and Lear (lines 273–286.1). This means that the body would not have been "buried" on stage— although the trap could have been used—and makes Gloucester's return to despair into a soliloquy. Even though a general reader would be untroubled by these admittedly fine points, by accepting what the Oxford editor suggests, that reader is given an interpretation of the scene that is open to question. And, those of us who refer to the textual notes for a discussion of these conjectures will not find even so much as an acknowledgment that they are new to this edition.

During the reunion of Lear and Cordelia she says: "O look upon me, sir, / And hold your hands in benediction o'er me. / You must not kneel" (4.6.50–52). The Oxford text indicates that Cordelia is "(*kneeling*)" as she speaks and, given that Lear seems to be reclining, this is likely the case. But if dialogue is to be an indicator of action, what is suggested by "You must not kneel"? It seems as possible that Lear moves to do so as that Cordelia actually does, raising the question of when a stage direction is required and when it is not. Furthermore, when does Cordelia rise? Presumably when she says "Will't please your highness walk?" (line 75), but no follow-up direction is given. Dead bodies need to be remembered but kneeling ones, it seems, do not.[8]

III

Similar to directions for characters kneeling and the removal of bodies are those describing action involving sitting and standing and, as already indicated, for the use of the gallery. A look at several examples of how both matters are treated should help to illustrate the peculiarities of this edition while also indicating that the kind of issues raised in *King Lear* are not restricted to that one play.

The first example of conjectures about when characters sit and stand deserves praise rather than criticism. In the third scene of *Richard II* the Oxford editor prompts a greater awareness in the reader that the ceremony of the challenge is one of dialogue supported by action.[9] Taking a cue from Richard's words at the end of the ceremony: "Let them lay by their helmets and their spears, / And both return back to their chairs again" (1.3.119–20), the Oxford editor adds "*[He sits]*" after first Mowbray and then Bolingbroke speak the words of the challenge (lines 25.1, 41.1), and conjectures that both stand again when elaborating on it later (lines 45.1, 84.1). Such additions not only contribute to the reader's sense of the ritualistic nature of the event but also indicate how the subtle battle for control begun by Bolingbroke in the first scene continues here both verbally and visually.

More problematic is the suggested staging of *1 Henry IV* 3.1, when the fractious rebels meet to divide the map of England. The scene begins with invitations to sit by both parties. First Hotspur asks Mortimer, Glendower, and Worcester to sit and the Oxford conjectures that they do so—which is likely the case. Then, after assuring Hotspur that he has the map, Glendower says, "Sit, cousin Percy, sit / Good cousin Hotspur." The Oxford editor says, "*[Hotspur sits]*" (lines 6–7.1).[10] This, given Hotspur's restless nature and the verbal jousting to follow, seems less likely, or more conjectural, than that the others sit. In both cases the textual note is merely: "This edition; *not in* QF." Notably, in the Oxford English Texts edition, which uses the same editorial principles, as is the usual practice there are no conjectures about anyone sitting or standing here.[11] According to the *Complete Works* Hotspur does not rise again until he threatens to leave and go to dinner (line 47.1). While it is certainly possible that he sits when Glendower invites him to, it is at least equally possible that he does not, but the stage direction added in the *Complete Works* virtually eliminates consideration of that possibility—despite the difficulty of imagining Hotspur sitting for that long on anything but his horse.

A third piece of sitting and standing business is found in the second scene of *The Tempest*.[12] Again there is an Oxford English Texts version different from that of the *Complete Works,* but both call attention to something this reader had never consciously considered before. In the *Complete Works,* after Prospero says to Miranda, "Sit down / For thou must now know farther," we read *"Miranda sits"* (1.2.32–33.1). Then a hundred lines later, it is conjectured that Prospero is "⌈*sitting*⌉" when he says, "Hear a little further" (line 135). It seems necessary that both sit at some point since as he concludes his exposition he says: "Now I arise. / Sit still, and hear the last of our sea-sorrow" (lines 170–71). Editors usually do not indicate these actions, and I have always imagined Prospero standing, commanding attention and exerting power throughout the scene, which goes against what the dialogue indicates. Thus the issue is not whether Prospero sits but when he does so, and it is on this that the two Oxford versions differ. In the single-play edition Prospero's "Sit down, / For thou must now know farther" is followed by an unconjectural *"They sit,"* and the only acknowledgment of the emendation is in the collation. There is no note to explain a decision that would significantly alter the visual effect of the scene and, as a consequence, a reader's—but especially an audience's—impression of Prospero.

In Stanley Wells's previously quoted discussion of the treatment of stage directions in the *Complete Works* he says that he is "more willing to add directions than many editors" (*Re-editing* 76). In the addition of stage directions indicating a use of the gallery, Wells and his colleagues have demonstrated this willingness. Richard Hosley, in his study of Shakespeare's use of the gallery, finds that in twenty plays it is required at least once (77–78). A check through the *Complete Works* will find all the uses of the gallery Hosley cites plus ten more in the twenty plays, as well as conjectures for its use in five others. Of the numerous suggested additional uses of the gallery I should like to look at four that seem particularly provocative.

According to Hosley, and to most editors, there is only one use of the gallery in *Othello*: when Brabantio comes to his window in the

first scene. In the *Complete Works* two more are conjectured.[13] The
first is at the top of 2.1: *"Enter below Montano, Governor of Cyprus;
two other gentlemen [above]."* A satisfyingly detailed textual note explains: "Perhaps one or both of the *Gentlemen* should be on the upper
level. This would explain Montano's opening question and add vivid-
ness to 2.1.11–17 (which would become a direct reaction to the spectacle)." This kind of observation scene certainly recurs in plays of the
period, and such a staging would make the dialogue more vivid without
working against any of the scene's effects. Unfortunately this is not the
case with the second added use of the gallery in the play, when, to the
original direction *"Enter Othello"* after the wounding of Cassio by Iago,
the *Complete Works* adds *"[above]"* (5.1.27.1). On this occasion there
is nothing in the textual notes to indicate either that this is a new
suggestion or that it is extremely doubtful, since there is no dialogue
support for this staging and no dramatic reason to have Othello observe
from above. Furthermore, the absence of any references to walls or
windows—which usually establish the location of such scenes—here
or in the previous instance, increases the speculative nature of this
unexplained conjecture.

In the second scene of *Troilus and Cressida* the Oxford editor conjectures that Cressida enters *"[above]"* at the beginning of the scene,
Pandarus joins her *"[above]"* (line 36.1) to promote Troilus as a suitor,
and, after some hundred and eighty lines of dialogue between them,
with no one on the main stage, they watch and comment as the various
men pass by in succession *"[below]"* (lines 180.1, 184.1, 194.1, 205.1,
213.1, 222.1).[14] At first this seems to make an effective scene; however,
it would have been most unusual to have a long and important exchange between two characters above and none below.[15] As well, there
is no specific indication that Cressida and Pandarus are above, and,
given the probability that those above on the Renaissance stage were
both less visible and less audible than those below, it is doubtful that
Shakespeare would have arranged the scene as this modern editor suggests. Once again the single-volume edition differs: Cressida and Pandarus are on the main stage throughout the scene, as is usually suggested.

But this significant additional use of the gallery is less of a problem
than what is conjectured for *Richard III* 5.5, where the *Complete Works*
has each of the ghosts enter *"[above]"* to speak over the sleeping Rich-

ard and Richmond in their respective "tents."[16] The textual notes tell us that this conjecture is based in part on the premise that a main-stage entrance would be "prosaic" and "most atypical of supernatural figures." After considering various other possibilities, the editor concludes: "Entry above would be natural for supernatural figures; would put them in a theatrically commanding position, reflecting their power as the spokesmen of God and destiny; and would allow them to address both sleepers as well as the audience without difficulty." It is worth noting that even in the *Complete Works* the ghost of Hamlet's father does not appear above. Furthermore, while Richard's description of his dream: "Methought the souls of all that I had murdered / Came to my tent" (lines 158–59), does not explicitly contradict such a staging, neither does it invite or support it. Once again a provocative staging change calls attention to itself rather than subtly elaborating dialogue implications.

For anyone in the Shakespeare business the publication of the new Oxford *Complete Works* has been eagerly awaited. Indeed, the Oxford reputation has probably fostered expectations that cannot possibly be met. However, it seems to have been the intention of the general editors and their colleagues to establish new editorial practices as a standard for the future. As the new broken brackets and examples of emendation and conjecture demonstrate, this aim is especially apparent in the treatment of stage directions. And with the amount of time and people involved the final product is clearly the result of careful consideration. This care is obvious in the always interesting and often provocative emendations and additions that are proposed, even if unexplained. For all these reasons I have been reluctant to question the results. If the problems were incidental and attributable to carelessness, they would be easy to discount, but they are fundamental and obviously the consequence of deliberate editorial practices. Perhaps in time the methods developed for handling stage directions in the *Complete Works* will come to be accepted; certainly their simplicity makes them appealing to the general reader of a Shakespeare play, but once again the question arises about whether this is at whom the edition is aimed. These same methods make it very difficult for the student to get at the original text, and for the academic who has come to expect, indeed requires, a more cumbersome but more informative system, the *Complete Works* seems idiosyncratic: worth consulting for its intelligent conjectures but not to be used as a primary text, especially regarding stage directions.

Notes

1. The New Penguin single-volume editions dispense with brackets altogether and list original stage directions and editorial emendations in an appendix.

2. The term used by Stanley Wells, speaking on editing at the Shakespeare Association of America meeting, April 1, 1988.

3. See Long.

4. On this issue see Dessen, chap. 8: "Conclusion: Elizabethan Playscripts and Modern Interpretations."

5. Edited by Gary Taylor.

6. The phrase is from the book jacket.

7. See the textual introduction to the quarto (*Textual Companion* 510).

8. Bevington also notes this ("Determining" 514).

9. Edited by John Jowett.

10. Edited by John Jowett.

11. Curiously, in Bevington's own complete edition of the plays he says "[*They sit*]" for the threesome but nothing about Hotspur doing so.

12. Edited by John Jowett.

13. Edited by Stanley Wells.

14. Edited by Gary Taylor.

15. See Hosley 81.

16. Edited by Gary Taylor. Stage directions to this effect appear at lines 70.1, 77.1, 84.1, 92.1, 99.2, 107.2, 112.2, 120.1.

Works Cited

Bevington, David. "Determining the Indeterminate: The Oxford Shakespeare." *Shakespeare Quarterly* 38 (1987): 501–19.

Dessen, Alan C. *Elizabethan Stage Conventions and Modern Interpreters*. Cambridge: Cambridge UP, 1984.

Hosley, Richard. "Shakespeare's Use of a Gallery over the Stage." *Shakespeare Survey* 10 (1957): 77–89.

Long, William B. "Stage-Directions: A Misinterpreted Factor in Determining Textual Provenance." *TEXT* 2 (1985): 121–37.

Shakespeare, William. *The Complete Works*. 3rd ed. Ed. David Bevington. Glenview, Ill.: Scott, Foresman, 1980.

———. *The Complete Works*. Alfred Harbage, gen. ed. The Pelican Text Revised. Baltimore: Penguin, 1969.

———. *The Complete Works*. Stanley Wells and Gary Taylor, gen. eds. The Oxford Shakespeare. Oxford: Clarendon, 1986.

———. *The First Part of King Henry IV*. Ed. A. R. Humphreys. The Arden Shakespeare. London: Methuen, 1960.

———. *Henry VI, Part 1*. Ed. David Bevington. The Oxford Shakespeare (Oxford English Texts). Oxford: Clarendon, 1987.

———. *King Lear*. Ed. Kenneth Muir. The Arden Shakespeare. London: Methuen, 1972.

———. *King Richard II*. Ed. Peter Ure. The Arden Shakespeare. London: Methuen, 1961.

———. *Mr. William Shakespeare His Comedies, Histories, and Tragedies*. Ed. Edward Capell. 10 vols. London, 1768.

———. *The New Penguin Shakespeare*. T. J. B. Spencer and Stanley Wells, gen. eds. Harmondsworth: Penguin, 1968– .

———. *Othello*. Ed. M. R. Ridley. The Arden Shakespeare. London: Methuen, 1958.

———. *The Riverside Shakespeare*. G. Blakemore Evans, textual ed. Boston: Houghton, 1974.

———. *The Tempest*. Ed. Frank Kermode. The Arden Shakespeare. London: Methuen, 1958.

———. *The Tempest*. Ed. Stephen Orgel. The Oxford Shakespeare (Oxford English Texts). Oxford: Clarendon, 1987.

———. *Troilus and Cressida*. ed. Kenneth Muir. The Oxford Shakespeare (Oxford English Texts). Oxford: Clarendon, 1982.

———. *Troilus and Cressida*. Ed. Kenneth Muir. The Oxford Shakespeare (Oxford English Texts). Oxford: Clarendon, 1982.

Wells, Stanley. "The Editor and the Theatre: Editorial Treatment of Stage Directions." *Re-editing Shakespeare for the Modern Reader*. Oxford: Clarendon, 1984. 57–78.

Wells, Stanley, and Gary Taylor et al. *William Shakespeare: A Textual Companion*. Oxford: Clarendon, 1987.

Textual and Sexual Criticism:
A Crux in The Comedy
of Errors

GARY TAYLOR

WOMEN MAY read Shakespeare, but men edit him. So it has been from the beginning, and so it remains. As early as 1605 a jealous husband in Thomas Middleton's *A Mad World, My Masters* felt compelled to take "all her wanton Pamphlets"—including *Venus and Adonis*—away from his young lascivious wife (B2v). In a manuscript dating from about 1635,[1] Richard James reported that "A young Gentle Ladie ... having read ye works of Shakespeare, made me this question. How Sir Jhon Falstaffe, could be dead in Harrie ye fifts time and againe liue in ye time of Harrie ye sixt to be banisht for cowardize." In a letter to a friend, written on January 21, 1639, Ann Merricke regretted her lack of access to other "gentile recreationes": "I must content my selfe here, with the studie of Shackspeare, and the historie of woemen" (Munro 1: 443).

The texts these first women readers read were all created and mediated by men. The works were written by Shakespeare and various male collaborators; copied by male scribes; annotated in the theater by male prompters, regulating the performances of male actors; edited in the printing shop by male publishers; set into type by male composi-

195

tors; corrected by male proofreaders; supplied with prefatory matter by male literati.[2]

The pattern established before the English civil war continued after it. The first prose critical essay on Shakespeare was written by a woman, Margaret Cavendish, in 1664. The poet, novelist, and translator Charlotte Lennox wrote the first full-length book on Shakespeare by an American-born critic (1753–54). Early in the eighteenth century *The Spectator* was already satirizing the reading habits of women, with their neglect of moral tracts and practical handbooks in favor of English plays and fiction; late in the nineteenth century women constituted two-thirds of the students in the new Modern Languages school at Cambridge, and seventy-nine percent of those who took the English examination in its first five years at Oxford (Baldick 69). As a parliamentary commission reported in 1868, "English literature occupies a more prominent position in the education of girls than of boys" (Beale 145).[3]

But men retained their monopoly on editing. As Lewis Theobald declared in 1733, "the Ladies" could not be expected to engage in textual criticism, because they "cannot form a true Judgement of its Effects, nor can penetrate into its Causes" (1: xlii). All the great eighteenth-century editions were prepared by men, and in this as in other respects the eighteenth century defined the rules which have governed Shakespeare's texts for three centuries. The collations of the 1980 New Variorum edition of *Measure for Measure,* for instance, do not award a siglum to a single text of that play edited by a woman (Eccles xii–xv). To my knowledge no edition of Shakespeare's complete works has ever been prepared entirely by a woman.

When women first dared to edit Shakespeare, they did so anonymously, or under the covering fire of male authority. *The Family Shakespeare,* first published in 1807, contained twenty plays of Shakespeare; this edition was actually prepared by Henrietta Maria Bowdler, but the first edition did not name any editor, and the second, eleven years later, credited it to her brother Thomas Bowdler, MD (who was in fact only responsible for changes in the second edition). Mary Cowden Clarke, best known for her *The Girlhood of Shakespeare's Heroines,* later collaborated with her brother Charles on an edition of Shakespeare's works (1864). In the 1930s R. B. McKerrow, at work upon an old-spelling edition for Oxford University Press, made Alice Walker his assistant;

McKerrow died before completing the edition, and with some nervousness the press appointed Walker as his successor, under the condition that her work be vetted by a board of male scholars headed by W. W. Greg. Walker never finished that edition, though she did prepare texts of *Othello* and *Troilus and Cressida* for Cambridge University Press. Her work on those plays, published in 1957, was overseen by John Dover Wilson.

In the last two decades women have been responsible for important editions of a few plays—*All's Well That Ends Well* (Everett 1970), *As You Like It* (Latham 1975), *The Taming of the Shrew* (Thompson 1984), *Twelfth Night* (Donno 1985), *The Merchant of Venice* (Mahood 1987)—and less important editions of a few more.[4] The Oxford, New Cambridge, and revived Arden series promise a smattering of further editions by women before the end of the century. But women remain, in our own time, a disproportionately tiny minority of the editorial clan; when they do edit, token women are almost always confined to the comedies, usually to plays which present few textual problems.

Quite apart from any effect it might have on the editing of the texts themselves, this underrepresentation of women in the Shakespearean editorial club tends to perpetuate various myths about editing and about gender. Textual scholars generally believe that textual scholarship is the most important activity of academic humanism: it constructs the foundation upon which all other literary interpretation is built. Textual scholars—by recovering, editing, and publishing classical texts—made possible the Renaissance itself. Within this value system, editing is work, criticism is play; editing is primary, criticism is parasitic. This value system can easily overlay another: men work, men are primary; women are idle, parasitic, secondary. The paucity of female editors reflects and reinforces the sexist myth that men do the scientific problem-solving, while women indulge in various forms of "appreciation": men make, women interpret.

This sexual bifurcation of labor can be seen as early as 1808: a year after the debut of Henrietta Bowdler's *Family Shakespeare,* a twenty-five-volume collection of popular English plays was published, called *The British Theatre.* The texts of these plays were "printed under the authority of the managers" of the Drury Lane, Covent Garden, and Haymarket theaters, "from the promptbooks." In other words, the texts were printed under the authority of, and prepared by, men. But each play was supplied "With biographical and critical remarks" by the novelist, dramatist, and actress Elizabeth Inchbald. Late in the twentieth century women are still performing the function Inchbald performed early in the nineteenth: the text of *The Riverside Shakespeare* was edited by G. Blakemore Evans, but the individual introductions to the comedies were written by Anne Barton. Barton likewise wrote the critical introduction to T. J. B. Spencer's posthumous edition of *Hamlet*. Inchbald and Barton play a part which can be characterized as "the good hostess," introducing readers to editors. The man does the work, and the woman takes care of the social arrangements.

In itself, the mere biological distinction between a male editor and a female editor should not make any difference to the resulting text of Shakespeare's works. We do not edit with our genitals, but with our eyes and minds and hands, organs shared by both sexes. But the minds with which we edit can harbor dubious assumptions about gender, dubious assumptions which influence the editorial choices we make.

Such prejudices can be shared by both sexes. Henrietta Bowdler, Mary Cowden Clarke, and Alice Walker were females, and they did some editing, but they could hardly be called feminist editors. Bowdler did justify her edition by quoting a woman author, the famous Elizabeth Montagu; but the quotation she chose—"every approach to obscenity is an offence for which wit cannot atone, nor the barbarity or the corruption of the times excuse"—displays Montagu at her most prudishly neoclassical. Acting on Montagu's principle, Bowdler selected "Twenty of the most unexceptionable of SHAKESPEARE'S plays," and then "endeavoured to remove every thing that could give just offence to the religious and virtuous mind," thereby producing a text fit "to be placed in the hands of young persons of both sexes" (1: vi, vii, xi).

Bowdler wanted to make Shakespeare safe for young women, by removing from his works anything to which a young woman should not be exposed. But this righteous ambition subjected her to an embarrassingly unrighteous paradox: she could only protect other women by exposing herself to material to which women should not be exposed. She almost certainly published her edition anonymously in order "to avoid the odium of admitting that she, an unmarried gentlewoman of fifty, understood Shakespeare's obscenity well enough systematically to remove it" (Perrin 76). If we want a feminist alternative to Bowdler's anxious anonymity and anxious prudery we have to go all the way back to Aphra Behn. In 1687, in the preface to her play *The Luckey Chance,* Behn also drew attention to the amount of what Bowdler would call obscenity in plays like *Othello:*

> If I should repeat the Words exprest in these Scenes I mention, I might justly be charg'd with course ill Manners, and very little Modesty, and yet they so naturally fall into the places they are designed for, and so are proper for the Business, that there is not the least Fault to be found with them; though I say those things in any of [my Scenes] would damn the whole Peice, and alarm the Town. (A4)

Behn, in her own name, declares that she understands such obscenities, but she also defends them as artistically appropriate and objects to the double standard which limits her own freedom of literary maneuver.

Unfortunately, Behn never edited Shakespeare, and Bowdler's attitude has been more common among the few women who have. Unlike Henrietta Bowdler or Mary Cowden Clarke, Alice Walker was a formidable textual scholar, who has profoundly influenced later editors. But she had a neoclassical attitude toward verbal and sexual decorum. Exactly a century and a half after publication of *The Family Shakespeare,* Walker was objecting to what she called "vulgarization" and "perversion" in the 1622 text of *Othello,* condemning its "dramatically objectionable oaths," and attributing such indecorous readings to "a licentious transcript."[5] The 1622 quarto has Desdemona declare that her heart is subdued to the "utmost pleasure" of Othello; the 1623 Folio reads "very quality" (537/1.3.251)[6]; Walker prefers the less physical, more abstract reading, asserting that "Othello's 'pleasure' has nothing to do with the argument." Later in the same speech Desdemona complains that, if her newlywed husband leaves her behind when he goes to Cyprus, "The rites for why I loue him, are bereft me" (543/1.3.257); Walker insists that "rites" has nothing to do with conjugal rites, asserting instead that "What Desdemona is asking for is the privileges ('rights') of sharing the hazards of war" (*Textual Problems* 140–41). Walker, like Bowdler, labors to chasten Shakespeare's text.

Such attitudes could of course be illustrated from the work of many male editors, too; I have quoted female editors simply in order to demonstrate that the biological distinction matters less than an ideological one. The physical fact of sex matters less than the psychological attitude toward gender.

Editorial attitudes toward gender matter, because editorial decisions directly impinge upon the representation of gender in Shakespeare's plays. E. A. J. Honigmann has demonstrated that a series of variants in the 1623 text of *Othello* consistently strengthens the role of Emilia, and that the 1623 text deliberately increases and heightens the play's "sexually specific" language. Likewise, Beth Goldring argues that, in *The Tragedy of King Lear,* the ambiguous speech prefix *"Alb.Cor."* (162/1.1.161), which editors have all but invariably interpreted as a male pair (Albany and Cornwall), actually creates a thematically important male and female pairing (Albany and Cordelia). Randall McLeod contends that *The Tragedy of King Lear* (the revised text) portrays Goneril more sympathetically than *The History of King Lear* (the unrevised text). In one version of *Troilus and Cressida,* Troilus's final bitter dismissal of Cressida goes unchallenged; in the other, it does not (Taylor, *"Troilus and Cressida"* 128). In one version of *Hamlet,* an important speech in the scene of Ophelia's funeral is assigned to Gertrude; in another version, the same speech is assigned to Claudius (3252–56/5.1.283–86).

At the end of *The Patriarchy of Shakespeare's Comedies* Marilyn Williamson takes comfort from the recognition that "The social constructs human beings invent, they may also change" (183). Shakespeare's text is just such a social construct. If we want to change the way Shakespeare's text is read, we—women and men—will have to start changing the way Shakespeare's text is made.

II

Shakespeare's text is made in part by editorial choices about which of two early versions to print, or whether to conflate two early versions to produce a third. But it is also made, more ubiquitously, less conspicuously, by editorial decisions about how to emend or interpret texts which only survive in one authoritative early edition. As an illustration of the interrelationship between textual and sexual criticism, I will spend most of the rest of this essay considering one such passage, a complicated crux in *The Comedy of Errors*. I quote this passage, below, as it appears in the first and only substantive text (1623). Adriana, the aggrieved nagging wife of Antipholus of Ephesus, is speaking to her sister Luciana. (For convenience of reference in what follows I will number each line in the margin.)

I see the Iewell best enamaled	371
Will loose his beautie: yet the gold bides still	372
That others touch, and often touching will,	373
Where gold and no man that hath a name,	374
By falshood and corruption doth it shame:	375

(371–75/2.1.109–13)

This does not make sense; at least, I myself have not been able to make sense of it, and neither, apparently, have other readers, male or female. It seems reasonable to assume, therefore, that the passage is in some way corrupt. "It is possible," as Louis B. Wright says, "that the confusion is a deliberate reflection of Adriana's jealous state of mind";[7] in other words, "you can't expect women to be coherent, especially when they are complaining about men." Perhaps Shakespeare deliberately wrote lines that do not make sense, in order to demonstrate that women do not make sense. However, I am personally inclined to suspect textual corruption.

The Comedy of Errors has, I believe, never been edited single-handedly by a woman. Bowdler excluded it from her collection, perhaps because a courtesan is inextricably entangled in its plot. The play was included in Inchbald's collection of plays from *The British Theatre;* but her introduction does not even mention the character of Adriana. Regarding the play as a whole, she complains, "Of all impossible stories, this is the most so"; she also objects particularly to its rhyming passages (1: 3, 4). In the play as Shakespeare wrote it, of course, this crux is one of those passages, and most critics have felt that Shakespeare was not at his best when composing couplets. But in the text Inchbald's essay introduces, this passage does not rhyme, because *The British Theatre* prints an eighteenth-century adaptation (1: 21):

> I see the jewel best enamelled
> Will lose its lustre—So doth Adriana,
> Whom once, unwearied with continual gazing,
> He fondly call'd the treasure of his life!

This does at least make sense. In the theater, if the passage is not adapted, in some such fashion, it disappears altogether: as Stanley Wells recommends, "The corruption of this passage is such that it is best omitted in performance" (137). By omitting it, of course, a performance diminishes Adriana's role. And since this passage comes in Adriana's final speech of this scene, in the climax of her indictment of male behavior, omitting this passage diminishes both the quantity and the intellectual quality of that indictment. The omission or abbreviation of this passage is one of many theatrical cuts, traditional since the eighteenth century, by which women characters are "denied the power of reasoning" (Dash 115).

I shall therefore, in my capacity as a reader and a literary critic, assume that the passage is corrupt, and that the passage is important enough to warrant some effort at correction. I must therefore lead you into the thorny wood of textual criticism.

This passage appears in the middle of the left column of sig. H2v (p. 88 of the Comedies section), apparently set by a workman conventionally identified as Compositor C.[8] Nothing about the immediate bibliographical context offers a mechanical explanation for the difficulties of this passage; there is, for instance, no sign that the text was adversely affected by the compositor's need to squeeze too much text into a narrow column. We are not sure what kind of manuscript the compositor was looking at. Most investigators have concluded that the text was set from Shakespeare's own foul papers, but Paul Werstine has recently challenged this hypothesis; the whole matter remains *sub judice*. In short, the bibliographical expertise accumulated by the last half-century of textual scholarship offers us, apparently, no help whatever in solving this problem. We are left with the text and our own intelligence.

In order to find or make sense in this speech, we have to engage in a close reading of the text. We have to consider every possible meaning of the words that are present; but we also have to consider every possible source of textual corruption in the passage. We need to examine the words that are there now, and the words that are not there now, but might once have been there. We have to consider not only the different available ways of *reading* the passage, but the different available ways of *writing* it.

Editors do this all the time, even when considering the simplest and most self-evident of emendations; but they usually do it intuitively. In a passage like this one, however, the original meaning seems to have been rather complicated; so much we can infer from the complexity of the context, and the difficulty of the lines in question. Moreover, the passage seems to have been corrupted in some complicated way; at least, most editors who have attempted to correct the text have been forced to assume multiple error. In order to solve a problem of this complexity, we have to slow the whole process of editorial reasoning down; we have to proceed step by step, word by word, like a mathematician working on a problem in multivariant analysis.

Step One. Theobald (3: 15) proposed that the first word of line 374, *Where,* is an aural error for *Wear,* and virtually every editor since 1733 has concurred.[9] Fausto Cercignani confirms that the two words sounded alike in Shakespeare's lifetime (145, 147, 162), making it easy enough for a compositor to substitute one for the other. A few conservative modern editors retain *Where,* but in order to do so they must assume a complicated double ellipsis: "will [continue to abide] Where [it is indeed genuine] gold". This meaning is difficult to convey to a scholarly reader (do you understand it?), and would be impossible to communicate in a theater. Moreover, editors who retain *Where* must still repunctuate the passage, thereby presuming that the compositor was thoroughly bewildered about its meaning.[10]

In short, no one has been able to make convincing sense of *Where* without altering the text in some other way. For instance, Quiller-Couch and Wilson (1922) retained *Where* by positing that two whole lines have been omitted:

                                   and often touching will,
Where gold and . . . . [rhyme word]
. . . . [rhyme word]
. . . . no man that hath a name

Copyists can commit such errors; but eye-skip of this kind occurs much
less frequently than simple aural error. Moreover, it is hard to see why
the image or the argument here should be dragged out so much longer,
or what might have been said in the two extra lines. Indeed, forty years
after he had made this suggestion Wilson silently buried it.

Although I have scrupulously examined every other option, in the
end I have arrived at the same conclusion Theobald reached two and
half centuries ago: *Where* should be changed to *Wear*. Like every other
emendation, this one is based upon a calculated judgment of probabilities: the probabilities of certain kinds of meaning and certain kinds of
error. As the Cambridge editors William Clark and John Glover declared
in 1863, "The only correction of this passage which we believe to be
quite free from doubt is" *Wear* for *Where* (1: 463). If you are not willing
to accept that *Where* is probably an error for *Wear*, then you may as
well stop reading this essay right now.

Step Two. Even with this emendation, however, the passage remains
obscure, not to mention metrically irregular. Metrical irregularity is
particularly suspicious when, as here, it occurs in an early play and
coincides with difficulties of interpretation.[11] The last line and a half
can hardly be taken at face value.

> no man that hath a name,
> By falshood and corruption doth it shame.

R. A. Foakes and other male commentators have defended this statement, but as it stands the generalization is not only false but wildly
uncharacteristic of Adriana. According to Foakes, Adriana is saying that
Antipholus's "true value as her husband cannot be violated by falsehood
and corruption"; this paraphrase is logically and morally obnoxious,
and difficult to extract from the words of the text. And if that is what
Adriana means, why does her sister Luciana respond by exclaiming
"How manie fond fooles serue mad Ielousie"? Luciana elsewhere defends the conventions of gender; she appears here to be criticizing
Adriana's speech; but in Foakes's interpretation Adriana's speech is itself
unimpeachably orthodox.

As they stand, Adriana's words are neither true nor characteristic.
Since she has no reason to lie to Luciana, it seems almost certain that

something is wrong with the text. Most editors since Theobald have located that something in the first word of the last line of this passage. Theobald emended *By* to *But;* since *But* could be used in Elizabethan English to mean "except, unless," this emendation exactly inverts the sense of the Folio text: falsehood and corruption do shame a man's name.

I am not convinced by this solution. If we emend to *But,* then Adriana must be likening the worn gold to the worn reputation: often touching will erode gold, and falsehood and corruption will erode a man's reputation. But if the worn gold and the worn reputation are alike, then a contrast seems to be required in line 373. Line 372 tells us that "the gold bides still"; lines 373–75, as emended by Theobald, tell us that the gold and the reputation do not abide. We need a disjunctive between these two assertions. Theobald supplied that disjunctive by emending the word *and* (in the middle of 373) to *yet:*

> I see the Iewell best enamaled
> Will loose his beautie: yet the gold bides still
> That others touch, [yet] often touching will
> [Wear] gold, and no man that hath a name
> [But] falshood and corruption doth it shame:

But even this is unsatisfactory. The repeated *yet,* in the same position in consecutive lines, is obviously awkward. This problem could be cosmetically removed by emending to *but* instead of *yet;* unfortunately, that would involve supposing that Compositor C twice in three lines substituted some other word for *but.* Such memorial substitutions are not at all common in Compositor C's work (O'Connor).

Besides, the more important difficulty created by such an emendation is less obvious, and less easily resolved, than the awkward repetition of *yet.* The passage contains four separate propositions:

1. The jewel best enameled will lose his beauty.
2. The gold bides still that others touch.
3. Often touching will erode gold.
4. Falsehood and corruption shame (or do not shame) a man's reputation.

As here emended, three of these four propositions involve erosion (1, 3, 4); but the anomalous proposition which does not involve erosion (2) is not syntactically assimilated, subordinated, or clearly related to the others. Nor have we been given any plausible explanation for the error which turned an original *yet* into *and*.

Solving these difficulties entails further emendation. Having emended *and* to *yet* in 373, Theobald was forced to emend *yet* to *and* in 372— assuming that *and* and *yet* had been transposed across adjacent lines. Thomas Hanmer then improved upon this solution by emending *the* to *tho'* (1: 394). Finally, in order to mend the meter Theobald inserted an extra word into 374. If we put all these emendations together—as many editors have—we get:

> I see the Iewell best enamaled
> Will loose his beautie: [and] [tho] gold bides still
> That others touch, [yet] often touching will
> [Wear] gold, and [so] no man that hath a name
> [But] falshood and corruption doth it shame:

This is an intelligible metrical statement. But it has been achieved by emending six words in a mere three and a half lines of verse, in the process supposing an irrational substitution of *By* for *But* and an unlikely transposition of two single words in the middle of adjoining lines. Even after all this tinkering, the sense is still not entirely convincing. As emended, propositions 2 and 3 are relative: gold will abide some touching, but too much touching will cause erosion. But proposition 4, which apparently derives from 2 and 3, is absolute: any falsehood or corruption whatsoever shames a man's reputation.

While printing this passage "as amended by the ingenuity of several editors," Alexander Dyce had to admit that "I must greatly doubt" whether these interlocking emendations had succeeded in restoring "the very words of Shakespeare" (2: 57). Most modern editors have refused to go so far; they have contented themselves with emending *Where* to *Wear* and *By* to *But,* then remarking on the corruption and obscurity of the whole passage. But once you have made the emendation to *But,* other emendations logically follow, if sense is to be wrung from the text. That emendation therefore cannot be accepted or rejected in isolation; it must be evaluated as part of a system of emendations. That system is not convincing.

I conclude that we should leave *By* intact. This means that we must reject the whole network of re-readings and re-writings of the passage generated by the emendation to *But*. This also means, in effect, that we must reject almost all previous editorial discussions of this passage, which have been trapped since 1733 in the rut made by *But*. *But* is a dead end.

Step Three. Editors have been led into that dead end by the apparent falsehood and corruption of Adriana's assertion that "no man that hath a name, / By falshood and corruption doth it shame". If the difficulties created by this statement do not originate in the word *By,* then perhaps they originate in the word *man*.

This innocuous word can, of course, conceal a variety of meanings; but the essential structure of its meanings is oppositional. A *man* is defined by contrast with something else. Thus, when Hamlet says of his dead father, "A was a man take him for all in all / I shall not looke vppon his like againe" (*Ham.* 342–43/1.2.186–87), or Antony says of the dead Brutus, "That Nature might stand vp, / And say to all the world; this was a man" (*JC* 2443–44/5.5.73–74), *man* is being defined ideally and qualitatively: Brutus, or Hamlet's father, was a *"real* man," a rare epitome of true maleness, in contradistinction to the many inadequate specimens of humanity which litter the planet. When Beatrice exclaims, "O that I were a man!" (*Ado* 1949/4.1.302), she defines the explicit *man* in contradistinction to an implicit *woman*.

Adriana's use of *man* here in *The Comedy of Errors* may therefore depend upon an implicit contrast with something else. The noun might be used, as in *Caesar* and *Hamlet,* normatively: Adriana might be saying, "no real man would act this way." No real man would shame his name by acts of falsehood and corruption; since Antipholus has done so, he is not a real man. As a condemnation of her husband, such a paraphrase of Adriana's statement is both logically acceptable and in character.

However, this paraphrase is difficult to extract from the actual words of the text. Adriana modifies the noun *man* with the clause "that hath a name". *Name* clearly means "reputation" and/or "high social rank." But a real man, by Elizabethan convention, always has both rank and reputation. (Witness Brutus and Hamlet's father.) If Adriana is using *man* in the normative sense, her modifying clause is redundant, and therefore confusing. Besides, if a man does *not* have a name, then he cannot do "it" shame: you cannot shame what you do not have. The words of the text, so interpreted, seem to imply a logically contorted contrast between real men who, having something, don't shame it, and unreal men who do not have it (because they have shamed it out of existence?). There may be a meaning here, but it cannot easily be communicated to an audience by the words the Folio text has given to Adriana.

Even if this paraphrase could be extracted from the last line and a half of the passage, it creates problems for the passage as a whole. It forces us to interpret the argument in terms like this: "If overused, gold will erode, and consequently, in order to avoid this kind of thing happening to the gold of his reputation, no real man behaves badly." This logical connection is, again, difficult to communicate. More important, this interpretation runs into a difficulty we have already seen in Step Two: the third proposition is relative, and the fourth absolute. Gold will only erode if touched *too much;* a real man will not let his reputation be touched by *any* falsehood or corruption.

I therefore conclude that Adriana is not using *man* in the normative sense. She is not contrasting "real men" with other men; she is instead contrasting the entire category "man" with some other category. In context, the direct and obvious contrast is between *man* and the immediately preceding noun *gold.* This contrast occurs within line 374, and we would expect it to be marked by a disjunctive. Logically, the middle of line 374 needs a disjunctive, which the printed text does not contain; metrically, the middle of line 374 needs an extra syllable, which the printed text does not contain. By remedying the logical deficiency of that line we can also remedy its metrical deficiency:

> and often touching will
> [Wear] gold, and [yet] no man that hath a name,
> By falshood and corruption doth it shame:

I am doing the same thing here that Theobald did: inserting a word to mend the meter of line 374. But Theobald inserted a logically superfluous connective; I am inserting a logically necessary disjunctive. This emendation presupposes that a single short word has been accidentally left out of the text; this is the most common kind of omission, and in this case the omission might have been assisted by the fact that the compositor had already set the same word two lines above.

This emendation does, I believe, make sense of the last half of this passage: "too much touching will erode gold, but in contrast no man with a rank or reputation can erode it, however falsely and corruptly he behaves." Moreover, the explicit contrast between *gold* and *man* clearly implies a second contrast, between *man* and "woman." That second contrast is, as Beatrice's exclamation demonstrates, deeply engrained in the structure of our language: *man* means "not woman," just as *woman* means "not man," each term defined by reciprocal opposition to the other. And that contrast between man and woman is the subject of the entire scene. The debate begins when Luciana declares that "A man is Master of his libertie", to which Adriana retorts "Why should their libertie then ours be more?" (270, 273/1.2.7, 10). Throughout, Adriana objects to the inequality of the contrast between man and woman. The passage we have been considering comes at the end of Adriana's final speech in the scene; in that context, it is hard not to read "no *man*" in bitter and emphatic contrast to an implied "any woman." No man will wreck his reputation, however badly he behaves; any woman will wreck her reputation, if she behaves badly at all. As one of Shakespeare's female contemporaries complained, "So in all offences those which men commit, are made light and as nothing, slighted ouer; but those which women doe commit, those are made grieuous and shamefull" (Sowernam 24).

Step Four. If we accept this reading of *man,* the whole passage can be divided into two sections, each two and a half lines long.

> I see the Iewell best enamaled
> Will loose his beautie: yet the gold bides still
> That others touch,

>   and often touching will
> [Wear] gold, and [yet] no man that hath a name,
> By falshood and corruption doth it shame:

The second section, as emended, now makes sense; the first section also makes sense. But we still need to relate these two sections to one another and to the larger context. In isolation, as individual statements about a jewel and gold, the first three clauses seem fairly straightforward and intelligible. But the dramatic context makes it clear that these statements must have a larger significance, that *Iewell* and *gold* must be taken as symbolic referents for something else. An editor must define that something, in a way which makes satisfactory sense of all three clauses and of the transitions between them. In the fourth clause, our problem was to make an apparently false statement true; for the first three, our problem is to make several true statements relevant. More specifically, we need to explain two transitions of thought: from the first proposition to the second ("beautie: yet"), and from the second to the third ("touch, and").

The first transition involves a contrast between two pairs of terms: "Iewell" against "gold", "loose his beautie" against "bides still". The meaning of the contrast must reside in an explanation of why the gold abides when the jewel loses its beauty. Logically, two alternatives are available. The explanation derives either from a contrast between the two nouns, or from a contrast between the two verbs. We need to examine both contrasting pairs in detail.

Step Five. I will begin with the nouns, because in both propositions the nouns precede their verbs. *Iewell* may refer to a brooch or other ornament,[12] or (more specifically) to a gem. But this object, whether ornament or gem, must itself be a metaphor for some other object or idea. If we literally identify this jewel with the chain Antipholus has promised Adriana, the only possible contrast the object could afford with *gold* would be one between the ephemeral love-token (chain) and the lasting love which "bides still"; neither "gold" nor "others touch" can possibly accommodate such a contrast. So the literal sense— which would in any case offer an uncharacteristically impoverished meaning for the passage as a whole—seems ruled out.

If *Iewell* has some metaphoric reference, then the context insists that the noun be taken as part of the man/woman debate which has dominated the entire dialogue. *Iewell* is frequently used elsewhere of or for a woman;[13] it may occasionally be applied to a man, but such usages are much rarer, and Shakespeare's works contain no examples. Besides, if we interpret the jewel as a vehicle for the tenor "man," we are left with a series of incongruities. How or why has the man—presumably

Antipholus, but also "man" in general—lost his beauty? (For a woman, the loss is, as Adriana complains earlier, quite literal.) The contrast with gold also creates difficulties. Presumably the man retains his intrinsic value ("gold") even though he has been unfaithful. But how can this paraphrase be extracted from the text? How can the intangible "intrinsic value" be touched by others? Moreover, this interpretation eventually forces on us the unlikely emendation *But* for *By,* and cries out for a strong disjunctive in line 373. In short, in addition to its other difficulties, the interpretation of *Iewell* as a metaphor for "man" leads us back to the blind alley which we examined in Step Two. For a whole range of reasons, then, it seems likely that *Iewell* is intended as a metaphor for "woman," *not* "man."

"Even the finest jewel loses its beauty; so does even the loveliest woman." The idea is commonplace; the metaphor, common. The first proposition thus seems relatively straightforward.

The noun *gold* could refer to the setting of a gem, to the brooch itself, or to the material of which the brooch (or its setting) is made. None of these alternatives gives us any reason for interpreting *gold* as a metaphor for "man" (in opposition to *Iewell* as a metaphor for "woman"); nor is there any intrinsic association of gold with men.[14] Adriana is therefore presumably still talking about women.

If *gold* refers to the setting of the gem, it is difficult to infer any metaphoric interpretation of the image which would explain why a gem deteriorates when its setting abides: in fact the reverse is more likely. (Gold deteriorates before diamonds.)

If gold refers instead to the material of the brooch or of the gem's setting, then the contrast must be one between the loss of exterior beauty and the retention of intrinsic value. Foakes, for instance, believes that "the passage contrasts an enamelled surface which wears away in use, with the gold underneath, which still 'wears gold', i.e. remains." But this interpretation, though initially attractive as a moral commonplace, cannot easily be reconciled to the actual words of the passage. The subject of the first proposition is *not* "an enamelled surface," but "the Iewell"; we are not told that the enameling deteriorates, but that the "Iewell" itself deteriorates. The key contrasting words in Foakes's paraphrase—"surface" and "underneath"—do not appear in the Folio text. Further problems are created by the modifying clause "That others

touch". How is intrinsic value touched? How does touching relate to
the contrast between perishing beauty and abiding value? The image
becomes desperately muddled.[15]

Given the difficulty with these alternatives, it seems to me almost
certain that *gold* must refer to the brooch itself: *gold* must be taken as
metonymic for *Iewell*. *Iewell* and *gold* are thus apparently being used
as two names for the same object (a brooch or other ornament); this
object is being treated, in an elaborate conceit, as a symbol of women.

The difficulties of this interpretation for a modern reader are chiefly
anachronistic, stemming from unfamiliarity with the obsolete sense of
Iewell as "brooch" and as a term of endearment for a woman. But the
difficulty is also caused in part by the change of noun—as becomes
evident if we rewrite the second line:

> I see the Iewell best enamaled
> Will loose his beautie: yet the Iewell bides still
> That others touch . . .

If Shakespeare had written the passage in this way, no one would have
doubted that the first and second propositions both refer to a single
object. But the reasons for this change of noun, and for the metonymic
use of *gold,* are fairly obvious. Gold erodes but does not corrode. Gold,
unlike other metals, is not subject to corrosion, and therefore operates
as an appropriate symbol of something which "bides still"; gold was
tested by being "touched"; gold readily provides a symbol for something which can be eroded by contact (it "wears" as a result of "often
touching"). The shift of noun in line 372 thus prepares for the shift of
thought in line 373.

The contrast between the first and second propositions, then, signaled by the disjunctive *yet,* cannot reside in the nouns, which both
seem to be used as symbolic referents for women; the contrast must
reside in the verbs.

Step Six. The jewel loses its beauty in one set of circumstances, but
abides in another set of circumstances. We are not surprised that the
jewel in the first proposition loses its beauty; long before the second
law of thermodynamics had been discovered, human beings had learned
that the mere passage of time causes deterioration. Decay, in itself,

requires no explanation. But when we pass to the second proposition, the disjunctive *yet* promises us some means of staving off, slowing down, halting, or even reversing the ravages of time, and this expectation is abundantly confirmed by "bides still". What distinguishes this second, abiding jewel, the recipe for its persistence, is "That others touch" it. The presence of this crucial single modifier in the second term of the contrast retrospectively implies the importance of its absence from the first term. The second jewel abides, because it is touched; the first jewel does not abide, presumably because it is not touched.

The verb *touch* includes the sense of mere erosive friction (*OED v.* 6a), of testing for value (*v.* 8), and of erotic contact (*v.* 2a). More generally, of course, touching involves tending, taking care of, expressing affection or interest or concern; it is a gesture of contact, closeness, affinity. The relevance and importance to a spouse of such attentions is the subject of Adriana's preceding speech.

> His company must do his minions grace,
> Whil'st I at home starue for a merrie looke:
> Hath homelie age th'alluring beauty tooke
> From my poore cheeke? then he hath wasted it.
> Are my discourses dull? Barren my wit[?]
> If voluble and sharpe discourse be mar'd,
> Vnkindnesse blunts it more then marble hard.
> Doe their gay vestments his affections baite?
> That's not my fault, hee's master of my state.
> What ruines are in me that can be found,
> By him not ruin'd? Then is he the ground
> Of my defeatures. My decayed faire,
> A sunnie looke of his, would soone repaire.
>
> (349–61/2.1.86–98)

The jewel, which is being offered as an image of women, loses its beauty—just as, Adriana complains, she has lost hers. Adriana has lost her beauty, not only or mainly through "homelie age" or "decay," but primarily because of her husband's unkindness and neglect. Therefore, when the first jewel is compared with another which "bides still" because "others touch" it, the inference is surely inescapable that this abiding results from the very attentions which Adriana—and, implicitly, the first jewel—have been denied.

This interpretation is supported by a passage in *Pericles;* it comes from the part of the play apparently written by George Wilkins, but it at least demonstrates the contemporary currency of the thought, and at most might be considered one of several passages where Shakespeare has touched up his collaborator's text:

> As Iewels loose their glory, if neglected,
> So Princes their Renowne, if not respected:
>
> (713–14/sc. 6, 12)

This parallel contains both the jewel and the loss of glory (beauty); it also relates this to renown (a name) and its potential loss (shame). And it makes explicit what seems implicit in *The Comedy of Errors:* neglect will accelerate the decay of a "Iewell."

This interpretation has the further advantage of explaining Adriana's insistence that the first jewel is "best enamaled". Enameling is both a decoration and a preservative. As decoration, it contrasts with the plain gold which, because it is prized and tended, preserves the beauty which the enamel loses. As a preservative, enamel attempts to forestall the decay wrought by time, but fails, partly at least for lack of the attentions which the gold receives: even the best enameled gem or ornament loses its luster and becomes tarnished if not regularly polished.

Moreover, if the jewel is a woman, then enameling, as both preservative and decoration, may suggest the use of facial makeup, which Shakespeare and his contemporaries frequently describe as a kind of "painting." Even the best cosmetics will not forestall decay. And since misogynistic writing often indicted the very use of cosmetics as a sign of female vanity and lechery, Adriana's apparently superfluous stress on enameling draws attention to ambiguities in the two following verbs.

Modernized texts—including my own—always interpret *loose* as "lose," which is undoubtedly its primary sense here; but in Elizabethan English the same spelling can also mean "let loose, release" (*OED v.* 1a). Shakespeare uses this verb more than once of a woman being made available to a man, always in contexts with a strong sexual undertone.[16] The sense of unrestrained and immoral movement suggested by *loose* contrasts with a secondary sense of the following phrase: *bides still* not only means "lasts forever," but also—satisfying the orthodox prescription for a worthy wife—"remains motionless," "stays at home quietly."

This second interlocking set of meanings reinforces the first. The woman who is touched retains her beauty, and also refrains from excess movement or speech; the woman who is not touched loses her beauty, enamels herself, and wanders illicitly.

The first two and a half lines of Adriana's conceit are thus complex, but coherent and intelligible. The jewel/gold is a metaphor for women. The difference between the first proposition and the second, between "loose" and "bides still", depends upon whether the woman/jewel is "touched", taken care of, cherished. Antipholus's neglect of precisely such attentions was the theme of Adriana's preceding speech.

Step Seven. Having successfully deciphered the first transition, we can now confront the second: the movement of thought between "yet the gold bides still that others touch" and "often touching will [wear] gold".

These two statements are almost certainly contrasting propositions. Foakes glosses *wear* as "remain"; this is lexically possible, but it disregards the proverb "Gold by continual wearing wasteth" (Tilley 192). It also requires a relatively unusual interpretation of *wear,* and imposes a very awkward construction on the preceding line. If *wear* means "wear away, erode" (the usual interpretation), then "often touching" is the subject of the verb; but if *wear* means "remain," then the subject must be "gold" (two lines before), with "often touching" construed absolutely in the sense "being often touched." These difficulties are surely in themselves insuperable. In addition, if my reasoning about the final proposition is valid, then Foakes's interpretation of *wear* is even more unlikely, because it destroys the contrast between *gold* and *man.*

I will therefore proceed on the assumption that the second and third propositions contrast each other. Why, then, is there no disjunctive between them? Because we do not really need a disjunctive: the repetition of both *touch* and *gold,* combined with the contrast between *bides still* and *will wear,* makes the logical structure clear enough. The force of the opposition is unmistakably located in the difference between *touch* and *often touching:* some touching is necessary, too much touching is undesirable. In the 1623 text, the absence of a disjunctive in 373 is awkward, because there is no disjunctive in 374 either: "and often touching ... and no man" is flaccid, and leaves the reader or listener without any logical signposts to the movement of thought. This deficiency reinforces the arguments (already advanced in Step Three) for inserting *yet* in line 374. But once we have a disjunctive in 374, we don't need one in 373. The entire passage resolves into a pair of contrasts, each hinging on *yet:* between decaying jewel and abiding gold, then between eroding gold and unshamable man. The four propositions align in a symmetrical rhetorical and logical pattern: A B A B, with each B marked by an introductory *yet.*

Adriana's reasoning could be paraphrased thus: "I see that the best enameled ornament (like a woman) will lose its beauty (if neglected)—yet a golden ornament (or a woman) that others touch and cherish will remain beautiful; and gold (like a woman) loses its value if touched too often—but a man, however false and corrupt, never loses his reputation."

If this interpretation is correct, then in line 373—in the middle of the middle line of this conceit—Adriana takes up and expands upon one of the terms of her own previous metaphor: she revises her own image. What prompts this shift of thought, verbally, is the unintended ambiguity of the phrase "others touch", which can suggest (sexual) contact with more than one partner. What prompts this shift, dramatically, is Adriana's own jealousy, her recurrent complaint that others have touched Antipholus. Women lose their beauty, if neglected; on the other hand, if they are touched too often, they lose their value. But men, however licentious, keep their rank and reputation. Adriana first develops a conceit on brooch-as-woman (a conceit prompted by remembrance of the ornamental chain Antipholus had promised her and not delivered); she then, abandoning that conceit, contrasts the predicament of women which it had bodied forth with the unfair invulnerable liberty of men. This passage, this speech, this scene, analyzes the sexual double standard.

Step Eight. This interpretation does, I believe, make communicable, coherent, dramatic sense of the entire passage. It assumes that the jewel, whose larger significance we set out to define, is a symbol of women—a usage very common in the period, a usage supported by both the immediate and the larger context. However, this metaphor is obscured and contradicted by a single letter of the Folio text. If the jewel is a symbol of women, it should not be assigned a male gender. The beauty of the jewel belongs to a her, not a him. I therefore propose to emend *his,* in line 372, to *hir.* The whole passage would then read (as it does in the Oxford edition):

> I see the Iewell best enamaled
> Will loose [hir] beautie: yet the gold bides still
> That others touch, and often touching will
> [Weare] gold, and [yet] no man that hath a name,
> By falshood and corruption doth it shame:

This final emendation is required by all of the arguments contained in Steps Five, Six, and Seven. It presupposes an exceptionally easy mis-reading, well attested elsewhere[17] and especially probable where, as here, the compositor had no clear guidance as to gender. In an Eliza-bethan secretary hand, terminal *s* was often almost impossible to dis-tinguish from *r,* and in contemporary orthography *her* could be spelled with a medial *i;* in such circumstances, a "hir" and a "his" are materially identical, and can only be differentiated by cultural context.

I therefore suppose that this passage, as printed in the Folio, contains three errors: one an aural error, almost universally accepted (*Where* for correct *Weare*), another a small omission (*yet*), the third an easy misreading (*his* for correct *hir*). The Theobald/Hanmer solution to the crux—the only one, heretofore, which has made something like com-prehensive sense of the whole passage—postulated six errors, not three. Theobald and I agree about one emendation (*Where* for correct *Weare*); as for the remaining emendations, my two presuppose much easier and more common errors than the five proposed by my eighteenth-century predecessors.

Errors tend to come in batches. Compositor A, for instance, com-mitted four major errors in three adjacent lines of *Macbeth,* errors corrected by all modern editors.[18] Compositor C himself committed three errors in eight lines of *Love's Labour's Lost* (644–51/2.1.167–74). Compositor C was more prone than his fellow compositors to omission, especially in verse (as here), especially of minor parts of speech (like *yet*); he elsewhere—as with *his* for correct *hir*—reversed the gender of pronouns (*LLL* 537/2.1.60); most of the known substitutions in his

work might (like *Where* for correct *Weare*) be due to memorial confusion (O'Connor 60–61, 69–70). Of course, we would all prefer not to
emend the text at all if we could avoid it. But if the logic of the preceding analysis is correct, *hir* and *Weare* and *yet* not only make better
sense of the passage than any previous interpretation, but provide the
only reconstruction which the logic of the lines and their context will
permit.

III

Let us assume for the moment, hubristically, that we have solved this
crux. Let us assume that we can now see what Shakespeare meant, and
how that meaning was corrupted, and how it can be restored. We are
then in a position to ask two questions, one about interpretation, one
about editing.

First, a question about interpretation: what difference does our new
understanding of this passage make to our understanding of the scene
and the play? Obviously, in their emended state the lines give Adriana
a clearer, stronger, subtler, more intellectually compelling statement;
they give her a critique of the double standard which most modern
feminists could endorse. This statement is given considerable structural
emphasis. The scene as a whole is divided into three parts: an opening
and closing conversation between Adriana and Luciana, interrupted by
an episode in which both confront Dromio; in the first and third sections, Adriana and Luciana debate the proper relationship between the
sexes, with Luciana supporting the sexual status quo. But in the third
section of the scene, the orthodox Luciana speaks only three lines,
broken up into three separated speeches; the discontented Adriana
speaks twenty-eight lines, in two long speeches which develop and
sustain a complicated argument. Structurally, Adriana dominates the
conclusion of the scene, and this emended passage contributes to that
domination. Much of what Adriana says in this scene could be quoted
and endorsed by a modern critic like Juliet Dusinberre, laboring to
demonstrate Shakespeare's credentials as a proto-feminist (77, 82,
111–12, 127,), or Marilyn French, applauding Adriana's "deeply felt
speeches" with their "probing of an unhappy marriage from the point

of view of the wife" (74). Our emended passage would give such critics one more passage to quote. So far, so good.

But the farther we go, the worse things get. The passage we have been considering is not the end of Adriana's speech; she continues:

> Since that my beautie cannot please his eie,
> Ile weepe (what's left away) and weeping die.

After her attack on male falsehood and corruption, Adriana returns, finally, to the subject of her own beauty. She leaves the stage crying: feminist argument dissolves into "womanish teares" (*Jn.* 1524/4.1.36). And the last word is left to orthodox Miss Luciana: "How manie fond fooles serue mad Ielousie?" On behalf of the audience and the author, Luciana interprets Adriana's entire argument as a mere symptom of irrational jealousy. The first woman critic to comment in any detail on this scene, Elizabeth Griffith, did not see in it Shakespeare's dramatic endorsement of female equality; two hundred years before Dusinberre, Griffith interpreted the scene as an argument for "the duty and submission which ought to be shewn to a husband" (1: 160, 165–66).

The play's larger structure even more disastrously undermines Adriana's position. Her arguments in the third section of the scene are precipitated by an encounter with her servant Dromio, who has himself had an encounter with the wrong Antipholus; Shakespeare makes her accusations result from a misunderstanding (which the audience understands). Shakespeare also demands that Adriana, in her first scene, beat her male servant, thus visually stereotyping her among the shrewish women who commit physical violence against men (Woodbridge 193). And at the end of the play, of course, Shakespeare turns the tables on Adriana, by asserting that she is responsible for her husband's misbehavior: "The venome clamors of a iealous woman, / Poisons more deadly then a mad dogges tooth", and so on for eighteen lines, culminating in the conclusion that "thy iealous fits / Hath scar'd thy husband from the vse of wits" (1419–36/5.1.70–87). This rebuke comes from another woman, so that it cannot be dismissed as male prejudice; it comes from an abbess, literally invested with all the authority of religion; and it is endorsed and accepted by Adriana herself.

Some of Shakespeare's female contemporaries would not have accepted it:

Drunkards, Leachers, and prodigall spend-thrifts: These when they come home
drunke, or are called in question for their riotous misdemeanours, they pres-
ently shew themselues, the right children of *Adam*. They will excuse themselues by their wiues, and say that their vnquitenesse and frowardnesse at
home, is the cause that they runne abroad. (Sowernam 44)

Ester Sowernam complains that, since Adam, men have been blaming
women for their own faults; Shakespeare does better, by having women
blame women for men's faults.

Looked at from this larger dramatic perspective, the more compelling
Adriana's argument appears to be, the more effectively Shakespeare
demolishes feminist criticism of male behavior. No matter how good
her arguments are, Adriana is doomed to lose. Shakespeare seems to
give Adriana her due—only so that he can, with an appearance of utter
impartiality, do her in. A feminist textual criticism can deconstruct the
sexist assumptions of centuries of Shakespeare editing; but it cannot
save Shakespeare from his own prejudices.

Second, a question about editing: why has this crux defeated so many
editors? It would be satisfying to conclude that the crux has defeated
editors because those editors were men, men who themselves accepted
the double standard which the passage complains about, men who did
not think Adriana's speech was important enough to warrant prolonged
meditation, men who did not see the implied woman or appreciate that
the word *man* might be the source of the text's difficulty. No doubt
that is part of the truth; but since I am a man, and claim to have solved
the problem, I do not want to think that it is the whole truth. Biology,
in this context, matters less than sociology. Thanks to two intense decades of feminist scholarship, it is now possible for any critic, suitably
informed, to see details which previous critics missed: we are collectively, as an academic culture, much more sensitive than our predecessors to the representation of gender.

But the crux has also defeated editors, in part, because of the extent
of the corruption: three errors in proximity are harder to correct than
one. And it has defeated editors, in part, because the thought itself is
difficult, and the conceit in question a species of poetry which all eighteenth-century editors—and many since—have regarded with irritation or at best impatience.

Editors prefer cruxes which permit them lightning strikes of ingenuity which—like Theobald's famous "[babeld] of greene fields" (*H5* 814/2.3.16)—suddenly and brilliantly illuminate a whole verbal landscape. Such emendations hardly need to be defended or explained: for most readers they are so obviously "right" that to utter them is to make them canonical. Such emendations are created, and appreciated, intuitively. But it should be apparent that, however emended, a passage like this one in *The Comedy of Errors* will never succumb to such an editorial blitzkrieg. Such passages depend upon the progressive logical and rhetorical unfolding of a conceit; if a passage like that gets corrupted in transmission, it can only be restored by painstakingly retracing, rethinking, reinventing, its argument, specifying and then evaluating the range of logical possibilities opened up by each stage of the conceit.

Editors always engage in a particular kind of intercourse with an author's discourse: they engorge the text, and simultaneously intrude themselves into it. The male editorial tradition has preferred cruxes which offer opportunities for a quick, explosive release; if an emendation does not provide such a quick fix, it leaves editors feeling dissatisfied. But a crux like this one presents us with "falshood and corruption" which can only be overcome by "often touching": prolonged exploratory attentiveness. Neither of these methods should have a monopoly on the text. A good editor, like a good lover, should be capable of both.

Notes

1. The date and circumstances of this manuscript are discussed in my "William Shakespeare."

2. For a full accounting of these activities see my General Introduction in Wells and Taylor (1–68).

3. Most histories of Shakespearean interpretation ignore or slight the contribution of women readers and writers; for an attempt at a more balanced assessment—with many more examples than I can offer here—see my *Reinventing Shakespeare: A Cultural History, 1642–1986* (New York: Weidenfeld & Nicolson, 1989).

4. Among the less important editions I include Mahood 1968 and Barton (in the New Penguin series), Doran and Bennett (in the Pelican series), Everett 1964 and Rosen (in the Signet series). The series to which these individual editions belong are, in general, not textually ambitious, and none of these specimens contributes anything of importance to the editorial history of the play in question.

5. Walker and Wilson 124–25. Although this edition of *Othello* was attributed to both scholars, Wilson was only responsible for the Introduction; these views on the text are Walker's own, and echo her *Textual Problems*.

6. References to Shakespeare's works are keyed to *The Complete Works*, Stanley Wells and Gary Taylor, gen. eds. (1986), citing first the continuous line number from the old-spelling edition, then the act-scene-line number from its modern-spelling counterpart.

7. Wright 16. I attribute this statement to Wright, as general editor; it is of course possible that it was written by his "Assistant," Virginia A. LaMar. In either event, the collaboration of Wright and LaMar is another instance of female editorial work being subordinated to and legitimated by men.

8. A summary of work on Folio compositors is contained in Wells and Taylor, 148–52; for textual problems in *Errors*, see 266–69. (The essay you are now reading is the one referred to, as forthcoming, in the textual note on this passage.)

9. The emendation is so obvious that it would probably have been made long before 1733, were it not for the fact that lines 374–75 were accidentally omitted by the second folio (1632), and hence continued to be omitted by every subsequent edition until Theobald's.

10. Evans follows Peter Alexander in retaining the Folio's words but thoroughly altering its punctuation: "yet the gold bides still / That others touch and, often touching, will / Where gold;". Because Alexander's edition has no notes, he did not have to explain what he thought this meant. C. J. Sisson guessed that Alexander meant "others touch and, often touching, will touch where there is gold to touch" (1: 91).

11. Shakespeare nowhere else treats *wear* (or *where*) as disyllabic. To my knowledge no one has defended the irregularity here as "expressive." For a full discussion of metrical criteria for emendation see my "Metrifying Shakespeare" (forthcoming in *Shakespeare Studies*).

12. *OED sb.* 1: "An article of value used for adornment, chiefly of the person; a costly ornament, *esp.* one made of gold, silver, or precious stones. *Obs.* in *gen.* sense; now restricted to a small ornament containing a precious stone or stones." The modern sense (*OED sb.* 2) developed late in the sixteenth century, and during Shakespeare's lifetime the two senses are often difficult to distinguish; but Shakespeare unequivocally used the more inclusive primary sense at least once (*TN* 1679/3.4.203), and it remained current into the eighteenth century.

13. *OED sb.* 3: "*fig.* Applied to a thing or person of great worth, or highly prized; a 'treasure', 'gem'." Shakespeare uses this sense at *Wiv.* 1417/3.3.39, *2H4* 273/1.2.19, *Oth.* 480/1.3.194, and *Cym.* 416/1.4.150. Compare also *MV* 979–80/2.7.54–55: "neuer so rich a Iem / Was set in worse then gold."

14. The only connection I have been able to find between *man* and *gold* is that both were at the top of their respective orders in the "great chain of being" (Tillyard 42–43). But I have found no examples of this parallel explicitly used; here it would have to be entirely inferred, without any assistance from the context.

15. By interpolating a full stop after "still" we could momentarily divorce the gold from the troubling clause "That others touch"; but this simply postpones the problem

to the following sentence ("others touch that"). Such an emendation in effect simply emphasizes the anomalous modifier.

16. *Wiv.* 731/2.1.172 ("I would turne her loose to him"), *Ham.* 1092/2.2.163 ("Ile loose my daughter to him"), *Tmp.* 704/2.1.131 ("loose her to an Affrican").

17. Control-text "his" is usually or always emended to "hir" at *R3* 2115, 2116, 2117/3.7.125, 126, 127, *LLL* 1897/5.2.147, *H5* 1423/3.6.29, *AYL* 1286/3.2.142 and 2609/5.4.112, and *Son.* 102.8. The reverse emendation—"his" for control-text "hir" (or "her")—is made at *TGV* 1674/4.2.110, *Tit.* 1162/3.1.146, and *Ham.* 1072/2.2.143. Editors usually emend "his" to "hir" at *1H6* 2253/5.5.13; I instead emend "her" to "his" at 2252/5.5.12. (I would not claim that this list is exhaustive.)

18. Within three lines, Compositor A set *sides* for correct *strides, sowre* for correct *sure,* and *they may* for correct *way they* (*Mac.* 533–35/2.1.55–57). These errors could derive from the manuscript that the compositor was working from; but in that case, either the scribe who prepared that manuscript was guilty of committing four errors in three lines, or the presence of some errors in the manuscript precipitated further errors by the compositor. Similar concatenations of error occur in other texts.

Works Cited

Alexander, Peter, ed. *William Shakespeare: The Complete Works.* London: Collins, 1951.

Baldick, Chris. *The Social Mission of English Criticism, 1848–1932.* Oxford: Clarendon, 1983.

Barton, Anne, ed. *The Tempest.* The New Penguin Shakespeare. Harmondsworth: Penguin, 1968.

Beale, D., ed. *Reports Issued by the Schools' Inquiry Commission on the Education of Girls.* London, [1869].

Behn, Aphra. *The Luckey Chance.* London, 1687.

Bennett, Josephine Waters, ed. *Much Ado about Nothing.* The Pelican Shakespeare. Baltimore: Penguin, 1958.

[Bowdler, Henrietta, ed.] *The Family Shakespeare.* 4 vols. Bath, 1807.

Cavendish, Margaret. *CCXI Sociable Letters, written by the Thrice Noble, Illustrious, and Excellent Princess, The Lady Marchioness of Newcastle.* London, 1664.

Cercignani, Fausto. *Shakespeare's Works and Elizabethan Pronunciation.* Oxford: Clarendon, 1981.

Clark, William George, John Glover, and William Aldis Wright. *The Works of William Shakespeare.* 9 vols. The Cambridge Shakespeare. London, 1863–66.

Cowden Clarke, Charles, and Mary Cowden Clarke, eds. *The Works of William Shakespeare.* 4 vols. London, 1864–68.

Cowden Clarke, Mary. *The Girlhood of Shakespeare's Heroines.* 3 vols. London, 1850–52.

Dash, Irene G. *Wooing, Wedding, and Power: Women in Shakespeare's Plays.* New York: Columbia UP, 1981.

Donno, Elizabeth Story, ed. *Twelfth Night.* The New Cambridge Shakespeare. Cambridge: Cambridge UP, 1985.

Doran, Madeleine, ed. *A Midsummer Night's Dream.* The Pelican Shakespeare. Baltimore: Penguin, 1959.

Dusinberre, Juliet. *Shakespeare and the Nature of Women.* London: Macmillan, 1975.

Dyce, Alexander, ed. *The Works of William Shakespeare.* 8 vols. London, 1864.

Eccles, Mark, ed. *Measure for Measure.* New Variorum Shakespeare. New York: MLA, 1980.

Evans, G. Blakemore, textual ed. *The Riverside Shakespeare.* Boston: Houghton, 1974.

Everett, Barbara, ed. *All's Well That Ends Well.* The New Penguin Shakespeare. Harmondsworth: Penguin, 1970.

———, ed. *Antony and Cleopatra.* The Signet Classic Shakespeare. New York: Signet-NAL, 1964.

Foakes, R. A., ed. *The Comedy of Errors.* The Arden Shakespeare. London: Methuen, 1962.

French, Marilyn. *Shakespeare's Division of Experience.* New York: Summit, 1981.

Goldring, Beth. "*Cor.*'s Rescue of Kent." Taylor and Warren 143–51.

Griffith, Elizabeth. *The Morality of Shakespeare's Drama Illustrated.* 2 vols. Dublin, 1777.

Hanmer, Thomas, ed. *The Works of Shakespear.* 6 vols. Oxford, 1744.

Honigmann, E. A. J. "Shakespeare's Revised Plays: *King Lear* and *Othello.*" *Library* 6th ser. 4 (1982): 142–73.

Hull, Thomas. *The Comedy of Errors. With Alterations . . . by Thomas Hull.* London, 1793.

Inchbald, Elizabeth. Introductions. *The British Theatre.* 25 vols. London, 1808.

James, Richard, ed. "The legend and defence of ye Noble knight and Martyr Sir Jhon Oldcastel". Bodleian Library, MS James 34.

Latham, Agnes, ed. *As You Like It.* The Arden Shakespeare. London: Methuen, 1975.

Lennox, Charlotte. *Shakespear Illustrated.* 3 vols. London, 1753–54.

McLeod, Randall. "*Gon.* No more, the text is foolish." Taylor and Warren 153–93.

Mahood, M. M., ed. *The Merchant of Venice.* The New Cambridge Shakespeare. Cambridge: Cambridge UP, 1987.

———, ed. *Twelfth Night.* The New Penguin Shakespeare. Harmondsworth: Penguin, 1968.

Middleton, Thomas. *A Mad World, My Masters.* London, 1608.

Montagu, Elizabeth. *An Essay on the Writings and Genius of Shakespear.* London, 1769.

Munro, John, ed. *The Shakspere Allusion-Book: A Collection of Allusions to Shakspere from 1591 to 1700.* 2 vols. London: Chatto, 1909. Rev. London: Oxford UP, 1932.

O'Connor, John S. "A Qualitative Analysis of Compositors C and D in the Shakespeare First Folio." *Studies in Bibliography* 30 (1977): 57–74.

Perrin, Noel. *Dr. Bowdler's Legacy: A History of Expurgated Books in England and America.* New York: Atheneum, 1969.

Quiller-Couch, A., and J. D. Wilson, eds. *The Comedy of Errors.* The New Shakespeare. Cambridge: Cambridge UP, 1922. 2nd ed., rev., 1962.

Rosen, William, and Barbara Rosen, eds. *The Tragedy of Julius Caesar.* The Signet Classic Shakespeare. New York: Signet-NAL, 1963.

Shakespeare, William. *Comedies, Histories, & Tragedies.* London, 1623.

———. *Comedies, Histories, & Tragedies.* London, 1632.

———. *The Complete Works.* Stanley Wells and Gary Taylor, gen. eds. The Oxford Shakespeare. Oxford: Clarendon, 1986.

———. *The Complete Works: Original-Spelling Edition.* Stanley Wells and Gary Taylor, gen. eds. The Oxford Shakespeare. Oxford: Clarendon, 1986.

Sisson, C. J. *New Readings in Shakespeare.* 2 vols. Cambridge: Cambridge UP, 1956.

Sowernam, Ester. *Ester hath hang'd Haman; or, An Answere To a lewd Pamphlet.* London, 1617.

Spencer, T. J. B., ed. *Hamlet.* The New Penguin Shakespeare. Harmondsworth: Penguin, 1980.

Taylor, Gary. "*Troilus and Cressida:* Bibliography, Performance, and Interpretation". *Shakespeare Studies* 15 (1982): 99–136.

———. "William Shakespeare, Richard James and the House of Cobham." *Review of English Studies* 38 (1987): 334–54.

Taylor, Gary, and Michael Warren, eds. *The Division of the Kingdoms: Shakespeare's Two Versions of* King Lear. Oxford: Clarendon, 1983.

Theobald, Lewis, ed. *The Works of Shakespeare.* 7 vols. London, 1733.

Thompson, Ann, ed. *The Taming of the Shrew.* The New Cambridge Shakespeare. Cambridge: Cambridge UP, 1984.

Tilley, M. P. *A Dictionary of the Proverbs in England in the Sixteenth and Seventeenth Centuries.* Ann Arbor: U of Michigan P, 1950.

Tillyard, E. M. W. *The Elizabethan World Picture.* London: Chatto, 1943.

Walker, Alice. *Textual Problems in the First Folio.* Cambridge: Cambridge UP, 1953.

Walker, Alice, and John Dover Wilson, eds. *Troilus and Cressida.* The New Shakespeare. Cambridge: Cambridge UP, 1957.

———, eds. *Othello.* The New Shakespeare. Cambridge: Cambridge UP, 1957.

Wells, Stanley, ed. *The Comedy of Errors.* The New Penguin Shakespeare. Harmondsworth: Penguin, 1972.

Wells, Stanley, and Gary Taylor et al. *William Shakespeare: A Textual Companion.* Oxford: Clarendon, 1987.

Werstine, Paul. " 'Foul Papers' and 'Prompt-Books': Printer's Copy for Shakespeare's *Comedy of Errors.*" *Studies in Bibliography* 41 (1988): 232–46.

Williamson, Marilyn. *The Patriarchy of Shakespeare's Comedies.* Detroit: Wayne State UP, 1986.

Woodbridge, Linda. *Women and the English Renaissance: Literature and the Nature of Womankind, 1540 –1620.* Urbana: U of Illinois P, 1984.

Wright, Louis B., and Virginia A. LaMar, eds. *The Comedy of Errors.* The Folger Library General Reader's Shakespeare. New York: Washington Square, 1963.

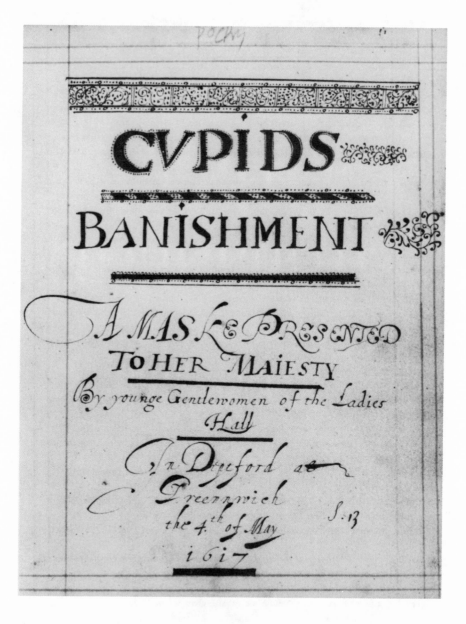

Original title page of *Cupid's Banishment*.
Courtesy of The Pierpont Morgan Library, New York.

Cupid's Banishment: A Masque Presented to Her Majesty by Young Gentlewomen of the Ladies Hall, Deptford, May 4, 1617

Edited by C. E. MCGEE

THE MANUSCRIPT OF Robert White's *Cupid's Banishment,* "lost?" according to the Harbage-Schoenbaum *Annals of English Drama,* has been found. I wish that the rediscovery of the unique manuscript of the masque made for an intriguing case of bibliographical sleuthing, but it does not. Once Hazlitt's error had been spotted (R. S. Turner's books were sold in 1888, not 1881),[1] the trail of the manuscript through Sotheby's catalogues was easily followed: Turner, who purchased the manuscript from William Upcott, an assistant librarian of the London Institution, sold it to James Toovey; Toovey, who sometimes acted as the agent for other collectors, bought this book for himself (fortunately) and passed it on to his son, who sold it to J. Pierpont Morgan in 1901. In his splendid library it remains.[2]

Cupid's Banishment has some significance as a book that it did not have as a performance. It is a small, handsome volume of twenty-two leaves wrapped in a vellum cover. Each page has been carefully ruled, the text beautifully set forth, and the prose passages describing the

227

action, characters, and set laid out in the shape of inverted pyramids. The manuscript may have been prepared as a presentation copy or as the basis for the publication of a handsome souvenir booklet of the occasion. It certainly became a souvenir book: Richard Browne, one of the boy actors, kept the book for his library and passed it on to his daughter, the wife of John Evelyn. As a performance, the masque was both a celebration of the development of the girls of Ladies Hall into graceful and worthy young women and a gift of their affection and reverence to the queen. As a fine book, the masque paid, and pays, fitting tribute to the patronage of Lucy, countess of Bedford, whose support, both moral and financial, made *Cupid's Banishment* a splendid affair.

The Morgan Library book of the masque has more importance still: apart from it, scarcely any other record of *Cupid's Banishment* remains. Henry Colborne and eight assistants earned £7.16 for eight days making ready the hall at Greenwich, but no details of the work are given.[3] Andrew J. Sabol (23) has noted that Charles Coleman and George Lippet, who played Hymen and Bacchus in the masque, were members of the King's Music. Their involvement, understandable given the grand scale of the masque and the slim resources of Ladies Hall, suggests that other "professionals" may have participated, such as dancers of the Inns of Court for those demanding, amusing dances of the "seuerall humers of drunkards" (514), but there is no positive proof of such collaboration. Who was Robert White?—"probably," says Gerald Eades Bentley, "master at the school" (5: 1258).[4] What was Ladies Hall? At this time, according to Peter Clark, there was marked growth in the number of "smart private academies in the metropolitan suburbs" (198), and "it was also thought increasingly important for a gentlewoman to have a modest degree of social education" (199). Still, we lack the solid evidence of Deptford records (most of the earliest of which date from the eighteenth century) to go much beyond Enid Welsford's description of Ladies Hall as "a kind of finishing school for aristocratic girls."[5] Typically, only the notorious John Payne Collier is certain about the reception of the masque at court; he affirms, "It was, of course, very graciously received by her Majesty" (1: 389). Such is the claim; of course, it is open to dispute, for there is no record of the book's publication, no account of the performance, and only one letter in the *Calendar of*

State Papers, Domestic alluding to Anne's activities during her husband's progress to Scotland. On May 9, 1617, George Gerrard wrote Dudley Carleton to say: "The Queen stays at Greenwich, and never missed one Lent sermon" (*C.S.P.D.* 464). Perhaps she was paying her dues for a night of masquing in May.

That masquing, *Cupid's Banishment,* remains in several respects—costuming, set, and theme—quite conventional. Its handling of time is: the masque defines itself as a precious moment in time passing, a moment in which timeless truths are made manifest. The theme of the superiority of chaste love recurs throughout Jonson's masques; in the *Masque of Beauty* (1608), there are Cupids, but "these being chaste Loues, they attend a more diuine beautie, then that of Loues commune parent" (7: 192, lines 340–48n). The characters, their costumes, and their properties are largely derived from Cesare Ripa's *Iconologia* (1611), whose emblem of Chastity standing in triumph over Cupid sums up nicely the action of the first part of the masque.[6] The set is relatively simple in design and operation. Diana's flowery arbor stands on a mountain flanked by groves from which the Driads enter to banish Cupid. The mount opens to loud music early in the show, either to reveal Diana more fully or to allow for the procession of Hymen with the King and Queen of Fortune. None of these features of the masque is new.

Nor is the masque/anti-masque contrast, which White develops thoroughly. The "Ante-maske" (437–38) is not the banishment of Cupid but the boisterous dancing of the children of Bacchus. Less volatile than Cupid, Bacchus accepts the boundaries of propriety fixed by Diana for the occasion and grants Occasion's request for "some quicke inuention to grace these Ladies reuells" (422–23). First a grand Bacchus skips in; hardly an embodiment of grace, he wears flesh-colored buckram and has a gross belly and a red, swollen, pimply face (434–35). He is the presenter of the anti-masque, a series of drunkards whose sports show their "seuerall humers" (514).[7] This anti-masque presents an array of characters, colors, fashions, forms of action in dance, and humors—from that of the cocksure belligerent drinker to that of the self-deprecating melancholy one. In this array, the anti-masque sets off the main masque sharply.

Diana's nymphs, on the other hand, comport themselves with brilliant simplicity. Their costumes embody the harmony of the group in its devotion to chastity. Their dresses are all alike in design and in color—all wear the white and silver of Diana. Her colors are also those of the Queen of Fortune and, for this occasion, those of Hymen, who comes "cladd all in purity / to shew the blessed chaine of amity" (270–71). The color and the brilliancy of the cloth along with the masquers' jewelry give literal sense to the metaphor used both for these nymphs and for the ladies of Anne's court: they are "starrs of women" (600), bright constellations about Anna and Diana. The procession from the mountain to the dance floor and the dances themselves reinforce the impression of harmony created by costume. Led by Fortune, the young ladies "pace with maiesty tawards the presence and after the first strayne of the violins they daunce Anna Regina in letters" (536–38),[8] then "Iacobus Rex," then "Charolus P." Diana describes these as a "whisperinge measure" (521) to "charme harts and eyes with neuer ending pleasure" (522)—the source of which was both the grace of the dance no doubt, and the royal family identified by it, a family in which the ideal of chaste matrimonial love was realized.[9] At least no one would have denied that suggestion on this occasion.

In contrast to this, each drunkard dresses in his own fashion, and the children of Bacchus, as a group, present a kaleidoscope of color: four Bacchanalians in flesh-colored suits with red fiery faces and red pumps; the drunk Fencer in yellow and blue; the mischievous ape in red and white with a hat of yellow and white; the tinker in leather, his face all besmeared. Their number includes one luminary: the tinker's trull wearing "a pare of leather bodies hir neather coate of yellow cotten a blacke hatt with fiue wax lights in it" (509–11). In contrast to the "whisperinge measure" of the main masque, the anti-masque revelry should make "the welkin rore" (449). It is fun, lively, and loud—especially loud when the melancholy drunkard bemoans his faults or when the tinker keeps time by beating a hammer against a kettle. They *are* drunk, after all, and when they are that is how they act and what the audience hears—all of which makes it livelier and louder. In dancing, Diana's nymphs, even while displaying their own grace and worth, coordinate their movements to spell out a lasting source of pleasure beyond themselves. The Bacchanalians, on the other end, enter separately; each one figures forth in dance only the humor which rules him when he is ruled by alcohol. Their pleasure, like the pleasures afforded by alcohol, is not everlasting.

Though conventional in many respects, *Cupid's Banishment* is unusual in blending the customary revels of the school with the lavish display of the court masque. Each year the young gentlewomen celebrate "with due solemnity" (108) the selection of a king and a queen "by Fortunes doome" (58). The solemnity involves a coronation and a ceremony symbolizing a union of chaste hearts. The coronation provides a metaphor by which White controls the meaning of the masque. Cupid expresses his initial excitement in terms of this metaphor when he says, "now Kinges and Queenes doe crowne the houres of time" (127). As Hymen comes to "crowne our sports with sweete delight" (234), so Fortune promises to "create / some vnexpected ioy to crowne thy howers" (261–62). The coronation ceremony prompts Occasion to pray that "Perpetuall ioy and tru delight, / crowne this howre with sweete content" (343–44). Most important, the coronation prompts Cupid to stamp and storm "What a marriage and Cupid no actor in it" (353). In this tantrum Cupid looks quite like the boy Diana calls him, little like the god he styles himself. His insolency leads to another coronation, a mock coronation of Cupid with Actaeon's horns, to symbolize Diana's triumph and Cupid's banishment. The annual Candlemas ritual of Ladies Hall, in other words, provides the form both for the celebration of Diana's ideal of chastity and for the banishment of Cupid.

Whatever the origin of these coronations and revels,[10] they were popular enough to be the butt of one of Jonson's jokes in *Christmas His Show* in 1616 and to provide the basis for the major show for Elizabeth I at Sudeley in 1592. On the latter occasion, a king and queen of the bean were chosen by cutting a cake; whoever got the bean was king, whoever got the pea, queen. But most like the revels of Ladies Hall was the annual Twelfth Night celebration of the Queen of the Bean by Mary Queen of Scots and her ladies. These precedents for the Candlemas revels of Ladies Hall shed some light on *Cupid's Banishment*. Both at Sudeley and at Mary's court, the selection of a queen by Fortune's doom was important because it created a situation in which two ruling monarchs were present at once. After noting that Mary Fleming's comportment as Queen of the Bean in 1564 showed "how fit a match

she would be" (*Cupid's Banishment* may have done the same for some
of its young masquers), Thomas Randolph summed up the significance
of the solemnities by remarking that, "Two such sights in one state, in
so good accord I believe was never seen as to behold two worthy
Queens possess without envy one kingdom both upon a day."[11] At
Sudeley, the shepherds *playing* king and queen turned their meeting
with a real queen into a lovely gift-giving ceremony in which a gift
really produced by real shepherds of England was presented; or, as they
put it:

> ... pardon, dread Sovereigne, poore Shepheards pastimes, and bolde Shep-
> heards presumptions. We call ourselves Kings and Queenes, to make mirth;
> but when we see a King or Queene, we stand amazed.... For our boldenes in
> borrowing their names, and in not seeing your Majesty for our blindnes, we
> offer these Shepheards weeds; which if your Majestye vouchsafe at any time to
> weare, it shall bring to our hearts comfort, and happines to our labours.[12]

Cupid's Banishment capitalizes on this meeting of monarchs as well,
to present what we might call a mirroring of majesties.

To see how this works itself out in the masque, it may help to bear
in mind another oddity of this show which Enid Welsford notes. The
masquers, she observes, "were revealed at the beginning of the proceedings, and remained in full view of the audience until the end of
the masque..." (197). In his first speech, Occasion describes the place
as a circle—the "circle of this sacred spheare" (94) within which Occasion can repose. Anne herself is the "bright spheare of greatness"
(86) whose fair beams define that circle, revive Occasion's muse, banish
all doubt, and protect true meaning. Near the end of the show, Diana
returns to this imagery and addresses the queen as the "bright shininge
lampe that in humane shape / showst heauens perfection" (560–61),
and in the concluding speech Occasion extends the praise by referring
to Anne and her train as a "bright Goddesse" among "starrs of women"
(607, 600). Anne is the cynosure mirrored by Diana, whose silver robe
makes her appear, as White says, "like the Moone amonge the lesser
Starrs" (158–59). Chastity's presence functions in a way similar to
Anne's in defining that special circle for this occasion. As the masque
unfolds, Diana is characterized as the mistress of "sacred sisters" (518)
and the focal point of a "sacred place" (133) profaned by Cupid's blind

intrusion. The circle in which Occasion can repose is that defined by the conjunction of the constellation of Anne and her ladies with that of Diana and hers.[13]

This mirroring of majesties is reinforced by the repetition of certain actions. Queen Anne's "free acceptance" (80) of Occasion's efforts to bring forth the masque stands as a model for Diana's "free acceptance" (245) of Hymen when he arrives for the coronation of Fortune's king and queen. Diana's graciousness then stands as a model for Anne to emulate when she is asked to bring the entire masque to a happy close by accepting the "timely fruits" (559) of the chaste labors of Diana's nymphs. The masque endows Queen Anne with powers of the deities in the masque as well. Bacchus, Fortune, and Hymen all strive to effect leagues between characters, human and divine. Bacchus fails to reconcile Jove's progeny; Fortune and Hymen succeed, and Anne can bring about a similar union of hearts—simply with a smile. As Occasion says:

> ... lett the sylent rhetoricke
> of that Gracious looke
> that workes a league betwixt the state of harts
> voutchsafe to shine vppon our childish sports.
>
> (601–04)

The magnificence and might of the gods and goddesses of the masque reflect the magnificence, power, and beauty of the queen. I have called this a "mirroring of majesties" because visual aspects of Diana's court reappear in Anne's, but Cupid's metaphor—"with maskes and musicke and sweete harmony / each Courte doth *eccho* forth hir melody" (124–25; italics added)—may be more apt. It makes clear, at least, that the wonderful show originates in the real court. "Anna" is origin of Diana.

Lest the pursuit of "more remou'd mysteries" falsify the tone of *Cupid's Banishment,* two other aspects of the show should be noted. First, the masque was supposed to provide an evening of enjoyment, and there *is* lots of fun in it. There is fun in the lively music and in the dancing (the four Bacchanalians with big bellies up front and barrels on their backs must have presented a surprising, amusing illustration of one way to move through space). For those admirable spectators of

Ben Jonson, who "beside inquiring eyes, are vnderstood to bring quick eares, and not those sluggish ones of Porters, and Mechanicks . . . ,"[14] there is levity in the continual punning and wordplay. However disreputable Bacchus and Cupid must be judged, they are also agents and victims of comedy. Cupid creates a fine comic effect when he boasts,

> you know full well that Cupids conquests
> ringe round aboute the world and will do still
> as longe as there are thinges calld women.
>
> (182–84)

In the context of this masque, and its audience, that is asking for trouble. The overall mood is festive—and more festive because it accommodates Bacchus, who is true both to the occasion and to himself in drinking a hearty toast "vnto these Ladies round" (325).

Second, *Cupid's Banishment* is a masque without a traditional "divisoring," unless we take the meeting of the queen and her goddaughters as such. And we might do so, for it is the moment when Anne and the two girls "reveal themselves as persons as well as personages" (Sabol 11). They are Diana's nymphs and Anne's goddaughters; they present fruits of their "chast labors" (559) because of their special ties to the queen, and their gifts remind all of the real identity of the recipient—a needlepoint acorn and a needlepoint rosemary, an *A* and an *R*, for Anna Regina—a great lady who likes needlepoint. In this culminating bit of business, *Cupid's Banishment* appeals to the human side of the queen and highlights the special, personal ties between her and these young gentlewomen of Ladies Hall.

The personal dimension adds a different kind of delight.[15] Queen Anne may have felt it as she watched her goddaughters approach. Other ladies, and men, may well have felt it as they watched daughters or nieces dance. They would not likely have expressed it as directly as Venus did in *Christmas His Show* (1616), but her excitement and theirs and the cause of that excitement were the same. As Venus said, "Yes forsooth, I can sit any where, so I may see my Cupid act; hee is a pretty Child. . . ."[16] This delight, arising from personal ties with those in the masque, provided some pleasure too—I imagine. In the personal note, *Cupid's Banishment* was most like early Jonsonian wedding masques which expressed "a most reall affection in the personaters,"[17] most like the civic shows which share with this masque a strong sense and pride of place, most like the manor house shows prepared for Queen Elizabeth I by Burleigh or the Norrisses or Lord Montague—shows in which the conventional love and dread of the sovereign were informed by real affection and real fear.

A Note on the Text

The Morgan Library manuscript of *Cupid's Banishment* is unique. Enclosed in a plain vellum wrapper, the manuscript consists of twenty-two leaves of paper 200 mm × 160 mm. The watermark, two columns 49 mm high and 25 mm across (resembling most closely No. 525 in W. A. Churchill's *Watermarks in Paper* [Amsterdam: Menno Hertzberger, 1935]), appears on folios 1, 3, 9, 13, and 17. The person who assembled the book appears to have first cut full sheets of paper in half, then sewn each half-sheet in separately. As a result, the first two quires have watermarks, the second do not. The text is neatly framed and the margins defined by lines in ink, now brown ink. These make columns 5 mm wide above, below, and to the right of the text; to the left an 18 mm column sets off the speech prefixes. Beyond the columns, there are approximately 10 mm to the outside edges of each page.

This edition reproduces the spellings, lineation, punctuation, and format of the original manuscript. Only the page of music, a facsimile of which has been published in Verlyn Klinkenborg, Herbert Cahoon, and Charles Ryskamp, *British Literary Manuscripts: Series I from 800 to 1800* (New York: The Pierpont Morgan Library and Dover Publications, 1981), plate 32, has been presented in a modern format.[18] In the original, the bass has been squeezed into two lines at the bottom of f. 18v. Preliminary information, added after the occasion of the masque, has been omitted: (1) the title on the outside of the cover, "Cupid's Banishment. / a Masque. / 1617—"; (2) the Morgan Library bookplate on the verso of the leaf to which the vellum cover is attached; (3) the Morgan Library catalogue description of the manuscript and the query "?John Evelyn's autog. on orig. cover?" on the recto of the first folio; (4) the following in black ink on f. 2r: "William Upcott / London. / 1817. Purchased from the library of the learned and amiable John Ev-

elyn of Wotton, *whose writing* is on the outside cover—also on the
reverse of this leaf—W.U.—"; and (5) on the verso of that folio, in faded
brownish ink: "12 yeare old Richard Browne 1617 / Acted herein before
Queene Anne." followed by a note in pencil: "(this refers to Sir Richard
Browne 1605–1683 of Sayes Court, Deptford. father-in-law of John Evelyn)". The title appears on f. 3r; different styles of lettering and several
fancy ways of underscoring are used for various parts of the title. Some
vignetting follows the title on f. 3r and the author's name of f. 7r. Folio 3v is blank but for "MA 1296" in pencil in the lower right corner.
Folios 1v, 4r, 4v, 5v, and 7v are blank.

The scribe has used abbreviations occasionally; these have been extended and appear in italics. Emendations appear in square brackets.

Notes

I am grateful to Elise Jorgens and Walter Davis for the opportunity to present an earlier
version of this work at the Sixteenth International Congress on Medieval Studies, Ka-
lamazoo, 1981. Thanks are also due to Len Bick, John Meagher, Andrew Sabol, Laura
Moyer, Rita Raccanelli, and the staff of the Morgan Library for contributions of various
kinds to this published version.

1. See Hazlitt 55.

2. MS. MA 1296, published with the permission of The Pierpont Morgan Library, New
York. The manuscript was still in the keeping of William Upcott when John Nichols
prepared an edition of the masque; see Nichols 3: 283–96. He silently altered the format,
normalized the spelling, added capitals to the first lines of the verse, and punctuated the
entire work.

3. See Wilson, *MSC* 6: 114 (Chamber Accounts, Apparellings); *MSC* 10: 27.

4. Perhaps the author of the masque was the Robert White who received his BA from
Merton College, Oxford, in 1608; see Foster 3: 1616. White's connection with Merton
College may have prompted Richard Browne to study there too.

5. See Welsford 197, and below "Commentary" line 1n. John Evelyn's sketch map of
Deptford in 1623 does not show Ladies Hall. Nathan Dews speculates that the school
was "probably in the rural thoroughfare leading from the Globe Inn to the Water-gate"
(177).

6. See Ripa 74. Ben Jonson's Cynthia sums up the central opposition of this masque
in another show, also performed by a group of children, *Cynthia's Revels* (1600): "Such
is our chastitie: which safely scornes / (Not *Loue,* for who more feruently doth loue /
Immortal honour, and diuine renowne? / But) giddie CVPID, VENVS franticke sonne"
(Jonson 4: 162–63).

7. *Love's Triumph through Callipolis* (1630) includes a similar anti-masque, in which the "confus'd affections" of depraved love are danced and banished from the royal presence in order to make way for a procession of perfect lovers; see Jonson 7: 736.

8. As the performance of a similar dance in the *Masque of Beauty* at the Sixteenth International Congress of Medieval Studies demonstrated, the easy alternation of quick, intricate movements and moments of stillness when the letters take shape is quite engaging. For the observer in a position to see the letters formed, there are additional pleasures: the pleasure of guessing what letter(s) will follow and what word they will spell—and, of course, the pleasure of guessing correctly.

9. The motif is central to Caroline mythology; see Orgel and Strong 1: 58.

10. See Strutt 343–44.

11. See Historical Manuscripts Commission 11–12; the account of the festivities appears in a letter, dated January 15, 1564, from Randolph to Lord Robert Dudley.

12. See Nichols (3: 143), who transcribes the anonymous *Speeches Delivered to her Maiestie this last Progress* (Oxford, 1592); *STC* 7600.

13. See Orgel and Strong, who describe the climax of *Love's Triumph through Callipolis* (1630) in similar terms: "Venus and Henrietta Maria are thus placed at the apex of opposite perspectives, like mirror images; the earthly Queen of Love reflects the divine" (1: 56).

14. See Jonson 7: 287; Jonson makes the remark when describing a change of scene early in *The Masque of Queens* (1609).

15. The eyewitness account of *Tethys Festival* (1610), that by Mr. John Finett in a letter to Mr. Trumbull, suggests that simply the youth of the participants could enhance the appeal of the masque: ". . . and the little Ladies performed their dance to the amazement of all beholders, considering the tenderness of their years, and the many intricate changes of the dance; which was so disposed, that which way soever the changes went, the little Duke was still found to be in the midst of these little dancers" (Nichols 2: 360).

16. See Jonson 7: 441.

17. See Jonson 7: 249; the phrase is taken from Jonson's introduction to "The Haddington Masque" (1608).

18. See Sabol 666–67 for a modern setting of the music.

Works Cited

Bentley, Gerald Eades. *The Jacobean and Caroline Stage.* 7 vols. Oxford: Clarendon, 1959, 1968.

A Book of Masques; In Honour of Allardyce Nicoll. Ed. T. J. B. Spencer and Stanley Wells. London: Cambridge UP, 1967.

Calendar of State Papers, Domestic Series. Vol. 9. *James I, 1611–1618.* Ed. M. A. E. Green. 1858. Nendeln: Kraus, 1967.

Clark, Peter. *English Provincial Society from the Reformation to the Revolution: Religion, Politics and Society in Kent, 1500–1640.* Hassocks, Sussex: Harvester, 1977.

Collier, John Payne. *The History of English Dramatic Poetry to the Time of Shakespeare, and Annals of the Stage to the Restoration.* 2nd ed. London: George Bell, 1879.

Dews, Nathan. *The History of Deptford.* 1884. London: Conway Maritime Press, 1971.

Foster, Joseph. *Alumni Oxonienses . . . 1500 –1714.* Oxford: Parker, 1892.

Harbage, Alfred. *Annals of English Drama, 975 –1700.* Rev. S. Schoenbaum. London: Methuen, 1964.

Hazlitt, W. Carew, ed. *A Manual for the Collector and Amateur of Old English Plays.* London: Pickering & Chatto, 1892.

Historical Manuscripts Commission. *Report on the Pepys MSS. Preserved by Magdalene College, Cambridge.* Ed. M. E. K. Purnell. London: HMSO, 1911.

Jonson, Ben. *Ben Jonson.* Ed. C. H. Herford, Percy Simpson, and Evelyn Simpson. 11 vols. Oxford: Clarendon, 1925 –52.

Nichols, John. *The Progresses, Processions, and Magnificent Festivities, of King James the First. . . .* 4 vols. London: J. B. Nichols, 1828.

Nicoll, Allardyce. *Stuart Masques and the Renaissance Stage.* 1938. New York: Blom, 1963.

Orgel, Stephen, and Roy Strong. *Inigo Jones: The Theatre of the Stuart Court.* 2 vols. London: Sotheby, 1973.

Ripa, Cesare. *Iconologia, Padua, 1611.* New York: Garland, 1976.

Sabol, Andrew J. *Four Hundred Songs and Dances from the Stuart Masque.* 1978. Hanover, N.H.: UP of New England, 1982.

Strutt, Joseph. *The Sports and Pastimes of the People of England.* London: Haddon, 1838.

Tilley, Morris Palmer. *A Dictionary of the Proverbs in England in the Sixteenth and Seventeenth Centuries.* Ann Arbor: U of Michigan P, 1950.

Welsford, Enid. *The Court Masque.* 1927. New York: Russell, 1962.

Whitney, Geoffrey. *A Choice of Emblemes, 1586.* Ed. John Horden. Menston: Scolar, 1969.

Wienpahl, Robert W. *Music at the Inns of Court.* Ann Arbor: UMI, 1979.

Wilson, F. P. "Dramatic Records in the Declared Accounts of the Office of Works, 1560 –1640." *Malone Society Collections* 10 (1977).

———. "Dramatic Records in the Declared Accounts of the Treasurer of the Chamber, 1558 –1642." *Malone Society Collections* 6 (1962): 1 –175.

CVPIDS   [3r]
BANISHMENT

A MASKE PRESENTED
TO HER MAIESTY
By younge Gentlewomen of the Ladies
Hall
In Deptford at
Greennwich
The 4th of May
1617

A note of all the Maskers   [5r]
names;

M^ris: Ann Watkins acted
    Fortune :
M^ris: Ann Chalenor :
M^ris: Ann Libb :
M^ris: Alice Watkins :
M^ris: Francis Graunt :
M^ris: Katherine Godschalk :
M^ris: Katherine Parkinson :
M^ris: Mary Draper :
M^ris: Elizabeth Madison :
M^ris: Elizabeth Cramfield :
M^ris: Elizabeth Bolton :
M^ris: Mary Chambre :
M^ris: Clasie Page :
M^ris: Lucie Mane :
M^ris: Ann Sandeland :
    The Wood Nimphs :
M^ris: Iacamote Brussels :
M^ris: Mary Als :
M^ris: Ann Tindall :
M^ris: Oungelo :

M^ris: Mary Cramfield :
M^ris: Elizabeth Ieffs :
M^ris: Susan Haruey :   5
M^ris: Lea Wadson:

Mr. Henry Iennor acted
    the Kinge :
M^ris: Debora Draper the   10
    Queene :
M^r: R W acted Ocasion :
John Burresan acted Cupid
M^r: Rich: Browne acted Di-
    ana :   15
M^r: Charles Coleman acted
    Hymen :
George Lippett Bacchus :
Paule Harbart acted Mer-
    cury   20

TO : THE : HONORABLE :   [6r]
AND : RIGHT : WORTHY : LADY   25
Lucy Countesse of
Bedforde:

MADAME:

   In regarde of the honorable furtherance and noble encour-
agement your La: gaue vs in presentinge our maske to hir   30
Magesty, I am bound yf our module of labor may attayne
to that happines of desarte to commit this shew to your worthy protection; deeming none more worthy then your Honor
to bee Patronesse thereof, for worth is best discerned by the
worthy, base and deiected mindes are destitute of that   35
tru influence which should [give] vigor to virtue! It is not from affected singularity, or from any conceite of worth in my labors, that they durst aspire soe hye but a confident opinion
of your fauorable acceptation, and an absolute resolution
of your milde and gracious censure, I confesse a lower Patro-   40
nage would haue serued a hyer worke, but duty herein onely
excuses mee from presumption I thought it iniustice to deuote
the fruits which your honor first sowed, to any but your selfe,
then from your honerable acceptance lett this draw a perpetuall Priuiledge, that it may still flowrish in the fayre   [6v]
Summer of your gentle fauor, and triumph in despight of
enuies raginge winter; butt lett the enuious spitt theire ve-
neme, and tipp theire toungues with gall; it matters not: this
is my comforte; enuie barketh onely at the starrs; and spight spurnes
at that shee cannot reach. I heare some curious Criticke allready,   50
whose hungry eares feedes still on other mens prouision, and perchance his teeth on other mens tables, hath spyed an error and as his
perspectiue informes him, a grosse one too! Hee abruptly demaunds
what should Hymen haue to doe, where Diana is? or why there
should bee a marriage solemnised by the Queene of Chastity; yf   55
his refined witt would bee confind with reason, I can awnsweare
him; but I thinke hardly satisfie him; the ground of our plott is,
choosinge of a Kinge and Queene by Fortunes doome; which is a
sporte our litle Ladies vse on Candlemasse night; againe it was

no marriage, but a forme of vnitinge chast harts, to shew a defi-   60
ance to Cupid, and his contracts, and that there could bee a chast
combination without his powers. yf this will not satisfie; I referre
him to the speeches; and thus Madame, holding you no longer with
preambles, and superfluous apologies, especialy to them that right-
ly vnderstand mee: I rest.   65

           Your Honours humbly   [7r]
              deuoted.

           Robert White

      OCCASION in a rich garment embrodered with   [8r]
        siluer a crimson mantle and a shorte cloake   70
          of rich tinsie with a white wand to signi-
           fy hir hast with a longe locke be-
            fore and bald behind alluding
             to the difficulty of recalling
              hir yf shee bee once past,   75
               hir speech to the
                Queene.

Occasion: Gratious and great Souueraignesse
           yf confidence and royall resolution
           of female worth, and free acceptance   80
           of noble fauor, had not armd my breast
           with that stronge temper of resisting proofe
           against Enuies hissinge adders
           Tymes handmayd had bene dumbe
           despayre and feare had ouercome our weake designes 85
           but bright spheare of greatness thy faire beames
           which shoote with splendor from thy maiesty
           reuiues our faintinge Muse with sweete reflection,
           and cheares our droopinge spirritts with vnacquainted [8v]
            light

thy presence frees each thinge that liues in doubt   90
no harmeles thought now feares the banefull stinge
of fell detraction nor here no carpinge god
bereaues tru meaninge of hir worth,
within the circle of this sacred spheare
Occasion doth repose,   95
and to this bright audience shewes
shee was addrest with full intention
longe before this to offer vpp times sacrifice
fleetinge houres to this faire company
but worthier obiects then they could produce   100
diuerted theire slight purposes
and yet Occasion cannot shake them off
againe shee is summond by that louely crew
of Ladies Hall an Academy
where modesty doth onely sway as gouernesse   105
these pretty Nimphs deuoted to your excellence
present a sport which they yearely celebrate
on Candlemasse night with due solemnity
and with greate applause
they haue a Kinge and Queene   110
of Fortunes choice   [9r]
these bee the reuells they intend
which yf your grace will deigne to see the ende
Occasion thinkes hirselfe most fortunate

       Occasion retiringe from the presence,   115
          Cupid meetes hir and snatches
             hir by the Locke.

Cupid: Come, come Occasion cease thy old complaints
        referre thy wrongs vnto an equall iudge
        summon younge spirritts to a iubile   120
        inuite fresch youth to some amorous sceane
        banish base dullnes for this night
        Reuells must bee the center of delight
        with maskes and musicke and sweete harmony

each Courte doth eccho forth hir melody   125
with Hymeneall ioyes and loue deuine
now Kinges and Queenes doe crowne the houres of time
and shall wee then bee sylent where such excellence
of worth and bewty will giue audience
and where such a Chorus   130
of louely Nimphs as these shall stand before vs.   [9v]

Occasion: Peace foolish boy thy blind intrusion
will not bee here admitted this sacred place
is only dedicated to chast Diana and hir louely Nymphs
no wanton subiect or immodest straine   135
can enter in for here they doe proclame
Chastety theire Queene and to hir they sacrifice
pure thoughts with lust abhorringe eyes
this is no tyme nor place for Cupids wiles
thy plotts and subtle shifts are all delusions   140
to mocke mortality and idle fict[i]ons
forgd by some Poets fruiteles brayne

Occasi-   Away lett goe thou dost depraue my houres
on shakes   With lust and rape and fowle incestuous acts
him off   vnder pretence of loue, begone   145
Ile lend thee not a minuite to produce
thy wanton subiect and laciuious Muse
see thou hast incenst the Goddesse
and Fortune with lowringe bewty frownes.

Diana in hir Arbor attird all in white to shew the   [10r]
   purity of Chastity richly deckt with iewells
   hir Kirtle embrodered with gold, hir mantle
of siluer tinsie a very rich girdle aboute calld
    the Zone of chastity to shew hir defiance
    to Cupid and to signify theire chast mee-   155
    tinge with a siluer wand in hir hand hir
   arbor adornd with flowers encompased
     round with hir Nymphs like the
      Moone amonge the lesser Starrs,

shee shewes hirselfe, whilst   160
the Mount opens, the
lowde musicke playes
shee speaks to
Cupid:

Diana: Cupid know thy daringe presence doth offend vs   165
and thy presumption hath incurd our anger
wee are displeasd and doe much distast
thy rash accesse without our high command
blind archer know wee are not subiect to thy tiranny
thy darts and chaines are of noe power with vs   170
nor are wee in the compasse of thy bow   [10v]
wee are free from thy bewitching philters
thy charmes and thy alluringe baytes
our vowes are heare entire
and are not subiect to thy lustfull fire   175

Cupid[:] What are wee goddes and beare no greater sway
is Cupid dead and Venus quite forgott
are all my dartes growne dull
my bow so weake that none will stand in awe
but contradict what wee command   180
why dull Tyme and you Lady Chastity
you know full well that Cupids conquests
ringe round aboute the world and will do still
as longe as there are thinges calld women.

Occasion: Boye leaue your waggish witt   185
putt vp your arowes in your quiuer
and bee gone
Fortune is the subiect of our sceane
and chast Diana the mistresse of the place
to which fond fancy may not haue accesse.   190

Cupid: And will all these Ladies banish Cupid thus   [11r]
is there neuer a tender hart that will relent
to thus disgrace me doe you all consent.

Diana: Cease fond idall thy presence heare is tedious
      steale to some amorous court and tutor   195
      wanton Ladies how to wo
      and ketch there seruants with a nimble glance
      inuent some anticke fashion how to please
      his M^{ris}: eye with vowes and endles protestations
      make him sweare hee loues hir dearely   200
      though indeede affecteth nothing lesse
      these are your practises and cheife exploits
      worthy atcheiuments for a God
      hence fond Boy
      thy very breath corrupts a Virgins vow.   205

Cupid: By all the powers that Cupid can command
      I'le vexe you women yf I ketch you
      in my pittfall:

Diana: Occasion post away and shake this copssmate of
      allot him not a minute space to breath here longer.   210

                Occasion hasteth away and   [11v]
                    Cupid after hir:

Cupid: Occasion sweete Occasion stay
      grant me but a paire of minnutes
      to rayle with bitter exclamations   215
      against these milkesopp Ladies

Diana: Mercury with wings of execution
      finish our command
      take thy Caduseus in thy hand
      and summon Hymen to our festiuall   220
      but not his fires; dispatch;

Mercury: With swiftest expedicion, I am gone;

      Two of Dianas Nimphes from the mounte singe
        call for Hymen; Hymen enters singinge

Occasion and Mercury before him, the   225
Kinge and Queene after him, his
followers attendinge him, with
lutes and theorboes and ex-
celent voices; the Musi-
cions all in greene   [12r]
taffaty Robes;
the Songe.

Hymen; Hymen; sacred Hymen; that our harts vnite,
Come and crowne our sports with sweete delight,
Banish Cupid that proud Boy,   235
That filles our harts with deepe annoy,
Lett vs chase him forth our gentle harts,
His deadly bow and cruell Darts.

Hymen: No spightfull God shall here remaine,
To crosse our sports and breed our paine;   240

The Song beeing
ended Diana
speakes.

Diana: Wee thanke you all with wellcome to our Court
our free acceptance shall declare our harts affection   245
and our ioy shall testify your presence acceptable
see Fortune congratulates your comming
and smiles wth cheerfull countenance at your approch.

Fortune at the bottome of the mount in a   [12v]
rich mantle wrought with changeable   250
coulors to expresse hir incertainty
with a vaile before hir face
to shew hir blindnes and in-
aequality in disposinge of
hir guifts, hir wheele   255
in hir hand to sig-
nify hir momen-
tary fauor.

Fortune: We are engagd to Tyme for this occasion
          that meetes our wishes with such good successe   260
          for this great curtesie Ile create
          some vnexpected ioy to crowne thy howers
          thy minnutes Ile soe turne vppon this wheele of mine
          that men hereafter shall call thee happy Tyme.
          Hymen Mercury how wellcome you are hither   265
          wee can no more expresse then wee allready haue.

Hymen: Chast and glorious Goddesses
          with chastest resolution wee are come,
          to further your intentions   [13r]
          cladd all in purity   270
          to shew the blessed chaine of amity.

          Enter Bacchus in a Chariatt hunge all with
          vine leaues and grapes draune by a Goate
          ridinge on a barrell with a truncheon in one
            hand and a bole of wine in the other; 2   275
            boyes Bacchanalians with wreaths of iuy
            red fiery faces and swelld cheekes
            wth torches in one hand and boles
            of wine in another; Cupid w^th
            him disarmed by Iupiter, Bac-   280
            chus comes to reconcile the
             Goddesse Cinthia and
             the God of loue and
             to make a league
             with the house   285
             of Ioue.

Occasion: What haue wee here more disturbers yet.

Bacchus: Come boy weele make you all freinds   [13v]
          with a bole of nectar crownd to the brim

Cupid: By Venus apron strings Bacchus meethinkes   290
          I am nobody now I am disarmd, I haue a spight

to these squeamish Ladies yet for disgracinge mee,
would I had my arrowes here;

Bacchus: Come you'le neuer leaue your wranglinge
          I thinke on my concience some Lawier was thy   295
          father and some scoldinge butterwife thy
          Mother thou wouldst sett all the world
          together by the eares yf thou hadst thy will
          come boy submit your selfe;

Cupid: Bacchus I am to stoute to yeeld bee thou   300
          my orator good Lyeus and I'le walke
          by like a sheepebiter ô here is fine
          sport for these scornefull Ladies
          they will laugh mee out of my skinn.

Bacchus: Come take courage boy and Ile repayre vnto the   [14r]
              throne,
          from the spatious Court of greate commandinge Ioue, wee
              here
          arriue, the anger to appease, of these incenced Goddesses
          against this little boy.

Cupid: You are to familiar Bacchus.

Bacchus: Come you are without your weapens now boy,   310
          my Father Iupiter who may command,
          intreats a league amongst his progeny,
          a truce a truce my litle rouer,
          you know you are confind to vse no trechery,
          against Cinthia and hir trayne,   315
          come letts conclude with loue,
          and drinke carowses to the house of Ioue.

Diana: Well on these conditions wee admitt you both,
          so you conteine with in the bounds of modesty,
          and not disturbe our sports with rude disorder.   320

Bacchus: Wee do obey
         yet graunt chast Cinthia that Bacchus may,
         in a castalean bole full fraught with wine,   [14v]
         squeesd in aboundance from the swellinge vine,
         carouse a health vnto these Ladies round.   325

Diana: Wee are content now Fortune it remaynes,
         that you do perfitt whats by vs begunn,
         descend blind Goddesse and with some worthy fauour,
         drawne from the aboundance of thy large lottery,
         grace the happy league of this thy choice.   330

     Fortune and Hymen to the Coronation, the Kinge and
      the Queene seated at the foote of the Mount vnder
       Fortune, the Kinge on hir right hand and the
        Queene on hir left; the Queene attird all in
         siluer tinsie showinge that shee was one   335
          of Dianas traine and that there reuells
          did wholly tend to Chastity bee-
           inge a sporte the Goddesse and
            hir Nymphs did vse in bow-
            ers and retird places wthout   340
            any preiudice to virginity or
            scandall to any entire vow.

Occasion: Perpetuall ioy and tru delight,   [15r]
         crowne this howre with sweete content:

         Cupid in a white loose garment girt close   345
          to him with a garlande of white
           and red roses disarmd of his
            bow and darts falls into
           a passion be[c]ause hee was
            excluded from theire   350
             Reuells hee stamps
             and stormes.

Cupid: What a marriage and Cupid no actor in it,
         what humane power can brooke this shame,
         shall wee that bee immortall then containe,   355
         and suffer this disgrace,
         wee that made Apollo rage with loue,
         Mars madd with dotinge fancy
         and great Ioue,
         a captiue with the conquering dart of loue,   360
         are wee now confind disarmd and scornd,
         with vildest imputations,
         yee coy dames, I'le make you raue   [15v]
         like belldames, teare your hayre,
         and curse your coynes,   365
         your squeamish affected nicenes,
         shall feele the fury of my vengeance;
         I'le torment you all.

                  The Goddesse beinge moued
                     with his insolency, cal-   370
                        eth to hir Wood-
                        nimphs to as[-]
                           sist hir.

Diana: Insolence thou dost profane our presence,
         thou shalt find and see,   375
         lust can neuer conquer Chastity,
         come all yee that loue chast Vesta,
         and chase this Bedlame forth.

         Enter the Driades or eight Wood nymphs rush out of a
         groue adioyninge to the Mount, 4, of one side and 4 of   380
         another with darts in theire hands to shew they had a
         dart could conquer Cupid, attird all in greene gar-   [16r]
         ments the vpper part close to theire bodies the lower
         full and loose with siluer and carnation lace from the
         brest to the foote theire armes halfe naked with brace-   385
         letts of berries aboute them, theire heads garlands with

greate variety of flowers theire hayre dissheueled hang-
inge careles aboute their shoulders bare with puffs of tif-
fany round aboute, greene pumps and gloues, after the mu-
sick playd ouer the first strayne they fall into their daunce
they enuiron Cupid in a figure and putt Ac-
teons head vppon him, they fall of threa-
tninge him with their darts when
hee offers to resist after many pret-
ty figures they chase him   395
forth into the wods
by violence and
banish him
that pre-
sence.   400

The Nymphs song in ioy
Cupid is gone.

Harke harke how Philomell   [16v]
Whose notes no ayre can paralell
Marke marke hir melody   405
Shee descants still on chastity
The diapason of hir song is Cupid's gone
Hee is gone, hee is gone, is quite exild
Venus bratt peeuish ape fancies child
Lett him goe with his Quiuer and his bow   410
Lett him know wee are not subiect to him though
Hee can command yet wee are free
From Cupid and his tiranny.

After this Occasion speakes to Bacchus
awakens him with hir wand   415
enioynes him to commit
no disordor.

Occasion: Bacchus looke to it see you do containe
least you bee branded with Acteons shame

come leaue your roringe this iouiall vaine   420
delights not Ladies mee thinkes your vine
should yeeld some quicke inuention to grace these La- [17r]
dies reuells, come bee not dull nor braynsicke now
rouse vpp thy spirites.

Bacchus: By Ioue Occasion I am horrible sleepy I could sleepe 425
           now with Endimion and snore with Epiminedes but at
           thy intreaty I will awake and show thee some of my
           delightfull sports come bullies my braue Bacchanali-
           ans make the wellkin rore with some reelinge vayne.

                 Enter a grand Bacchus skippinge in   430
                 with a belly as bigg as a kinderkin
                 all in flesh coulord buckram w^th
                 a wreath of vine leaues aboute
                 his head a red swolne face
                 full of pimples wth a base   435
                 lute in his hand singing
                 and describing the Ante-
                 maske all of Bacchus chil-
                 dren he describs them par-
                 ticular as they come   440
                 forth.

                 The Songe.   [17v]
        1   Bacchus at thy call
            they here come marchinge roundly
            that will not flinch at all   445
            but take their liquor soundly

            theyle do their parts, theyle drinke whole quarts
            a pinte with them is but a swallow
            they'll nere giue ore, till the welkin rore
            the house runn round and the sky looke yellow   450

4 Bacchanalians
2 Bacchus children come
    and at theire backes they haue barrells
    with bellies like a tunn
    muldsacke shall end all quarrells   455

The drunk- Next Swash appeares who stormes and sweares
Fencer.   yf that they bringe not better wine
    the potts hele maule, against the wall
    hele beate my host and breake his signe.
          The ape drunkard   460
3 Another drunkard skipps
    whose head is like a feather
    hele show as many trickes   [18r]
    as your ape baboone together

The drunk- The fidlers croud now squeakes aloud   465
Fidler.   his fudlinge stringes begin to trole
    hee loues a wake and a weddinge cake
    a bridhouse and a braue maypole.
          The drunk Tinker.
4 Next the roringe tinker   470
    as furious as a dragon
    hee sweares hele bee no flincher
    his carows is but a flagon.
    hee loues his punke but when hee is drunke
    his muddy braynes well muld with licquor   475
    hee then will rore and call hir whore
    and out of doores hee sweares heele kicke hir.
          The weepinge Drunk:
5 Armed all with claret
    the weepinge drunkard next   480
    hee is very sorry [for it]
    his soule is sore perplext
    these are the crew of drunkards trew
    that do belong to Bacchus court

soone see you shall theire humors all
yf you marke awhile theire drunken sporte

Bac-chus at thy call they here come march-ing round-ly that

will not flinch at _____ all but _take _their liq - - -uor sound-ly

they'le doe thayr parts thay'le drink _____ whole

quarts _____ a pint _____ with them is but a swal-low

thay'le ne're give o'er till the _____ wel - -kin roare

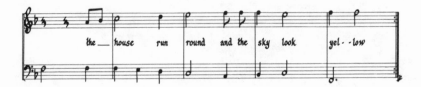

the _house run round and the sky look yel - -low

This songe beeing ended the Bacchanalians begin to   [19r]
   daunce
4 of them in flesh coulord buckram wreaths of iuy on
their heads and girdles with twists of iuy, barrells at   495
their backs with red fiery faces longe hayre great bellies
and red pumps. the Fencer with a sword and dagger
great slopps garded with yellow and blew cotten, a roring
band and a broad brimd hat with a low crowne buttend vp
in the fashion, the Ape drunkard in red and white cot-   500
ten his breeches one side a slopp the other side a trunke
with stockings of the same his short cloake reaching
halfe way to his backe his hatt garded with yellow
and white cotten. the Fidler with a blew coate with han-
ging sleeues on the left sleeue a ratt for his cullisan playing on a fidle with a great nosegay in his hatt. the Tinker in a leather pelt with a hammer and an old kettle
keeping time with the musicke his face all besmeard
his trull with a pare of leather bodies hir neather
coate of yellow cotten a blacke hatt with fiue wax   510
lights in it a posie pind to hir breast, the weeping
drunkard in blew and yellow cotten his breaches close
dauncinge a malancholy measure and bemoaning his
faults they shew the seuerall humers of drunkards
with many pretty figures befitting that vayne.   [19v]

The daunce beeing ended
Diana speakes

Diana: So now let these sacred sisters
       with their chast sceane begin
       aduance this howre with some sweete passage   520
       and with some whisperinge measure
       charme harts and eyes with neuer ending pleasure.

Twelue Nymphs descend from the mount attird all in white
tinsie to shew their defiance to Cupid and to signify their
chast meeting with rich mantles six of watched the   525
   other

six of crimson their hayre disheueld their breasts naked
with rich iewels and pearles necklaces on their heads coro-
netts of artificiall flowers with a puff of tinsie risinge
in the midst white pumps and roses and white gloues.
Fortune descends with them to daunce to grace this hir   530
choice and to signify shee is pleased with this chast fes-
tiuall shee is attird in rich garments of diuers coulers
a wastcote enbroadered with gold many curious flowers
wrought with siluer and silke with pleasant coulors a   [20r]
    rich
mantle a vaile before hir face hir wheele in hir hand   535
they pace with maiesty tawards the presence and af[-]
ter the first strayne of the violins they daunce Anna
Regina in letters their 2 maskinge daunce Iacobus Rex
theire departinge daunce is Charolus P with many excel-
ent figures fallinge off. by Mr Ounslo tutor to the La: hall.
haueing ended their daunces and fallinge of halfe of one
side and halfe of another Diana descends from the
        mount with 2 of the Queenes godaughters and
                presents them to hir maiesty
                    with this speech.   545

Diana: From our chast throne wee condiscende
         to greete your maiesty with this my trayne
         my Nymphs retird from the leauy wods
         haue left theire wonted habitts all of greene
         their sportiue quiuers and their huntinge weeds   550
         their loose girt garments which they vse to weare
         the hills and dales the brookes and fountanes cleare
         deckt all in virgins hue they come to see
         faire Albions Queene enthrond in Maiesty.
         and see two of all the rest do seeme to show   [20v]
         a deuine duty which they owe
         vnto your Highnes grace
         who to intimate their loues aboue the rest
         presente the timely fruits of their chast labors

of which bright shininge lampe that in humane shape
showst heauens perfection voutchsafe to accept
and Phebe with hir trayne
deuoted to your grace foreuer will remayne.

This speech beeing ended the Goddaughters
    presenting theire needleworke gifts   565
      one an Acorne the other rose-
        mary beginninge with the
          first letters of the
        Queenes name they re-
        tire all 2 by 2 ma-   570
        kinge their honors
        they ascend the
        mount with
        this songe.

The last   Thus Cinthias triumphs begin to cease   [21r]
Songe.   With true loue, and ioyfull peace
          Yf worth and honor haue content
          Times fleeting minutes are well spent
          And wee shall thinke what here wee do bestow
          Are things of duty which wee still do owe   580
          but cruell Time doth slide so swift away
          that wee must home vnto our shady bowers
          where wee will euer for your highnes pray
          that you in ioy may spend your happy howers

        The songe beeing ended Occasion   585
          speakes to the Queene.

Occasion.   Bright Pallas and royall M^{ris}: of our muse
          Occasion hath aduenturd to bestow
          some nimble minutes which yf they haue runn
          soe happily that they haue wonne   590
          the Olimpian prise your gracious fauor
          wee haue atcheiud a peece of worke

far richer then the golden fleece
which Iason stroue to purchase
but yf vaine oportunity   595
hath ought prophand your reuerent dignity
with tedious tyme and hath vtterd ought   [21v]
in preiudice of your most noble sex
pardon you glorious Company
you starrs of women   600
and lett the sylent rhetoricke
of that Gracious looke
that workes a league betwixt the state of harts
voutchsafe to shine vppon our childish sports
wee professe [our] stage no Helicon   605
our Muse is homespunn our action is our owne
then bright Goddesse with one sweete smile
grace all
our Nymphs Occasion and our
      LADIES : HALL :   610

         : FINIS :

Commentary

1 the Maskers> As one might expect, few records of these girls remain. Even when the *DNB* notes that a gentleman with the same surname as one of the girls had daughters, it rarely names them. Some possible kin have been suggested in the notes that follow; these possibilities would indicate that Ladies Hall was a school attended by the daughters of learned officers of the court.

5 Susan Haruey> Possibly the offspring of William Harvey, MD, the king's physician from 1610 on.
Ann Chalenor> Possibly the offspring of Sir Thomas Chalenor, tutor of Prince Henry and benefactor of the grammar school of St. Bees.

6 Lea Wadson> Possibly the offspring of Thomas, later Sir Thomas Watson, teller of the Exchequer.

7 Alice Watkins> Possibly a daughter of David Watkins, who was granted the Controllership of the Works at Windsor Castle and other places in 1618.

10 Katherine Parkinson> Possibly the offspring of John Parkinson, apothecary of James I.

12 Elizabeth Madison> Possibly the daughter of Sir Ralph Maddison/ Maddestone, knighted in 1603 and active at court throughout the 1620s.

13 Elizabeth Cramfield> Possibly a daughter of Lionel Cranfield, already an important official in James's court.

14 Elizabeth Bolton> Possibly a daughter of Edmund Bolton, who proposed a royal academy to James in 1617, or possibly a daughter of Robert Bolton (1572–1631), a fellow of Brasenose College whose father was one of the original governors of Elizabeth I's grammar school. The latter had four daughters.
Rich: Browne> His name is marked by a check mark in pencil in the right margin—by John Evelyn perhaps.

15 Mary Chambre> Possibly the daughter of Dr. James Chambers, one of the king's physicians.

16 Clasie Page> Possibly the offspring of Samuel Page, the poet and divine, who in 1597 was appointed vicar of St. Nicholas, Deptford.
Charles Coleman> Later an important musician at court who contributed to another masque presented by children, "The King and Queenes Entertainement at Richmond" (1636), ed. W. Bang and R. Brotanek, *Materialien zur Kunde des alteren Englischen Dramas* (Louvain: Uystpruyst, 1903).

18 Ann Sandeland> Perhaps the daughter of Sir James Sandilands.

19 Paule Harbart> Possibly the offspring of John Harbert, mayor of Sandwich.

22   Ann Tindall> Possibly kin of John Tindall, Master Gunner, granted a Gunner's place in the Tower for life in 1613 and 1616.

23   M^ris: Oungelo> Possibly kin of Signior Angelo, the Prince's musician.

26   Lucy> Lucy Russell, patroness of the major poets of the day, danced herself in Jonson's masques of *Beauty, Blackness, Queens*, and *Hymenei*. The book of the masque is dedicated to her because she patronized the show both financially and morally (see lines 55–56). White's reasoning is not unprecedented; see the dedicatory letters of *The Masque of Flowers* (1613) and Chapman's *Masque of the Middle Temple and Lincoln's Inn* (1613). A picture of Lucy in masquing attire has been reproduced in *A Book of Masques*, plate 44.

31   module> plan in little; that is, the slim book of the masque as opposed to the magnificent production of it.

35   deiected> lowered in estate or character; base.

36   give> Nichols's emendation; there is no verb in the ms.

39   resolution> conviction.

47–48   the enuious spitt theire veneme> Envy is portrayed with adders for hair in Whitney 4, 94.

49   enuie barketh onely at the starrs> proverbial; see Tilley D449. This envy is a recurrent motif in dedications of masques, and it reflects the censorious context in which they were performed. See for example Daniel's *The Vision of the Twelve Goddesses*, lines 184–212, Jonson's *The Haddington Masque*, lines 10–22, and Chapman's *The Masque of the Middle Temple and Lincoln's Inn*, lines 571–72.
          spight spurnes> proverbial; see Tilley E175.

50   curious> inquisitive; prying.

51   whose hungry eares feedes> see *Hymenei*, lines 20–26, in Jonson 7: 209, for a similar criticism of the feeding habits of Envy.

53   perspectiue> optical instrument for magnifying things; in this case, however, the grossness is a result of the critic's view, rather than the show.

56   refined> here in its most pejorative sense: affecting a high degree of subtlety.

69   OCCASION> See Ripa 390 (who makes no mention of Occasion's white wand, however) and Tilley T311, for the proverbial association of this character with Time.

71   tinsie> rich material with glittering gold or silver thread through it.

86   bright spheare of greatness> Queen Anne; the terms of praise are standard in masques up to 1617 and in neoplatonic lore.

88   faintinge> losing brightness.

94   circle> the sphere in which a heavenly body revolves.

95   repose> corrected by the scribe; the *o* is a superior figure located by a caret at the line.

119   equall>   equitable.

130   Chorus>   the girls of Ladies Hall who constitute an organized group of dancers on this occasion.

140   plotts>   sly plans.

        shifts>   fraudulent stratagems.

142   forgd>   both made or invented and counterfeited.

149   lowringe>   louring; frowning, threatening.

152   Kirtle>   outer petticoat.

154   Zone>   girdle, belt, encircling band.

159   Moone>   Diana, goddess of the moon. In *The Vision of the Twelve Goddesses*, silver half-moons adorned her robe. See Nicoll 175–76 for further details about Diana's portrayal in other masques and for a reproduction (fig. 138) of an Inigo Jones drawing of the character.

171   compasse>   the first of three nicely consistent images, for both "compass" and "bow" have special senses in archery. The "compass" is the curved path taken by an arrow.

172   philters>   love potions or charms; the verb *philter* reinforces the adjective used in this passage, for "to philter" means, figuratively, "to bewitch."

173   alluringe baytes>   a lure, like a bait, is a means of enticement.

176   Cupid:>   ms. *Cupid*;.

185   waggish>   wanton; mischievous.

188   subiect>   Fortune is subordinate to, ruled, and protected by Diana, the reigning figure.

190   fond>   foolish; infatuated; over-affectionate; doting.

        fancy>   amorous inclination; love.

194   idall>   pretender; false god.

198   anticke>   antic; grotesque, uncouth.

201   affecteth>   is fond of or has affection for something.

209   copssmate>   adversary; a person with whom one copes.

216   milkesopp>   effeminate; spiritless.

219   Caduseus>   Mercury's rod of office is clearly portrayed in Whitney 2.

228   theorboes>   large lutes, with double necks and two sets of strings.

231   taffaty>   taffeta; a glossy silken cloth.

232   Songe>   followed by a triangular flourish in the ms.

236   annoy>   disturbance; vexation.

240   crosse>   Both to contravene or to disrupt and to cause to interbreed are relevant here.

249   Fortune>   see Ripa 182–83; the blindness and the wheel noted by Ripa were proverbial.

259   engagd>   attached by gratitude.

261   curtesie>   favor, kindness.

272   Bacchus>   see Ripa 67–68.
           Chariatt>   see Inigo Jones's drawing of the chariot of Comus in *Plea-sure Reconciled to Virtue*, reproduced in *A Book of Masques*, plate 14.
274   truncheon>   Bacchus's rod of office—his thyrsus.
292   squeamish>   coy; cold; modest; prudish.
294   you'le>   the apostrophe is above the *o*.
295   Lawier>   an original *e* appears to have been changed to the *i* by the scribe.
296   butterwife>   a woman who makes or sells butter.
298   together by the eares>   fighting; set at variance.
300   stoute>   stubborn or rebellious.
301   Lyeus>   Lyaeus, an epithet for Bacchus that emphasizes his power to release people from cares and sad thoughts.
302   sheepebiter>   a dog which bites and worries sheep, and which, for that reason, is kept at a distance.
304   out of my skinn>   an appropriate image given the customary naked-ness of Cupid.
319   conteine>   an unusual use of "contain" as an absolute verb, meaning "to keep oneself" or "to remain"; see *OED*, 13b.
323   castalean>   of Castalia, or of the Muses.
325   carouse>   drink deeply, freely, and frequently.
327   perfitt>   perfect; complete.
342   entire>   unreserved; unfeigned.
349   because>   ms. *beause*.
357   Apollo>   Cupid's mastery of other deities is discussed by Hesiod, *Theogony* 120–122, and by Lucian of Samosata, *Gods* 12 and 19.
362   vildest>   vilest; most base.
           imputations>   charges.
364   belldames>   old hags, viragos—in both cases, opposites of the mod-est young girls of Ladies Hall.
366   nicenes>   modesty; coyness.
370   insolency>   behavior beyond the bounds of propriety.
372   as->   not hyphenated in the ms.
377   Vesta>   virgin goddess of health, a goddess associated with purity and chastity.
379   Driades>   see Ripa 377.
384   carnation>   flesh-colored or rosy pink.
388–89   tiffany>   transparent silk or gauze muslin.
391   enurion>   form a ring around; see Shakespeare, *The Merry Wives of Windsor* 5.5.85–100, for a dance similar in form and in effect.
395   figures>   dancing movements.
406   descants>   sings melodiously on a theme.
407   diapason>   a rich full outburst of sound; in this case, it is the climax of the chorus and expresses the gist of their theme.

409   peeuish ape>   mischievous, spiteful counterfeiter or mimic.
        fancies child>   the child of blind, unreasoning affection.
420   vaine>   vein; strain or style.
422   quicke>   lively or vigorous; in this case, the special sense applied to
        wine is relevant: brisk, effervescent, fit to drink.
423   braynsicke>   foolish; addle-headed.
426   Endimion>   in Greek mythology, the character whom Zeus gave
        eternal life and youth by allowing him to sleep perpetually.
        Epiminedes>   a teacher and wonder-worker of Crete who was re-
        ported to have fallen asleep in a cave for fifty-seven years.
428   bullies>   affectionate terms of address: good friends, fine fellows. See
        Oberon, lines 130–137 and note in Jonson 7: 346.
        braue>   another general epithet of admiration: stout-hearted, fine.
431   kinderkin>   half a barrel.
432   buckram>   coarse linen or cotton.
444   roundly>   directly, promptly.
446   soundly>   deeply, to the full.
454   tunn>   tun; a large cask.
458   maule>   to hammer, beat, strike.
463   trickes>   the scribe incorrectly ends the stanza at this point, leaves
        a space, then begins the next stanza with line 464.
464   ape baboone>   this baboon is a kind of ape with a long snout resem-
        bling a dog's and canine teeth; figuratively, the phrase is a term of
        abuse.
466   fudlinge>   muddling and intoxicating.
        trole>   troll; move nimbly.
468   bridhouse>   bridehouse; a house where a wedding is held.
469   Tinker>   mender of pots.
473   flagon>   large bottle.
474   punke>   harlot, prostitute.
475   muld>   dulled, stupefied.
481   for it>   ms. *forit*.
498   slopps>   wide, baggy breeches.
        garded>   trimmed.
498–99 roring band>   loud, colorful material around the hat?
501   trunke>   trunk-hose.
505   cullisan>   cognizance; crest or badge.
509   trull>   strumpet.
        bodies>   bodice.
525   watched>   light blue cloth.
536   presence>   Queen Anne.
        af->   not hyphenated in the ms.
540   Mr Ounslo>   Judith Edwards of Wadhurst, Sussex, hired a dancing
        teacher with the same name for her daughters in 1627. Regular quar-

terly payments to him of £3 are registered in her personal account
book until August of 1628. As yet unpublished, her account book is
in the Dorset Record Office, Dorchester, MS. D 124, Box 222. In addition, an Amaria Oneslowe undertook on October 21, 1618, "to serve
this howse Gray's Inn with musike for the next yeare following for the
ould wages . . . " (Wienpahl 155). It is hard to resist thinking that this
musician and that Mr. Ounslo the dancing master are related.

543   godaughters >   Nichols suggests Ann Chalenor and Ann Sandilands;
        see Nichols 3: 295.

547   condiscende >   descend.

550   weeds >   apparel.

554   Albions >   alluding to the white cliffs of Dover, and thereby associ-
        ating Anne with the girls in white.

575   triumphs >   solemn procession.

591   Olimpian prise >   heavenly or divine reward; again this aligns Anne
        with Diana.

594   purchase >   to earn or win; to gain possession of.

597   ought >   aught; anything.

605   our >   ms. *no*.

        Helicon >   part of Mount Parnassus and home of the Muses.

Notes on Contributors

JONATHAN GOLDBERG is Sir William Osler Professor of English Literature at The Johns Hopkins University; his most recent book is *Voice Terminal Echo: Postmodernism and English Renaissance Texts*. *Writing Matter*, a study in cultural graphology, is forthcoming.

ANNABEL PATTERSON is Professor of Literature and English at Duke University. Her most recent publications are *Censorship and Interpretation* (1984) and *Pastoral and Ideology* (1987). The essay published here is part of her forthcoming *Shakespeare and the Popular Voice*.

JOSEPH LOEWENSTEIN is an associate professor of English at Washington University. He is currently an NEH Fellow at the National Humanities Center, where he is completing a book on English Renaissance intellectual property and the cultural economy of authorship.

BARBARA MOWAT, Director of Academic Programs at the Folger Shakespeare Library, is editor of *Shakespeare Quarterly* and author of *The Dramaturgy of Shakespeare's Romances*. She is currently working on a book on Shakespeare as a reader of Renaissance texts.

DAVID BEVINGTON, Phyllis Fay Horton Professor in the Humanities at the University of Chicago, is editor of the Bantam Shakespeare (1988), the third edition of Scott, Foresman's *The Complete Works of Shake-*

265

speare (1980), and *Medieval Drama* (Houghton Mifflin, 1975). His most recent critical study is *Action Is Eloquence: Shakespeare's Language of Gesture* (Harvard University Press, 1984).

PAUL WERSTINE is Professor of English at King's College and the Graduate School of the University of Western Ontario, coeditor of the New Variorum *Romeo and Juliet*, associate editor of the annual *Medieval and Renaissance Drama in England*, and author of numerous articles on the Shakespeare text in such scholarly journals as *Analytical and Enumerative Bibliography, The Library, Papers of the Bibliographical Society of America, Shakespeare Quarterly, Shakespeare Studies*, and *Studies in Bibliography*. He is currently at work on a critique of twentieth-century Shakespeare textual criticism.

LESLIE THOMSON is an assistant professor of English at the University of Toronto. She has published articles on the staging of, and editorial treatment of stage directions in, *Women Beware Women, Hengist, King of Kent*, and *Antony and Cleopatra*. A current project is a study of window scenes in plays of the Renaissance.

GARY TAYLOR is an associate professor of English at The Catholic University of America, joint general editor of the new Oxford *Complete Works* of Shakespeare, coauthor of *William Shakespeare: A Textual Companion,* coeditor of *The Division of the Kingdoms: Shakespeare's Two Versions of* King Lear, and author of *To Analyze Delight: A Hedonist Criticism of Shakespeare*. His most recent work is *Reinventing Shakespeare: A Cultural History, 1642–1986* (Weidenfeld & Nicolson, 1989).

C. E. MCGEE is an associate professor of English at the University of St. Jerome's College, University of Waterloo. He is coauthor of "A Checklist of Tudor and Stuart Entertainments," the most recent section of which, that covering the years 1614–25, is to appear in *Research Opportunities in Renaissance Drama* in 1989, and coeditor of the *Records of Early English Drama: Dorset* (in progress).